An Actor's Business

First Sentient Publications edition, 2004

Cover design by Kim Johansen, Black Dog Design
Book design by Nicholas Cummings

Library of Congress Cataloging-in-Publication Data

Reilly, Andrew.
   An actor's business : how to market yourself as an actor no matter
where you live / Andrew Reilly.-- 1st Sentient Publications ed.
      p. cm.
   Includes bibliographical references.
   ISBN 1-59181-020-5
   1. Acting--Vocational guidance. I. Title.
PN2074.R45 2004
792'.023--dc22

                                        2004003956

Printed in the United States of America

10 9 8 7 6 5 4 3 2 1

SENTIENT PUBLICATIONS
A Limited Liability Company
1113 Spruce St.
Boulder, CO 80302
www.sentientpublications.com

An Actor's Business

How to Market Yourself as an Actor
No Matter Where You Live

Andrew Reilly

SENTIENT PUBLICATIONS

Contents

APPENDICES

The quotes from casting directors in this book were either made to me directly or are from Karen Kondazian's fine book, *The Actor's Encyclopedia of Casting Directors* (Lone Eagle Publishing, 2000), which has over one hundred interviews with casting directors and which I recommend that all actors read from cover to cover.

Preface to the Second Edition

After I wrote the first edition of this book in 1996 I went on to other projects that involved less acting and more producing, directing, writing, and teaching. I wrote a novel about Palestine while teaching there, started an English-language theater on the steppes of Russia while on a Fulbright, and now have my own production company. I do miss acting from time to time, of course, and perhaps one day I'll go back to the boards to do some classical theater, but as my friend and mentor Tom Williams told me when he published the first edition, "You can have anything you want in life, but you can't have everything." All things considered, I am happy with my choices.

I want to reaffirm something important, however. In revising this book for a second edition, I am both surprised and pleased at how little has changed with regard to the business of show business in eight years. To be more up-to-date I now use different movie stars as examples of points I want to make, and the dollar figures for film production have gone up—obscenely I believe in the case of movie star salaries—but the basic business and marketing principles for working actors have remained exactly the same.

If you decide to major in theater and your parents hit the ceiling when you break the news to them, just read this book and tell them afterward about how you are going to market yourself, and that if your acting career does not succeed, you will then be splendidly prepared for a lucrative career in sales! Mention also that a degree in theater will give you as fine a liberal education as any degree in the humanities, that a theater degree will make you a well-rounded, educated person, and that your degree in theater will also train you in how to walk and talk effectively with clarity and charisma, skills that will make you even more attractive to corporations willing to train young college graduates for entry-level management positions!

This should work very well in getting them to cut you some slack about what you'll eventually decide to be when you grow up. I hope, though, that many of you will become professional actors as a result of this book, especially those of you who leave school as educated idealists. I want to teach educated idealists how to hustle, because if you do get into this business you might just improve it some. I also hope that perhaps we will have a chance to work together one day.

Yours in the audition lines,
Andrew Reilly

What This Book Will Do for You

I f you are considering making acting a career, then I wrote this book for you. Read it, and when you are done you will have learned two very important things:

- Whether or not you really want an acting career.
- If you do, how you can build that acting career from the ground up, no matter where you live.

I am an actor myself, as well as a writer, director, and teacher of acting. I began acting in community theater some time ago, and for years acting was just an enjoyable hobby. When I finally decided to turn professional, I got some formal training, specifically a Master of Fine Arts in Theatre from the University of South Carolina, with further study in classical acting at the Folger Conservatory in Washington, D.C. I did regional theater work, TV commercials, and some day-player roles in feature films that were shooting on location in the Southeast, then saved some money and set out for Los Angeles. After a year there I got a notice from the Screen Actors Guild that I was going to have to pay an increase in my union dues because of my earnings as an actor.

I immediately called the union and told the lady in bookkeeping that there must be some mistake. My total earnings as a film actor for that year, I told her, came to only $6,800. She quickly informed me that this was, comparatively speaking, quite a large sum for an actor to earn. It seems that I had made more money in film that year than 85 percent of the members of the L.A. local of the Screen Actors Guild.

Needless to say, I was stunned, but I should not have been. For some months preceding this bit of news, I had been trading notes with other actors on the difficulties of actually earning a living as an actor. The consensus? Lacking the kind of marketing skills I will share with you in this book, such a career is virtually impossible. My conclusion? While professional training programs in this country are turning out some fine actors, most of these young actors don't have the faintest idea how to get started in the business once they graduate. As strange as it may seem, the marketing of one's talents is just not a part of the curriculum in most acting schools. This is a crucial omission. No professional training program should call itself that without a real study of the business of acting and of the proven ways that you can sell your talent, get work as an actor, and build a career in your chosen field.

This book tells you about self-marketing techniques that most actors have to pick up piecemeal, over a long period of time, if they manage to pick them up at all. It is actually a kind of marketing manual of the sort that would be used to sell insurance or real estate. This book will help you decide what you are selling, how to find and convince people to buy what you are selling, and how to keep track of it all.

An Actor's Business can save you three years of your acting life. An actor is really engaged in a kind of small business, and statistics show that 60 percent of small businesses fail before their third year. This is also just about the length of time it takes for most actors to leave New York or L.A. and return to Charlotte or Des Moines, disillusioned and unaware of why they failed.

> If you are in this profession because you think you're going to become a big star and make a lot of money, you are probably setting yourself up for a disappointment. If you are doing this for the love of it, the true passionate love of it, then that's where your commitment should lie, to yourself and your work.
>
> —April Webster, Casting Society of America

Before an actor becomes established and becomes one of the 5 percent of his peers who earn their entire living by acting, he or she has almost invariably stuck it out for at least five years. When you have finished this book you will be prepared to join that 5 percent, if you still want to, of course. It ain't going to be easy, but it will be doable.

- You will know how to turn yourself into a small acting business.
- You will have an understanding of how you fit into the larger stream of commerce that is show business.

And if you then decide to go for it, you will have at least a fighting chance of becoming that one professional actor in twenty that makes all of his or her money acting.

Chapter 1 | # The State of
the Art

People Who Become Actors

More people are afraid of getting up in front of an audience than of anything else, including snakes or heights. So why do we actors do it? Actually, yes, we are a bit nuts, like most creative people. There's even a theory that creativity is nature's compensatory mechanism for coping with madness, and perhaps some actors cope with life by dredging up very private parts of themselves for public display. Sometimes you can get paid for that; however, most professional actors prefer to make a living by advancing stories without causing distractions, and I will explain what this means later, very clearly I hope.

Laurence Olivier is reported to have said that there is only one reason anyone becomes an actor: "Look at me! Look at me! Look at me!" Actors are usually outgoing and seem to require a kind of regular validation of their worth from other people, and perhaps that is what makes us want to go into this business, but that impulse will need to be tamed and harnessed in order to be put into serving an actor's real work. This is what professional training is about, and it will be covered shortly.

> Acting is a profession. One should carry oneself like a professional, act like a professional.
> —Mike Fenton, Casting Society of America

Many pretty women give the business a try, "just to see," as they are fond of saying, and find that there are actually not that many roles for very pretty women and tremendous competition for such roles as there are. Cool guys who plan to become the next action hero will encounter the same sort of problem, whereas an actor who can play the romantic lead's friend and confidant actually has a much better chance of working regularly because there is less competition in that segment of the market.

> Remember that good looks aren't enough. There is a left-over myth from old Hollywood that all you have to be is good-looking.
> —Alice Cassidy, Casting Society of America

There are quite a number of gay men who become actors, but the necessary combination of being both sensitive and outgoing is probably more characteristic of the artistic community in general than of the gay community. (If you are a homophobe, you're not going to be particularly welcome in this business, by the way, as the business prides itself on tolerance in such matters.) Outgoing charactertypes find in show business a community that accepts them and might actually pay them for being fat or bald, assuming, of course, that they can act.

What is the main difference between an amateur and a professional actor? An amateur is defined in the dictionary as one who does something only for the love of it. The word *amateur* does not mean second rate. America's community theaters are blessed with people who act for the love of it, and some have more talent and more skill than many professional actors. After all, a professional can be defined simply as someone who does the same thing for money, with all that this implies, although an actor can rarely last long in show business if he or she doesn't do it at least as much for love as for money.

It is regrettable that many actors who decide to become professionals do so with the idea of becoming movie stars. They think that this is what making it means, and they are sadly wrong. A star is someone who can get his or her name above the title in a feature film, a TV show, or in lights on a Broadway marquee. This ability is not always because of talent, skill, beauty, or charisma, though these things certainly help, but rather because of an unpredictable desire on the part of the public to look at this person. Most people do not go to the movies to see a story so much as to see their

> The truth is, if you can make a living as an actor, take care of yourself and your family, then you have *made it*.
> —Phyllis Huffman, Casting Society of America

favorite stars in a given situation. The rest of the actors involved in the production just do their jobs and advance the story. If they advance enough stories they can make a good living, even though no one but people in the industry and the folks in their hometowns may know their names. Actors who work like this regularly have indeed made it, and often lead happier, fuller lives than stars. They retire with a pension from the Screen Actors Guild, or one of the other performer's unions, and a thousand memories of small victories, artfully achieved.

No one, including the heads of the seven major studios, can accurately predict who is going to become a star, or why. The decision makers at United Artists, for example, were sure that Kris Kristopherson was going to become a star, so they put him in a little something called *Heaven's Gate*. The public, however, didn't think Kristopherson was going to be a star, and the movie lost so much money that the studio went belly up. United Artists was later sold by its parent corporation, Transamerica, to MGM, which wanted to acquire UA's distribution network. And Kris Kristopherson? I'm told that Willie Nelson still returns his phone calls. Another example of a faded star is Ryan O'Neal, who was America's number one box office star in 1976. Do any of you young folks even know who he is now?

At any given time there are less than one hundred stars, and more than 120,000 union actors. The actual membership breakdown will be covered in a later chapter. There are also an estimated 250,000 more actors hoping to get into the unions at any given time, and most of them will have given up within three years, to be replaced by another quarter million more. Such people, as well as most union actors, might be called wannabees. You see them striking poses at parties and cafes, complaining that the entertainment industry doesn't appreciate real talent. If such a person is a friend of yours, suggest this book, even though he or she will probably not get past this chapter. I occasionally give marketing seminars for actors and have discovered a sad truth: most wannabees care more about clinging to their affectations about themselves than about doing good work or getting the check.

Actors who go into the business with the idea of becoming stars might as well base their careers on winning the lottery. "But," you say, "an actor needs to believe in himself!" That's true, son, but in order to make a living as an actor, he needs to believe the right things about himself. It's not enough to have a dream. He also needs a plan.

> Complaining keeps you stuck. It is far more productive to take an active responsibility for your career and your life.
> —Lindsay Chag, casting director

Want to act professionally? Read on, MacDuff, and keep your sense of humor. After all, it ain't nothin' but another job.

An Actor's Real Work

What does a professional actor do? "She acts," you say. Sorry, that response is too vague and is only part of the truth. That is like saying "a real estate salesman sells houses."

The successful real estate agent spends most of her time canvassing—on the phone, in the newspaper, behind the wheel of a car, or on foot. A very small portion of her time is spent showing houses to potential buyers, and an even smaller portion is spent watching contracts being signed in an

> Successful people are no different from anyone else except they are more focused, more driven, and work harder.
> —Anthony Barnao, casting director

actual sale. A real estate agent who goes to one such signing a month is doing very well and is probably among the 10 percent in the field that sell 90 percent of the real estate.

The parallels between a career in sales and a career in acting will become more apparent as we move along. A successful actor spends about as much time canvassing as does a realtor and as little time showing the product (auditioning) as a real estate salesman does showing houses and, in acting as in real estate, about 10 percent of the professionals get about 90 percent of the work. This is not because they are necessarily more talented than the rest. *It is because each has turned his or her talent into a marketable skill and has learned how to canvass the market for people willing to buy that skill.* Such actors do not wait for a talent agent to get them work, and the reasons for this will become clearer in the section on talent agents in chapter two.

> I hear actors saying "I'm not working. My agent never sends me out." Well, what are you doing to get work?
> —Julie Ashton, casting director

Ultimately, whether the actor or the talent agent arranges for an audition, the pro knows that the actor's job is to advance a story in the best possible way without causing distractions— no more, no less—and her ability to do that is what she is selling. This is true whether an actor has one line or a hundred lines of dialogue. It is also true for extras.

Playwrights and screenplay writers do not write stories to showcase actors. It's true that Hollywood development people often ruin stories in order to showcase stars, but we cannot help that. Besides, you will probably never be given the chance to sell out that way, but you may be given the chance—you have it now in fact—to sell your skill in order to advance a story.

> The whole cast has to be shown in a good light. The play's the thing, not the actor's vanity.
> —Natalie Hart, Casting Society of America

The story is more important than any of us, comrades. The best moments on stage or screen, especially for the actors who manage to keep loving it, come when everyone involved with the production stops looking in the mirror and looks together in the same direction. "The play's the thing," to quote a guy. It was the Greeks who gave us drama as an art form, and our word *drama* comes from the Greek word *dran*, which means *to do* or *to take action*.

Once trained correctly and cast in something, you will take the actions that your character takes in the story, sometimes without even moving at all, and this will be covered in the section on playing verbs. Acting, however, is only a part of what a professional actor does for a living.

What does a professional actor do for a living? An actor keeps his instrument—his body—in good condition. He doesn't ruin it with drugs, alcohol, junk food, or lack of sleep. If an actor ruins his instrument, he soon doesn't act anymore. An actor warms up his instrument so as not to strain his voice or muscles. He increases his performance capabilities through training and exercise. A professional actor learns to play his instrument like a musician and plays the song he is paid to play. A professional learns to deliver a performance on time and to the best of his abilities, regardless of personal preferences or personal problems. The professional continually puts in the hours, turning talent into skill, because talent, after all, is only a reservoir of potential, an ability to learn quickly. Effort is required to turn talent into skill, and that means putting in the hours. It means caring. It means loving the craft enough to want to do it for money, and that is a lot of love. An acting career can actually be described with a simple equation. Let T stand for talent, or how quickly you can learn something. Let E stand for effort, how much time and sweat you put into it. Let S stand for skill, which is your ability to do the job they are paying you for. Let P stand for persistence, or sticking it out for at least five years. C, of course, stands for career. Here's the equation:

> I think actors need to take more responsibility for their careers as opposed to relying on agents. Taking responsibility also means coming to auditions prepared and ready to work. Until you have a job, your work is getting the job. Taking responsibility also means keeping yourself well oiled by taking classes or being in a play. Unless you keep working at it, you get flabby.
> —Debi Manwiller,
> Casting Society
> of America

$$T \times E = S \quad S + P = C \quad \text{Got it?}$$

A professional actor continually looks for people to buy his or her skill. Just as a pilot is always looking for a place to land (and a lawyer is always looking for money about to change hands), an actor is always looking for the chance to perform.

A professional actor constantly asks to perform and constantly lives with the rejection of being told "no," time after time. Those old days in community theater may glow warm and

> Actors cannot afford to ever let a single day go by in which they don't do something to invest in and improve their craft.
> —Reuben Cannon,
> Casting Society
> of America

nostalgic in the actor's memories, but professional actors learn not to take rejection personally. They just move on to the next audition with curiosity and a positive attitude.

A professional actor prepares for auditions by getting all available information about what is called for in the role and by arriving at the audition with a rested, tuned instrument and carefully made choices to offer the auditors. She brings something to the table, so to speak, and it may be a revelation to the auditors, something they never imagined. Professionals also arrive calm and early for an audition.

If asked to change something in the audition, a good professional actor changes on a dime and offers what is asked for to the best of her abilities. As Michael Shurtleff points out in his wonderful book *Audition,* this usually means that an actor should try if possible to *add* the suggestion to what he or she has already done. (Read his book.)

A professional actor uses the good manners his mother tried to teach him and is courteous, though not obsequious or servile, to everyone involved with the project, both at auditions and when he eventually gets work. This means being courteous to all people, not only to important people.

> If an actor has talent and is willing to discipline himself and respects his craft enough to become trained and learn professional etiquette, he will not go unnoticed. Trust that.
> —Lindsay Chag, casting director

Finally, a professional actor does not wait by the phone or strike poses in sidewalk cafes. She gets on the phone, or gets to a desk to write letters or cards. He gets the trade papers and scours them for information about possible work. She gets off her butt and hits the street looking, always looking, perhaps with a bit of a whistle.

A professional actor also occasionally acts.

University Drama Schools

"Those with formal training tend to make a greater investment in the part, based on all the information they have been able to gather and that makes them more interesting. Theater actors know how to work, they know the technique of acting, they know the discipline of acting and how creatively to reveal the characters they are working on." Paul Weber, Casting Society of America

There are about three hundred accredited drama schools in this country. For a list of them, buy the *Directory of Theater Training Programs.* The address is in the appendix. The lady who began compiling this excellent directory, as well as several others, was Jill Charles. She died of cancer several years ago, and we are all poorer for this today. She was a pro and I highly recommend that you buy her resource books if you are considering going into this business. Her company is being carried on by her friends and colleagues who continue her fine work.

A prospective actor should make intelligent choices with regard to university training programs, independent acting classes, workshops, and seminars, and what follows is some information that I hope will help you do that. Another thing to consider when choosing a theater school is its location, as you can also be working that local market as an actor while you are still in school, and for a time afterward. The chapter in this book on regional markets will give you more information on that.

> I would recommend finishing high school and college and doing every play you can possibly do while you are in school.
> —Mike Fenton,
> Casting Society
> of America

It is sad to report that the overwhelming majority of university training programs for actors still do not train as many actors for the profession as does the School of Hard Knocks. University drama teachers often train potential actors to reteach their opinions about acting in repertory theater companies, a profession that does not really exist any more, much less thrive. It is also sad to report that, generally speaking, most university academic departments do not feel they have any responsibility to prepare their graduates for the jobs they will be trying to get in their chosen professions once they graduate.

Don't count on being able to teach with that degree either, unless you also get a teaching certification to teach in the public schools. Only a few graduates of drama schools will have careers as professional actors, and few will be able to get teaching jobs at the university level. We've touched on some of the statistics for actors. The stats for teaching jobs in university theater departments are equally grim. They were grim when I published the first edition of this book eight years ago, and remain so today. There is still a glut of acting teachers with terminal degrees out there looking for jobs. A case in point is that of a friend of mine who applied for

> I think someone should offer a class to actors on the business aspects of acting.
> —Jeff Gerrard,
> casting director
>
> Author's note: I offer such classes and seminars.

a teaching position in the drama department of a rather small college in the Southeast. The job description stated that applicants should have either an M.F.A. in acting or a Ph.D. in theater. My poor friend did not even make the final cut of those being considered. The little college received applications from over two hundred people who presumably had either an M.F.A. or a Ph.D. Among these applicants, those that had tried to make a living as actors had probably failed in that endeavor because, though they had been taught how to act, they had not been taught how to hustle and had left their drama schools on a children's crusade to New York or L.A. Unfortunately, this whole situation probably will not change for some time to come.

Let me describe two types of college drama departments that actors, disillusioned with their training, often complain about once they hit the streets. One might label these two types of drama departments the monastery and the romper room.

In the monastery the faculty members are stern and severe. They are often rude and abusive to their students, whereas the power players in the business rarely are. In the business they are nice to the actors they want and simply ignore the actors they don't.

Teachers at the monastery pontificate about art and rail against crass commercialism. Many have a lingering love of British accents and a kind of fetish for silk. (The women generally wear it around their heads and the men around their necks.) Let's call these folks shouldabeens in deference to their opinions about themselves. For the most part, what they say about art is valuable, but artists like Shakespeare and Molière would not share their opinion that real art cannot be brought successfully to the marketplace. Because these monastic types refuse to teach their students anything about marketing, they are like generals who send their soldiers into battle without ammunition while they remain sequestered in their tenured ivory towers.

> I do *not* teach my acting class as if it's high art, but I do tell actors that they are a marketable product and need to see that as the nature of the business. They have themselves to sell and they should be doing things that they could be cast in. I advise them not to do wasteful things.
>
> —Stanley Soble,
> Casting Society
> of America

The teachers at these monasteries, though, perform two important services to the industry and to the actors they send into it: they do trim actors' egos down to size, and they do teach actors to put themselves into the service of the work.

And the romper rooms? There the student's tuition buys the teacher's love.

A musician or an opera singer would never try to substitute "just feeling it" for years of practice to acquire at least a minimum skill, but America is full of actors and acting teachers who seem to think that just being themselves, being there and feeling it, is enough to do a good acting job. From time to time, though, that one in a million shot proves to be true, like the lottery, and someone who can't act becomes a star, thereby encouraging thousands of other fools to clutter up the business. The romper room schools encourage this kind of folly. They begin with the silly assumption that if an actor will only relax and be honest, then what he or she does on stage or film will be wonderful.

They teach lots of relaxation exercises at romper rooms. Acting students prowl around the room like angry alley cats, or twitch on the floor like sizzling strips of bacon. This is to unleash the actor's inner creativity, you see. Movement classes often look as though a group from the funny farm had been given happy drugs, bouncing about, skipping along, and flailing their arms in the air. This is to unblock the students, you see. At romper room you hear people say things like "Brian had a breakthrough today. He cried!" When an actor gushes with emotion in class, the instructor often beams, whether the emotion advances the story or not, because the actor is "getting in touch with his feelings," you see. Finally, the graduates are given one last hug (they have previously been given lots of hugs) and told to believe in themselves as they leave for Gotham and Tinsel Town.

Graduates of these schools should immediately get jobs in summer camps or with the Parks and Recreation Service teaching creative dramatics to children. Only a tiny percentage will ever work as actors. But their teachers will continue smiling, beaming, hugging, and drawing their salaries.

> I try to recommend acting teachers who don't mess with the psyche.
> —Penny Perry, casting director

In all fairness it should be remembered that theater departments are not very different from other departments in a university. No chemistry teacher can be expected to get all his chemistry majors jobs at Dupont, and a B.A. in theater is just another liberal arts degree, nothing more. However, many graduates of so-called professional training programs, whether B.F.A. or M.F.A. programs, seem quite bitter about not having been adequately prepared for entry into the profession. They have been given neither a realistic overview of the profession and how it works in real life nor specifics on how to become practicing professionals themselves.

My advice to anyone wishing to go into this business after college would be to double major in theater and anything else. I would advise taking the kind of theater classes, whether in college or privately, that stress technique and story analysis. I believe that classical training is still the best. Learn to do Shakespeare in iambic

> Realize this is a business and understand the business end of it as well as the artistic end of it.
> —Patrick Rush, Casting Society of America

pentameter, and film acting will be easy. It will be like a runner taking the training weights off his ankles and then running with his trained muscles.

By the way, don't let anyone tell you that film and stage acting are totally different. They are not. The creative process is exactly the same. It is the delivery that is different, just as speaking to someone at the dinner table is different from speaking to someone across the room. In film acting you usually talk as if the person were standing next to you, and in stage acting you always talk as if the person were across the stage, even in a love embrace. (This means that the person you are doing a love scene with may

> Theater acting is about talking to a person who may be sitting in the back row, while film acting because of the sensitivity of the camera and sound is revealing yourself to an intimate, ideal listener.
>
> —Rick Pagano,
> Casting Society
> of America

pop a plosive and put a pittle of spittle into your eye, but as a trained actor you will not register this until you get off of the stage, and then only with benign good humor.)

The stage is where you learn to act, and that is the only place where you really learn to act. You make money acting in film and TV, and that is probably the only place you will ever make much money acting. But first you have to learn to act, so take classes that teach technique, do as much stage work as possible, and get in touch with your feelings on your own time.

Classes that teach you story analysis will help both your acting and your auditioning, because the story provides guidelines for you. Story analysis helps an actor make good, clear choices about what is actually going on in a scene, and once an actor decides on the actions that are taking place, he will be able to advance the story better as part of the team. There is a clear and rather simple way to do this, and that is to play verbs, a technique that will be covered in the section on "Developing Your Craft in Academic and Community Theater" later in this chapter.

> Figure out with the context of the whole piece what sense your character makes in it. The most important thing is to concentrate on what the scene is about and what your character wants.
>
> —Alice Cassidy,
> Casting Society
> of America

If you study drama in an academic setting, it would also be an excellent idea to take at least one marketing course over in the business school if you can, perhaps as an elective. (This will look good to your parents too, remember.) Perhaps one day theater departments will offer such marketing courses, rather than pretending that "students get that kind of thing in advisement." This will, of course, require that someone in the department knows something about marketing.

You can also find many fine books on marketing at your public library, which will supplement what you are learning from this one. In the meantime, finish reading this book. Then instead of lending it to your friends, tell them to buy it. (I am a professional, and I wrote it so I could make money!)

Workshops and Seminars

Picking a workshop or deciding to attend a seminar is not as risky as choosing a college. Workshops and seminars are much cheaper and take less of your time, and they are easier to evaluate in terms of effectiveness. There are many respected independent acting schools, such as H.B. Studios and the Actor's Studio in New York. But you still need to be careful, folks. There are lots of people out there waiting to separate you from your money, including some actors whose names you might recognize.

Let's take a stroll through this territory, and while we're at it let's lighten our load by getting rid of a couple of widespread misconceptions. The first of these is that a person whose face you have seen or whose name you have heard will automatically have something valuable to teach you. (Does Pee Wee Herman teach now? He might, for all I know.)

The second false assumption is that such a person might be able to get you a job if you go to his seminar or take his class. Some of the 80 percent of American actors who make less than $5,000 a year acting spend more money under these false assumptions than they make acting.

You may have seen ads for seminars in your hometown paper, where for only $300 you can spend four hours with an actor who has actually been on a soap opera! When attractive females give these seminars they often print a photo of themselves in the ad, as if to say "See how pretty I am? I must be right!" and this kind of thing seems to be effective in getting people to spend their money. Wannabees plunk down their cash and leave such seminars as happily innocent as when they arrived.

Before paying for any class or seminar, try to talk to some people who have taken it, and insist that a syllabus of exactly what will be covered be sent to you before agreeing to spend a cent. If the material is not then covered to your satisfaction, demand your money back at the first opportunity and threaten to call the cops if you get any flak. Remember that you are paying for real information! Remember also that except for casting directors, a subject to be covered in a moment, people who give seminars and classes do not hire actors, so raising hell with them won't hurt you.

Due to past abuses on the part of agents, the Screen Actors Guild will not allow a franchised agent to charge for acting classes. Modeling agencies, like the ones in your hometown, usually make most of their money by giving classes rather then by getting people work, and so do many small, nonfranchised "agents." Please don't waste your money. Most of these modeling agencies shamelessly prey on the fears of mothers that their daughters will not be popular unless they learn poise at those schools, and such schools are rarely worth the money it costs to take those classes. They are scams, pure and simple.

There is another kind of "workshop" given by casting directors in New York and L.A. that as of this writing is still tolerated by the unions. Some actors claim to have gotten work through them. You will need to decide for yourself whether you want to spend your money on them. Here's how they work:

Someone reserves a conference room at a hotel and asks a casting director if she wants to make $500 for three hours of work teaching a cold reading workshop. If the casting director agrees, the promoter rents a room for $200 and spends about $100 promoting the workshop, then charges $50 a person tuition. Thirty people are "admitted," and after expenses the promoter makes about $700. (Once the casting director has successfully done a couple of these, she usually concludes that she doesn't need a promoter and does that part of the work herself.)

The actors arrive for the workshop, and the casting director breezes in a little late. Each actor is interviewed briefly by the casting director and is given a partner and a scene to read from a project the casting director has previously worked on. Scene partners go out to the parking lot and practice their scenes while the casting director takes a break. The actors return and the scenes are read. The casting director then offers some feedback after each one, but because the casting director may never have taken an acting class, such feedback may not be much real help. Still, you can learn lots of tricks by watching other actors work, and you do get seen by the casting director. This argument, that "It's a way to get seen," is the lame excuse that union board members give for allowing the practice to continue, although they write in union newsletters things like "Remember, union members, you are not allowed to give Christmas presents to casting directors, not even cookies!"

> I am very opposed to [casting seminars] if an actor has to pay a lot of money to attend. I don't think the casting director should be charging anything to provide the opportunity for actors to meet them.
> —Terry Liebling, casting director

If you were to go to a workshop with a different casting director in L.A. every night, assuming you could, it would take you almost a year and about $7,000 of your money to meet all of them. Many actors think these workshops are worth it. You make the call. If you stay in touch with the casting director, you may get some work out of this kind of workshop, but let's be clear about what this has really been about: you have paid for an audition.

Developing Your Craft in Academic and Community Theater

Acting is not so much about becoming a character as it is about figuring out and doing what a character would do in a given situation. Acting is not about being. Acting means taking action.

You cannot act convincingly by playing qualities such as nice, or shy, or snobbish, or bitchy. To do this is to give, or to present, your opinion of a character to the audience. This is called presentational acting and is also described as commenting on the character. When you try to do this you separate yourself from the character, and it shows.

By representing a character, however, and doing what he or she would do in a given situation, you wind up feeling as he or she might feel, not to mention advancing the story much more believably. This, in a nutshell, is the difference between presentational acting and representational acting.

Now, let me tell you a story that illustrates two main approaches to representational acting, one that is taught more in the U.K. and the other more in the U.S.

Laurence Olivier was on a talk show promoting *Marathon Man*, which he had just completed with Dustin Hoffman. Olivier said that one morning Hoffman showed up looking awful. He had apparently stayed awake for three days in order to look tired in the scene they were shooting that morning, and Olivier asked him "Dear boy, why don't you try acting? It's much easier." This is the difference between an inside-out approach to acting (Hoffman's) and an outside-in approach (Olivier's.) Now, Hoffman is certainly a wonderful actor, some say a better film actor than Olivier was, but he is also a star. At this point in your career there just isn't time for you to live the part in order to say a few lines as a day player.

The American practice of living the part rather than practicing the craft is the result, I believe, of a misinterpretation by Lee Strasburg about Stanislavsky's "method." I have heard Strasburg quoted as saying, "Stanislavsky doesn't know what he means; I know what Stanislavsky means." However, I was not there for that conversation, so I can't verify it.

Because Stanislavsky could presume classical training in most of his actors, he may have developed his method to breathe new life into techniques that had become two dimensional and glib. I personally doubt that he ever meant to eliminate technique.

Stanislavky's methods, such as sense memory, can enhance technique but not replace it, and passion will never be as clear or reliable a means of advancing a story as the making of conscious, intelligent choices about what the character is doing. For me, the best acting seems to be a blend of both passion and craft and is exemplified in the fine work of such actors as Meryl Streep. In *Sophie's Choice* she did live the part by losing about thirty pounds to play the concentration camp scenes, but to do a Polish accent she learned to speak Polish. She already spoke French and German, and when it came time for the dubbing of the versions of the film to be released in France and Germany, she did it herself, speaking French and German with a Polish accent. You see the kind of work that goes into a skill like hers? By the way, she got her M.F.A. at Yale.

Now, let's take a look at a quick, sure way of advancing the story using the technique of *playing verbs*.

Qualities, like shy or bitchy, are only clues to what a character will do in a given situation. Remember that characters in a story are not necessarily what they say they are. They are what they do, which includes both what they say and how they say it. Both depend upon what they wish to accomplish by saying the words. Isn't this also true of each of us at every moment of our lives? What characters do determines what goes on in a story. These actions are best described with verbs, and actors who have learned to play verbs can clearly advance the story without causing distractions.

Here's an example of the difference between trying to play a quality and actually playing a verb:

How would you play "reasonable"? Put on glasses and speak with mellow tones? Let's decide instead what a reasonable character does to get what he wants. Persuade, perhaps? Isn't it easier to take action, to persuade rather than parade around with a character's so-called qualities? And doesn't the action of persuading advance the story much better than someone showing off how well he can play a reasonable person? And don't you already know how to persuade? Sure you do. You also know how to threaten, entice, and plead, and with those four verbs you can play hundreds of scenes, right now.

Here is a list of some verbs you can use in different story situations, things that people really do in interacting with each other. Directors, please take note of these verbs, and when directing actors, ask them to do these things in the scenes you are directing. This will make your directing simple and clear and will be much less time consuming than trying to fondle an actor's psyche.

Playable verbs:
- accuse, advise, acquiesce, admit, agree
- blame, brag,
- comfort, challenge, coax, command, criticize, confide
- defend, denounce, deduce
- emphasize, encourage, entice
- fret, fib
- goad, grieve
- humiliate
- intimidate, inquire
- judge, justify
- kill, kibitz, kindle
- lure, lead
- mock, mollify
- nag, needle, notify
- order, object, oppose
- plead, persuade, pardon, pacify
- quibble, question
- retaliate, retreat, rectify
- sweet-talk, surrender, shame
- tantalize, tempt, threaten, test
- underscore
- verify
- warn

As acting practice, either alone or with a group in an acting class, use these verbs to change the meanings of lines of dialogue. Take a line of dialogue from a script and use one of these verbs to invest the line with meaning. Then use a different verb to give the line a different meaning. For example, use the line "The president's plane leaves in an hour" to threaten another character with the line, then to persuade, then to entice, then to plead. (These four verbs, as mentioned earlier, can be used in hundreds of situations in that they are probably the most common ways we get what we want.) You can also take the same line and notify, warn, or congratulate another character. It's a lot of fun with a group to take a sentence and invest it with a verb and have the others guess what you are playing, and it's a good way to hone your skill as well.

In a rehearsal or an audition, you should always be up to something, and if asked what you are doing, you should be able to answer "I'm trying to_____." Fill in that blank with an active verb and a direct object, and that will be the answer to what you are playing, i.e., what you are doing. The direct object will usually be another character in the story. "I'm trying to threaten Henry," or "I'm trying to persuade John." Practice until you can take a line from a script and say it many different ways by using different verbs. When you are able to do this, you will have developed a basic, marketable technique that will continue to get better and clearer with time and practice. It will also be a technique that will not be dependent on your own personal mood of the moment. Jim Belushi was in the middle of performing in a play when he learned his brother John was dead. He continued his performance and finished the show that night.

Chapter 2

The State of the Business

"Remember it's called show business and not show art."—Jeff Gerrard

The Film Studios

The seven major motion picture studios are Columbia, Disney, Twentieth Century Fox, MGM-UA, Paramount, Warner Bros., and Universal. For a fascinating account of the early days of Hollywood, there is a wonderfully readable book called *An Empire of Their Own*, by Neal Gabler. It tells the only-in-America story of studios and fortunes built by first- or second- generation Eastern European Jews who began as nickelodeon owners, became distributors, and finally movie producers. They moved to L.A. to take advantage of the weather, which was ideal for filming, and also to get away from Thomas Edison's thugs, who could easily be talked into smashing other people's movie cameras for a dollar or so.

The moguls are all gone now, but Yiddish is still a kind of second language of Hollywood, and people use it without even realizing it. The Italian financier Carlo Paretti is reputed once to have made the offhand remark that he was having trouble buying MGM because "the Jews are ganging up on me." *Variety* printed the remark, as well as the responses of several powers in the industry. One response quoted in *Variety* was: "If he said it, he's dead"—figuratively speaking, one assumes.

For some excellent accounts of modern-day Hollywood, I suggest *Adventures in the Screen Trade*, by William Goldman, and *Reel Power*, by Mark Litwak.

These days the studios are owned by parent corporations who own controlling interests in the studios' stock, and hire intermediaries to keep artistic temperaments in harmony with the bottom line, which is, of course, profits.

The film industry itself has always had its ups and downs, but the studios have managed to keep control of the box office even after the moguls have long since gone. Only approximately 5 percent of money taken in at the domestic box office goes to independently distributed movies, while 95 percent still goes to studio pictures. Here's a bit of recent history.

In 1948, the studios finally knuckled under to the antitrust division of the Justice Department and sold off their movie theaters. Until that time the moguls had kept thousands of people under contract on their lots and had turned out an unending stream of product to be shown at theaters that they also owned. The only limitation to the studios' aggregate output was the public's willingness to leave their homes and pay to sit in a dark room full of strangers to watch a movie. When the studio-owned theaters were sold, however, the studios not only had to convince people to leave their homes, which became even harder with the advent of TV, but also had to convince the new theater owners to show the movies they were making. Distribution became the key to profits. A product of the highest quality was worthless unless it could be sold.

As parent corporations gained control of the studios, operating expenses were cut to the bone. The contract system gave way to the present system whereby the studios use their solid assets—real estate, capital equipment, and film libraries—to generate income. They sell the television and other ancillary rights to the movies they own, use their real estate as collateral to finance independent productions, and then rent their capital equipment to the independent producers they agree to back financially. They also retain the right to distribute the independent producer's product. Mark Litwak has aptly pointed out that most of these so-called independent producers are nothing of the kind. They are dependent producers. A truly independent producer makes a film with his own money, and perhaps then makes a deal with the studio to distribute it, either with a percentage deal or by selling the negative to the studio outright. Such a deal is referred to as a negative pickup and is the route whereby an independent producer maintains the maximum financial and artistic control over his or her film. Few producers have the money to go that route.

When a studio agrees to make a picture, they borrow the $30 million or so from a bank at prime rate and then lend it to the producer at two points above prime to make the movie. The producer must also agree to change the script; hire certain stars; rent studio trucks, cameras, sound stages, etc.; and finally to put studio executives on the payroll to come to the set to hassle the director and to make sure everything else mentioned has been complied with to the studio's satisfaction.

The studio also gets the right to distribute the picture. The numbers work like this: unless a $20 million star is attached to the project, an average studio-backed picture costs about $30 million to get into the can, and another $10 million or so to make copies of the film (prints) and buy advertising, for a total cost of $40 million. The theater owner (exhibitor) gets half the ticket receipts and reportedly steals a bit more. (Remember that time they collected your ticket instead of tearing it in half? They might have sold that ticket again and kept the cash.) So if the entire population of the state of New York goes to see the picture and it grosses $120 million, the exhibitors keep (at least) $60 million and return $60 million to the studio distributor. The distributor takes a third, or $20 million for their distribution services. The producer is left with $40 million. After paying $10 million for prints and ads and then taking the remaining $30 million to repay the money used to pay the studios for equipment rental, etc., the independent producer is left with nothing except the salary he or she received up front out of that original $30 million. This is why everyone wants his or her money up front. Net profit points are considered worthless because, according to studio accounting, a picture almost never gets into profit. Yet the studio executives keep buying bigger houses anyway.

Some producers continue to search passionately for what the American audience wants in a movie. Some settle for the knowledge of what the American audience is willing to eat. Both types are pretty good at what they do. A few beautiful movies do get made, as well as a good deal of junk that the public seems happy enough to consume. In addition to taking in 95 percent of the domestic box office dollars, the studios, together with the TV networks, are the major players in creating America's third largest export, electronic media entertainment, which in terms of dollar volume ranks just behind weapons and food in U.S. exports.

Many American mothers have tried preparing gourmet meals for their families, only to learn that their families prefer hamburgers, so it shouldn't be surprising that many producers become disillusioned and cynical about putting a lot of care into their product when most of the audience seems to prefer junk food. It is simply not reasonable to expect the studios to have higher aesthetics than their audiences. If your film history professor disagrees, let him go make a movie instead of striking his own kind of poses from behind his little lectern.

The U.S. Audience

In terms of goods and services, Americans consume almost as much as the entire common market and Japan put together, so it should not be surprising that Americans also consume as much motion picture and television entertainment as well. We'll look at film first.

The end users of the products produced by the film industry are the people who buy tickets to see the movies, and it is the end users who determine which movies are hits and which actors become stars. Despite all the demographic studies and the millions of man-hours expended by development types, nobody knows anything for sure. The best the studios can do is to make educated guesses about what the American people want. H. L.

Mencken may have been right when he said that "no one ever went broke overestimating the vulgarity of the American people," but in fairness to ourselves we might add that very few have gotten very rich by overestimating our vulgarity either.

About half the people who go to movies are between the ages of sixteen and twenty-four, and about half of them are on a date. This is the reason that an "R" rating is the most sought-after one when a movie is submitted to the Motion Picture Association of America. Going to a movie provides a nice, neutral activity for people on a date and something friends can do to get together and share an evening.

People over twenty-four also still go to movies, but the numbers drop progressively with age until retirement, when it picks up again somewhat. Despite VCRs and one hundred cable channels and the ever-increasing sizes of TV screens, there probably will always be movie theaters because there is just something about the experience of looking up at that big screen in that darkened theater that takes a person away from the mundane world of his own existence.

If a group of guys go to see a movie, they will probably pick an action picture with car chases and things getting blown up. Their female counterparts will usually choose to see a romantic comedy. When a couple goes to see a movie, the one who is more involved in the relationship will usually acquiesce to what the other wants, as in other aspects of their relationship. These are only generalities, remember, with exceptions, of course, but generalities are important to studios for marketing purposes.

Horror pictures appeal mostly to teenagers. In fact, if you want to make a cheap independent film that actually might make some money, take ten kids out to the woods and chop them up, figuratively speaking, of course.

Period pieces and costume epics don't have much appeal to studios because they cost too much to make. This also tends to be true for science fiction, although both kinds of picture still get made when a big name like George Lucas wants to do one.

The word *drama* is anathema to studio execs because they know that most Americans do not go to the movies to have their minds engaged. If a movie forces people to think, they will often leave the theater as resentful as if someone had forced them to run around the block. Consequently, they will give the picture bad word of mouth. The word *thriller,* however, has been considered a very nice word ever since *Fatal Attraction* became a megahit.

A buddy picture can be either two men or two women in a comedy or an action picture. Guys will go to see two male stars as buddies in an action picture to see which one is the toughest. Gals will go to see two buddies, male or female, in a comedy to watch the interactions of their relationship. *Thelma and Louise* was a chick flick pitched as *Butch Cassidy and the Sundance Kid,* with two women! There are obviously exceptions to these things, and plenty of them. Again, generalizations are only generally true, but corporations make money with them.

There are also art films that get made. These pictures are seen by only a tiny minority of the population. They engage the mind and give the intellectuals that see them something to discuss after the movie. If you go to see one of these films with an intellectual, and afterward he asks you what you thought of the movie, you can always say, "It was such a deeply moving and personal experience for me that I would prefer not to talk about it."

Sometimes an art film will become a commercial success if it wins a couple of prizes and gets some publicity. Regular people may then go to see it, believing they can achieve some sort of status by going, but this doesn't happen very often, and I say so with regret. Personally, I prefer films that engage my mind as well as my emotions, though that does not mean that I automatically like foreign films.

Foreign films often have government financial help given in the name of art, thus permitting the enormous self-indulgence of some foreign filmmakers, who seem to be enamored with myriad camera angles that communicate no new information and symbols that do not advance a story but turn the story into a crossword puzzle. The scene opens and you see A FIELD. Then from another camera angle you see THE FIELD. Then from a third camera angle you see THE FIELD! One more shot of this FIELD and your butt begins to ask why you brought it to this movie.

When a picture has been filmed, edited, and is in the can, the studio will still not release it until such time as marketing studies have shown that it will appeal to moviegoers.

Here's what happens. There are companies, such as the National Research Group (NRG) in Hollywood, that specialize in determining audience reaction to movies before they get released. This gives the studio the chance to fix something before it is too late. NRG hires people (such as unemployed actors) to recruit members of the public who are not connected in any way with the film industry to go to a screening of a picture before it is released. These recruiters go to a supermarket parking lot or to a shopping mall—anyplace where there are lots of people—and ask folks if they'd like two free movie tickets. There is also occasionally a demographic breakdown that has to be adhered to, such as so many young teens, so many sixteen- to twenty-four-year-olds, so many in their thirties, etc. As I've said, no one connected with the film industry is supposed to be invited to these screenings. The studios know that they can get all the expert advice they care to listen to anytime. What they want to know is what the public thinks, because the public is the end user of the product. All corporations behave this way. Before Ford Motor Company puts a new car on the market, they commission a poll through Gallup or Louis Harris to determine what the public's reaction to it will be. They do not question car dealers. (Do you think Plymouth started manufacturing that PT Cruiser without doing some research first?)

On the night of the screening, the recruited viewers arrive at the theater and are questioned again about any affiliation they might have with the movies before being allowed to take their seats. The producer of the movie is usually there with two or three retainers. Typically, he is in his fifties, not very tall, suntanned, silver hair slightly over his collar, and wearing an expensive sport jacket with no tie. He is trying to look relaxed as his beady, Mediterranean eyes dart about, and his retainers, not at all looking like sycophants in their early thirties, try to look happy. When the recruited audience has been seated, the producer and his retainers take the seats in the back row that have been reserved for them. During the movie, the retainers take notes of all the audience's reactions—laughs, groans, gasps, etc.

When the movie ends and the credits begin to roll, an employee of the company doing the screening then hops onto the stage and asks the audience to please keep their seats for two minutes. At the same time employees are passing out questionnaires that ask the people in the audience specific questions about their reactions to certain scenes, about actors' performances, and most especially about the movie's ending. It is said in the trade that a movie is about what happens in the last ten minutes, because no matter how good the rest of the movie has been, if it ends badly it will get bad word of mouth.

To become a hit, word of mouth must take over from expensive advertising as the way a movie gets publicized. *Fatal Attraction* originally ended with Glen Close's character committing suicide like Madame Butterfly and making it look like Michael Douglas's character had killed her. This would have been perfectly consistent with Glen Close's character, but the preview audiences hated that ending. Consequently, the studio reshot the ending so that motherhood triumphed over the other woman, and the audience loved it. Women dragged their husbands and boyfriends to see the picture, possibly to show men that there is no such thing as free sex. *Fatal Attraction* became a huge hit, feminist objections not withstanding. Interestingly, when the movie was released in Japan, the original ending was used, and the Japanese audience liked it just fine.

Studios may be able to influence the public, as any large corporation can, but a studio cannot shove a $40 million product down the public's throat if the public does not want to consume it. The product must be tailored to suit audience tastes. Again, it is not reasonable to expect the studios to have higher aesthetic values than their audiences. Let's look now at how they put a product together.

Screenplay Structure

Film production accepts the tastes of its intended audience, and a good screenplay can accept such limitations and still thrive within them. Almost all studio pictures use the format that follows, and so should any budding writer who wants to write a screenplay. You will see this structure in most movies, and because an actor's job is to advance a story, an actor also should know something about story structure, n'est-ce pas?

Movies are typically two hours long. The human posterior begins to protest like a restless child after two hours, and moviemakers want the audience to leave happy. Exhibitors in one-screen theaters used to prefer movies that were a little shorter than two hours so they could have showings every two hours on the hour and still have time to get people in and out and sell them popcorn, because the concession stand actually accounts for more than half the exhibitor's profits. These days, single-screen movie theaters have mostly gone belly-up and been replaced by multiplex theaters that have continuous showings throughout the day and night, so there is somewhat more flexibility in the length of a movie, but not much. One hundred twenty minutes is still the average. (By the way, many of those old movie theaters are now community theaters that do amateur stage productions, and for this I am very glad.)

In that only a handful of film directors have what is known as final cut, the final decision on the length of a movie is determined by what the studio tells the editor to do. The editors are almost always told to bring the movie in at about two hours. Yes, some movies are longer, but if you don't bring up *Dances with Wolves*, I won't bring up *Heaven's Gate*.

One page of screenplay equals one minute of screen time. This is a phenomenon but one that for some reason continues to be the truth. We may as well accept this as one of God's laws, like gravity for instance, and so screenplays are 120 pages long. That is a screenwriter's limitation number one. If the final movie can neatly be cut to please exhibitors and help sell the movie, it is often cut despite the groans of the stars or the director. The screenwriter's reactions are not even considered.

A screenplay writer, one who works regularly at least, knows that in the first ten pages of a screenplay, three questions must be answered:

1. Who is the protagonist? (This role is played by a movie star.)
2. What kind of world is the protagonist living in?
3. Why should we care? What hooks our interest in this protagonist?

If the writer knows the answers to these questions, the story will be clear. I used a movie called *Working Girl* as an example in the first edition of this book, and even if some of you youngbloods haven't seen that movie, I would advise renting it. It's something of a classic and a pretty good movie too. After looking at the story structure of this movie, we'll look at some other more modern ones, which will show us that the structure has remained the same.

In the opening minutes of *Working Girl* we learn that Melanie Griffith's character works in a fast-paced investment firm dominated by men, many of whom don't take women seriously. A guy named Charlie tells Melanie that he has gotten her a job interview. On route to the interview with her potential new boss (Kevin Spacey in an early role), she learns that her interview will be taking place on the casting couch, so she demands to be let out of the car. She gets out, and as she is crossing the street, a passing car splashes mud on her. She is blond and vulnerable, rather than tough and dark, and the American audience feels sorry for her standing there drenched and humiliated, and they begin to care.

The next scene shows her going to work the next morning, and we learn that she is taking speech classes to better herself. Almost unconsciously, we admire her desire to grow. When she arrives at the office, she puts a new message on the electronic message board, which reads "Charlie is a slimeball with a tiny little dick," and she has won us over completely with her gumption. You bet we care.

Within the next fifteen minutes, the following three elements must be introduced if they have not already been introduced in the first ten minutes:

1. The antagonist.
2. The romantic subplot.
3. The complicating subplot.

In the case of *Working Girl*, the antagonist will turn out to be Sigourney Weaver, Melanie's new boss. The love interest will be Harrison Ford, who obviously likes her immediately. The complicating subplot involves her boyfriend, who will later remind her that she could leave the cutthroat business world and be "just a housewife" while he runs his tugboat business. This will tie into the action later, tempting her to give up her dreams.

I define a story as a narrative account of someone (or some people) trying to solve a problem, another reason why drama is conflict. Twenty-five minutes into the movie the problem is presented to the protagonist, and it must be something important enough to really challenge the protagonist or the story will not be interesting. The protagonist is going to have to rise to the occasion of impending events. He or she will need to be better, smarter, braver than before. Michael Hauge calls this the first inciting incident, and Syd Fields calls it plot point #1. (Their books are listed in the bibliography.) Whatever you choose to call the event, it is rise-to-the-occasion time. In the case of *Working Girl*, this event is Sigourney Weaver's ski accident because it places Melanie in the position of having to run the office while the boss is gone and thus prove herself.

Within five minutes the protagonist must accept the challenge, and his or her goal must be clearly understood by both the characters and the viewers, even if the audience understands the goal only emotionally. In *Working Girl,* accepting this challenge becomes even more serious five minutes after the accident, because Melanie looks at Sigourney's computer and learns that her boss is planning to take all the credit for Melanie's work and also might presumably get rid of her afterward. It thus becomes even more necessary for Melanie to prove herself, and we understand why Melanie must pursue the business deal behind Sigourney's back, and we do not fault her for this. End of Act I.

Act II is sixty minutes long and consists of the protagonist solving a series of problems of ever-increasing difficulty while trying to accomplish his or her goal. These problems can relate to the romance or the subplot as well as to the main goal. Three romance problems, three subplot problems, and six main-goal problems are a safe number to keep the action moving in a romantic comedy. That's an average of one problem every five minutes for the protagonist to solve. Action pictures will have more. A bad guy may get shot every two minutes in an action picture. Guys like that.

On page eighty-five an important event takes place after a whole culmination of other events. It is a new difficulty that must be introduced, which makes the protagonist pause and feel tempted to give up. We must be able to presume this, even if we do not see the protagonist's hesitation. When Sigourney Weaver's character returns to New York, we may presume that Melanie's character pauses before deciding to go through with the deal she has been pursuing behind Sigourney's back. The decision to go on must happen within the next five minutes, and the protagonist and antagonist then become locked in a collision course, resulting in a climax where the protagonist may fail, though he or she will usually succeed. In an action picture this climax is often a ten-minute battle full of special effects, such as in James Bond movies, for example. In a love story the climax might be a long scene where the boy concludes he just can't live without the girl and so makes a commitment. In *Working Girl,* the climax comes when Sigourney's character storms into the important business meeting on crutches and denounces Melanie as a fraud who is only her assistant. It seems as though the protagonist has failed, but remember this working girl's got spunk and doesn't give up easily. Leaving the meeting, she makes a last-ditch attempt to prove to Mr. Corporate Man that she was the one who conceived of the deal and actually put it together. Her voice has the ring of truth. Corporate Man inquires further, the truth is uncovered, and working girl has won after all.

The climax is usually followed by a few minutes of calming resolution, which reassures the audience that things are going to be fine. The movie version of *Working Girl* had a fairly short resolution, which contributed to the impression at the end that Harrison and Melanie were in a bit of a hurry to hop into the sack. The video version had him pack her a lunch before she went to work in her new job, where she learned that she wasn't a secretary anymore, but the boss.

After the resolution, the credits roll. Film buffs and people in the industry usually sit through them.

Let's look at a couple more movies now to show how things haven't changed.

I'm not asking you to watch *Legally Blonde* if you are lucky enough not to have seen it or its sequel, but just to consider the story structure described here. We'll then look at *Legally Blonde II,* followed by *Erin Brockovich.* Like *Working Girl,* all three of these movies are about a woman trying to get ahead in life, and although the society has changed, they still have the same story structure that *Working Girl* had more than a decade earlier. Let's take a look.

Legally Blonde begins with opening credits rolling over some long golden hair being brushed, then we see a coed riding a bicycle across a large university campus. She produces a card that will be for someone special named Elle, which a flock of seemingly air-headed sorority girls giggle and sign. Now that we're all supposed to be curious to learn who this girl is, the card is delivered to Elle, the president of her sorority. This is who the story will be about. It is now five minutes into the movie, and we have met the protagonist and know that the world she is living in is a sorority world at a large university.

The card is one of congratulations because Elle expects a proposal that evening from her boyfriend, Warren Huntington III. Two of the girls then accompany Elle to a dress shop, where she will choose a dress for the big night, and (surprise!) Elle proves in an exchange with the salesperson not to be a dumb blonde at all, but very clever. We are now six minutes into the movie. Although she is popular and smart, we still need a more personal reason to care about her, and the dinner with her boyfriend provides this. He doesn't propose. He dumps her, the cad! Then he lets her out of his car at her sorority house and drives off, not even walking her to the door! It is minute ten and we are supposed to care because we are supposed to feel sorry for her. Many did care. Hey, they made a sequel, right?

Well, Elle decides that to win him back; she must go to Harvard Law School, like Warren, in order to become the kind of woman he wants. She has a 4.0 GPA at her university, CULA, in Fashion Merchandising (!), and she crams for the LSAT entrance exam and scores very high on that as well. Needless to say, because everyone likes her (just can't help it!), she is admitted to Harvard Law School, where she's a fish out of water, of course, and on her first day she is kicked out of class by a tough woman professor for not doing her homework. It is close to minute twenty-five at this point, but neither the antagonist, the romantic subplot, nor the complicating subplot have been introduced. This all happens in the next three minutes, however.

Things need to hurry up a bit in this movie because it's only ninety minutes long. So, sitting on the bench outside, she is comforted by a handsome and sympathetic guy named Emmet, who will later become the guy in the romantic subplot in this movie. The antagonist's name, a professor named Callahan, is mentioned in some advice this nice guy gives her, though we don't know that Callahan is the antagonist yet. We assume it will be Professor Stromberg, the tough woman who kicked her out of class. Ex-boyfriend Warren comes over now, joined by Vivian, his former prep school sweetheart to whom he has become engaged. Elle, in tears, of course decides to get her nails done, and meets Paulette, the manicurist, about whom the complicating subplot will revolve. We are now twenty-four minutes into the movie. Elle pours out her heart to Paulette, they bond, and at Paulette's encouragement Elle makes the commitment to do well at Harvard Law School and show them all! Doing well in order to prove herself will be the main problem that Elle will try to solve in this movie, and this is the end of Act I, right on time.

This is a ninety-minute movie (God be praised), so Acts II and III will be shorter than in a two-hour movie, but nevertheless in Act II the protagonist will still overcome a series of obstacles of ever-increasing difficulty trying to achieve her goal, just like in a two-hour movie. In this movie she will parry insults from her peers with great comebacks that leave them speechless while she continues to smile. She will study hard and prove she can do the work, and she will help Paulette, still her only friend at this point, to get her dog back in the complicating subplot. Emmet will gradually fall in love with her, and even Vivian, Warren's fiancée, will be won over, conveniently getting prettier in the movie as she becomes nicer to Elle. At the end of Act II, Professor Callahan, who Elle thought admired her mind, tries to hit on her, which makes Elle feel like chucking the whole thing and just giving up.

"All anybody will ever see in me is a blonde with big boobs," she says in tears to Paulette in the nail salon.

Then Act III begins. Tough Professor Stromberg happens to be in the salon and hears this. She tells Elle, "If you are going to let one little prick ruin your career, then you're not the girl I thought you were." That word "girl" is apparently okay again these days, at least with the girls who liked this movie enough for a sequel to be made. Anyway, Elle reaffirms commitment to proving herself as a good law student, takes over a trial case from Professor Callahan, and based on her knowledge of hair permanents, she discovers the real guilty party in a Perry Mason kind of moment in court and wins the case! Then she steps out of the sun and makes the commencement address for her graduating class, where she tells everyone that it is important to believe in yourself, and we learn in the credits that everyone will either get what he deserves, like Warren, or will live happily ever after.

"It's a feel-good movie," I heard some girl say. Victor Garber played Professor Callahan, and I doubt he felt good about being in it because he deserves better movies than this. I suppose I have some personal feelings involved because I got my SAG card working with him in a TV miniseries called *Roanoke*, about the Lost Colony, but he also played the naval architect who designed the ship in *Titanic* and did some beautiful work in that movie. Maybe he had a dry spell after *Titanic* and needed the money. Raquel Welch was in *Legally Blonde* also, in a little cameo with about five lines. When I wrote the first edition of this book, she was still a major sex symbol, and I used her as an example of a movie star, imagining her paired with Schwarzenegger. Well, times change.

The sequel, *Legally Blonde II*, opens with Elle's loving friends going through a scrapbook of pictures of her at various stages of her life. There isn't any question as to who this movie is about. Reese Witherspoon, the actress who played Elle, is now a star and got executive producer credit on this movie, so this makes me think that she had her agent take a script to a studio to get the money for a sequel, and the studio decided the sequel would make a profit. Anyway, Elle is now a successful lawyer living in Boston and engaged to Emmet, as we learn at her surprise bridal shower, and the reason we like her, care about her, is that she is not stuck up but is very nice and thoughtful to the people she works with, personally bringing all of them coffee exactly as each one likes it!

Now the problem begins to take shape. She hires a private detective to find the natural mother of her Chihuahua, Bruiser, so Bruiser's mom can attend the wedding. This is very important to Elle. The detective finds out where the mother is, and it turns out the mother is the captive of an evil cosmetic company that does cosmetic testing on animals! And they won't release Bruiser's mom! Elle is certainly not going to take this lying down. Getting married without Bruiser's mom there would be unthinkable, so Elle contacts a congresswoman from Massachusetts, who once was a Delta Nu, Elle's sorority, and of course gets a job in the congresswoman's office. Elle is going to go to Washington to get the law changed in order to free Bruiser's mom and all doggies. This is the end of Act I, and throughout Act II she will struggle to do this. The romantic subplot will be her continuing wedding plans. The complicating subplot is a bit of a surprise. We assume that the antagonist is the young, black, female member of the congresswoman's staff who has contempt for Elle, but their relationship turns out to be the complicating subplot, and the antagonist turns out to be the congresswoman who hired Elle.

Anyway, three-fourths of the way through this ninety-minute movie, Elle is tempted to give up. Why? Because the congresswoman antagonist has arranged with the cosmetic company, who is the congresswoman's biggest financial contributor, to release Bruiser's mother and to give Elle a great job as their attorney. But Elle reaffirms her commitment to get the law changed to forbid cosmetic testing on all doggies in order to save them and enlists the aid of all the Delta Nu sorority sisters throughout the nation to do so. In the climax, Elle makes a resounding dog lover speech that wins over Congress, and Elle wins again. Ahem.

Having spent most of the past three years overseas teaching English through theater at foreign universities, I was happy to see a movie like *Erin Brockovich* when I got back. I like having my mind engaged, yes, but I also like seeing stories that don't trivialize women's efforts to find respect and a place in the sun, so, personally, *Erin Brockovich* is my idea of a feel-good movie.

The film opens with Erin, well played by Julia Roberts, doing her good-hearted best in a job interview. We learn from what she says that she is a single mom taking care of three kids, and when we see her outside on the city street of Los Angeles, not having gotten the job, she has our sympathy. She has a parking ticket on her car, breaks a fingernail opening the door, and then is broadsided by another car going through the intersection. Next we see her in a lawyer's office, orthopedic collar around her neck, and then in the courtroom, where we hear Ms. Julia use some of the foulest language of her career. Perhaps because of it, she loses the case. Back in her home, she takes off the collar and we see that her neck is okay, but there is hardly any food in the cupboard and so she takes the kids to a restaurant, where she orders nothing for herself, claiming that her lawyer took her out for a big lunch and she's stuffed. Cut to her alone in her kitchen, later, eating cold beans out of a can. It is now minute ten, and by this time virtually everyone who saw this movie was on her side.

Between minutes ten and twenty-five, the romantic subplot is introduced, and in this movie it involves a good-natured biker who moves in next door and offers to take care of her kids in the afternoon. The complicating subplot will continue to be her children because she can't spend enough time with them after she becomes engaged in solving the big problem, which is introduced at minute twenty-four. She's now working in the same lawyer's office who lost her case, and he gives her some files to work on. She notices that medical files are mixed up with real estate files involving the entity that will be the antagonist, Pacific Gas and Electric, a huge California corporation. She can't figure out what's going on with the files, so she asks a colleague, who refuses to help her. Determined to do a good job, she takes those files home, gets interested in them, and after five minutes of investigation out in the field, decides to do battle with the antagonist, PG&E. This structure represents a slight variation from the norm in that the antagonist and the problem are introduced at the same time, but it is still not much of a variation.

Some of the things that make this a very good movie, in my opinion, are the obstacles this gutsy little woman manages to overcome on her way to slaying Goliath. They are the kind of obstacles that we all face in our lives and that we often use to excuse ourselves for not being any braver than we usually are. In sequential order they are: taking personal responsibility for doing something about a social injustice, winning the trust of people she is trying to help and sometimes overcoming their hostility, not being accepted by colleagues because she is not their kind, enduring the boss's bad temper, feeling her son's resentment about spending so much time at work, overcoming her boss's worries about engaging a powerful antagonist, missing her children and not being there when her baby daughter speaks her first word, and seeing others profit from the work she has done, without thanks. Any of this seem familiar?

At minute eighty-five, right on schedule, her boyfriend threatens to leave her unless she quits, telling her he has his own needs too. This will also mean that she must find someone else to take care of her kids. She refuses, however, because in the past she has bent herself around a man's needs and is not going to do that anymore. She reaffirms commitment to her goal and takes the kids to work with her. She and PG&E are going to do battle, and only one is going to win.

The climax comes not in a courtroom but rather when a guy she thought was hitting on her gives her some photocopied memos that will seal the case against PG&E, who we learn in the denouement, or slow curtain, has been ordered by the judge to pay more than $300 million in damages. As I said earlier, this is my personal idea of a feel-good movie, and if anyone suspects that I am a liberal Democrat, let me hereby confirm that you are correct.

Let's now recap story structure. In the first ten minutes we learn who the protagonist is, what kind of world he is living in, and are given a reason to care about or be interested in him. Before minute twenty-five (usually) we meet the antagonist, and the romantic and complicating subplots are introduced. At minute twenty-five the problem is revealed, followed by five minutes of clarification about it, and at minute thirty the protagonist commits to solve the problem.

For the next fifty-five minutes, or for about half of the movie, the protagonist overcomes a series of obstacles of ever-increasing difficulty, trying to solve the problem and achieve the goal. Romantic and complicating subplot problems are interspersed. Eighty-five minutes, or three-fourths of the way into the movie, an event causes the protagonist to be tempted to give up, but he reaffirms commitment to the goal and becomes locked in a collision course with the antagonist. The climax usually comes about fifteen minutes later, and then there is a period of denouement during which things settle, and the story fades into the rolling credits.

I hope this section has been useful to would-be screenplay writers, and for them I recommend *The Screenwriters Workbook,* by Syd Fields, and *Story,* by Robert McCee. Watch a few studio movies with this structure in mind, and you will see that almost all of them follow it. If you want to sell a screenplay, you'd better follow it too. I did not put this chapter in only for writers, however. I wrote it hoping that actors will think in terms of story and how the characters they are playing advance the story, the way players on a football team move the ball down the field. That's what they pay you for, actors. A good exercise for you is to watch movies and rather than say to yourselves, "Boy, I would have been great in that movie," to ask yourselves instead, "How would I have helped to move that story along?" Answers to that question can be a big help to actors in auditions.

How Studio Movies Get Made

Deal making in Hollywood is no longer done by movie moguls, nor for the most part are deals even put together in the studios anymore. The major deals are put together over lunch by agents, especially from the big three talent agencies, which are Creative Artists Agency, William Morris, and International Creative Management.

At this point let me warn aspiring actors not to be foolish and think, "Gee, all I have to do is get represented by one of them and I've got it made." Wrong. You've got nothing they need, no matter how wonderful you are, and even if your connection gets one of them to accept you for representation, your headshot and résumé will sit on the bottom of their stacks gathering mold. The reason I am writing about these agencies is to show you how the business works. Getting the right agent for yourself will be covered in the section "Agents" later in this chapter.

These agencies package projects. They take a script by a screenwriter they represent, get stars and a director they represent to agree to do the picture, and then sell the package to a studio, thereby making not only a 10 percent commission off the fees paid to their clients but also a packaging fee for putting together the gross deal, pun fully intended. They perhaps may also get an executive producer credit for one of their executives. So, Michael Ovitz, head of CAA, might have lunch with Michael Eisner, assuming he's still head of Disney, and conclude a $50 million deal in less than an hour, and the first Michael might well return to his office a million dollars richer. (I can't give you exact figures, though, because he just won't return my phone calls.)

We're talking about show business now, so let's take a look at a typical project from conception to packaging, through production, and finally to release in the theaters and the ancillary markets.

The High-Concept Idea

The word *high* in *high concept* does not refer to high aesthetics but rather to high marketability. Advertising in the media is too expensive to be continued indefinitely, and sooner or later word-of-mouth advertising must take over the selling of the picture. That means that an ordinary person must be able to describe what a movie is about to another ordinary person, using a description that must not only be easy to understand but will also have some sizzle to it and some appeal. For example, John Q. Public might say something like, "We saw this great movie that was like a science fiction version of *Jaws* except that Jaws was inside a spaceship." That would be great word of mouth for the movie *Alien,* and the idea for the movie was literally pitched that way.

High-concept ideas are often fish-out-of-water stories like, "What if an African prince went to Harlem to find a wife?" That idea became *Coming to America.* (The courts later determined that Art Buchwald had been the first to submit this idea to Paramount and that Paramount had not paid Art for services rendered when they gave Eddie Murphy story credit for it.)

Here's another one: "What if a kid made a wish to be big, and got his wish, only he was still a kid in a grown-up's body?" That idea became the movie *Big.* Sometimes an ordinary story can become a high-concept idea because of the casting. "What if Arnold Schwarzenegger and Danny DeVito found out they were twins?"

High-concept ideas can be expressed and understood in very few words, both by ordinary people and also by studio development executives, who are themselves somewhat ordinary. Like the public, they have short attention spans. These ordinary qualities put the studio execs in much closer touch with the public's taste than does the erudition of your film history teacher, who is probably a malcontent. Their ordinariness gives them a much better intuitive feel for how the studios should invest their money to get the most bang for the buck.

So one morning a development type arrives at his office at one of the big agencies and finds to his delight that one of his readers, possibly a cute English major right out of college, has read ten screenplays over the weekend and has written coverage on all of them. Coverage entails filling out a form about each screenplay, giving genre, plot outline, recommendations, and a one-sentence summary of what the story is about, which is sometimes called the log-line.

Because the exec has never been crazy about reading, he usually reads the log-lines for scripts his readers have provided him, and if he likes one of them he will read the whole two paragraphs outlining the plot. If he likes the plot, he might actually read the screenplay, but there is no guarantee of that, and actually no necessity for it. A marketable idea, including a prize-winning piece of literature, can always be "fixed" by an established screenwriter for hire. (Would you refuse to bastardize another writer's work if they offered you $50,000 for a few weeks of your time? "All right, all right, $75,000.)

When they buy the movie rights to a story, they buy the right to do as they please with it. Sometimes they just want the idea and couldn't care less about the story. I know of one writer who claims he sold a story idea on a 3x5 note card for $55,000 dollars. The contract he signed, foreswearing all rights in all timewarps on all planets including, but not limited to, the planet Pluto, was more than sixty pages long.

So this morning the exec's nostrils tingle as he reads an idea. He picks up the screenplay and oozes into his boss's office. His boss, who these days may be named Samantha instead of Sammy, asks, "So what have you got for me?" and the exec pitches the idea to her. If Samantha's nostrils tingle, she might say, "Hmmm, this would be good for Tom Cruise," and so she takes the script down the hall to the agent who handles Tom. (In the first edition of this book, I used Arnold Schwarzenegger in this example, but as he is now the governator of California, I chose someone else to describe this moviemaking process. I also used Raquel Welch as Arnold's female counterpart, but she's not young anymore.)

The agent listens to Samantha's pitch, and if he likes the high-concept idea of the story, he will probably read the script, as he needs to imagine Tom Cruise saying the lines in order to decide if the script will keep Tom in the bucks. If the agent thinks the concept will be a winner, Tom is sent the script. Meanwhile, Samantha has had the script copied and is clicking on down another hall to give it to the agent who handles Julia Roberts.

The Bankable Elements

There are many people in the movie business who think they know everything, but as mentioned earlier, no one in this business really knows anything for sure. In speaking about bankable elements, we should remember that anyone's check can bounce. Still, when analyzing the take at the box office, certain patterns seem to emerge.

People generally go to see stars, not stories. Tell a development executive that you have a tragic story about two filthy, homeless people, and he will laugh if he's in a good mood and tell you he's got no time for bullshit if he's in a bad mood. Tell him Meryl Streep and Jack Nicholson want to do the picture, and he will put his hand on your neck and call you "baby." (That picture became *Ironweed*, a good movie but a financial flop in spite of the stars' fine work. Just too depressing.)

A studio will almost never back a picture without stars attached to it, because they know that when John and Mary Public pick up the paper to see what's playing at the movies, they are going to look for the names of the stars printed above the title of the movie and then look at the picture in the ad to decide if they want to see those stars in that situation. Americans often expect stars to act like themselves and not stretch very far out of their personas. They will be amused by an idea like, "What if Arnold Schwarzenegger had to pretend he was a kindergarten teacher?" but they don't want to see him play a shy, lonely hairdresser. His fans would actually become very angry if he did, no matter how good his acting job was. If Arnold made a picture like that, some critic would probably write an article pronouncing him "not hot."

Americans want to see what their favorite stars would do in certain situations. Just the idea of Jack Nicholson playing the Joker in *Batman*, for instance, was enough to make people want to see that movie. Sometimes the idea of what certain stars would do together becomes intriguing. "How about Arnold and Raquel Welch together?" was the example I used in the first edition. Now let's try "How about Tom Cruise and Julia Roberts together?"

Even if a bestseller has been made into a movie, the story still matters less to the public than who is in it. There are no truly bankable elements, but stars are as close as anything comes.

It is said that in Europe the director is a bankable element and is more important than the stars, but with the exception of Steven Spielberg and George Lucas, that is just not so, even in Europe. American movies outdraw European movies in Europe, and Europeans go to see American movie stars, though curiously it is not always the same American stars who draw crowds in other parts of the world. Charles Bronson was extremely popular in the third world, and Mickey Rourke was idolized in Japan. With the growing homogenization of the world, which some refer to as "the cultural imperialism of America," movie tastes are becoming more and more similar, though each country with its own film industry has its own favorite native stars as well.

Along with Spielberg and Lucas, Woody Allen can also be considered a bankable director. This is because he has a following. He makes intelligent movies that appeal to film buffs, intellectuals, and other urbane types. Film buffs all over the world watched Fellini, Bergman, and Woody Allen movies, but these directors still have not come as close to guaranteeing a packed house as movie stars do.

A director's status and reputation do help a project get the green light, however, because it is the director who must tell the story in pictures, and a bad story will get bad word of mouth, no matter what stars are in it.

Because any actor's job, including a star's, is to advance the story without causing distractions, stars who remember to act professionally help the story, and then the story in turn helps them. Not all of them do this, preferring to showcase themselves, and this puts them on the fast track to oblivion.

A director who is good at telling a certain genre of story is regarded as a kind of insurance by the studios. Directors get typecast too, as action-adventure directors, or mystery-thriller directors, or romantic-comedy directors, and studios are reluctant to trust them with $50 million unless they have a proven track record within a genre.

A high-concept idea that has been polished into a good story, plus a couple of stars who want to do the picture, plus a director who is good at telling that kind of a story in pictures, are the so-called bankable elements, and they often come in a package from the same agency.

There is one more professional who is as important as any of those already mentioned—the producer. If the movie gets an Oscar for Best

Picture, he will be the one to accept the award. This is not the executive producer, mind you, who actually executes nothing except helping to put the deal together.

The difference between the roles of these two individuals is important. In order to get an opening credit as executive producer, plus a handsome, up-front fee, all he needs to do is to put stars and a story together, which are the core of any movie deal. It is the producer who accepts the award for Best Picture because he is the one responsible for bringing the picture in, and to do that he has to do a lot more than lunch.

I have heard movie producers referred to as nothing but glorified personnel managers, but not by anyone who has ever tried to produce a movie. Would you call an admiral in the navy a personnel manager? Even though the director is often compared to the captain of a ship, and *Daily Variety* might say that a certain picture is being "helmed" by a certain director, it is the producer, not the director, who decides the course the ship will take, as he is the one accountable to the admiralty back at the studio. The guy at the helm, the director, can be sent to pack his duffle bag pretty much at the producer's pleasure. This must be done correctly to avoid problems with the Directors Guild, but it can still be done if the director becomes unsatisfactory.

Marketing the Film

Because films are actually marketed even before they are produced, we should look now at how films are marketed.

For a studio feature film to recover the costs of production and distribution in movie theaters alone, as films did in the days of the moguls, roughly the equivalent of the entire population of the state of New York would have to pay $8 each to see the movie.

Now, couple those statistics with these: the Motion Picture Association of America gives ratings (G, PG13, R, etc.) to more than six hundred pictures a year. Divide six hundred by fifty-two weekends, and you will understand why most of these pictures, two-thirds actually, will never make it into a movie theater at all, despite the millions of dollars spent to produce them. For all of these pictures to get into the theaters, the theaters would need to book about a dozen new releases each weekend, and there is not a single weekend of the year, including the weekends after Thanksgiving or before Christmas or the first weekend in June, that sees the release of a dozen new pictures. Making a movie is like mining for gold, and most miners fail. Most of the films that get made either sit in the can or go directly into the ancillary markets, which I'll explain in a moment. For a full-length feature film to be financially successful, it usually needs to get at least some kind of domestic theatrical release even if it doesn't make a profit there, and it must later make a profit in the ancillary markets.

Before the studio agrees to back a picture, studio executives must feel that theaters will agree to show it and people will want to see it. Sometimes a market survey is done. In addition to arranging preview screenings, the National Research Group does this kind of thing also, hiring Hollywood flotsam and jetsam to do telephone surveys that ask people if they would like to see a movie with Tom Cruise and Julia Roberts as lovers, for example.

A couple of industry mavericks, Golan and Globus, used to sell pictures in the film markets of Cannes, Milan, and L.A. before shooting a single scene. I've heard a tale that in one instance they contracted Bo Derek to appear in the nude in their next film and then invited buyers into their hotel suites at the film markets. They asked, "How many of you guys would like to see Bo Derek naked?" Many chains booked the film based on Bo's agreement to perform in the buff. Golan and Globus then borrowed the money to make the film on the basis of its presales, and the movie *Bolero* got made.

Roger Corman, another industry maverick, got into the film business by buying a bankrupt lumber company. The warehouses were just fine for sound stages because the lumberyard was in a rural area where there wasn't much noise at the time, and the high ceilings of the warehouses were fine for hanging lights. The warehouses were also full of lumber that Roger used to build sets.

Roger Corman became famous for developing pictures in reverse order. If he liked an idea, he'd have someone design a poster around the idea. The poster wasn't designed to express what was in the movie, because there was no movie yet. The poster was designed and evaluated according to its ability to attract people into the drive-ins, which were his primary market for low budget films at the time. He would then have someone write a story that expressed the poster. He was famous for not reading scripts and at development meetings would ask things like, "This story has plenty of violence—am I right? And plenty of sex?" Roger not only filled a niche in the market. He also gave some pretty famous people their starts: Frances Coppola and Jack Nicholson, for instance.

The studios, which are now owned by conservative parent companies, are naturally more conservative in their marketing approach. A guess is made (and that is all it is despite the market surveys and many meetings) of how many people will go to see the movie in the various parts of the country and what kind of advertising will best bring those people in. A certain number of copies of the movies, called prints, are planned, and ads are planned for TV, radio, and newspapers, while publicists get ready to work on creating as much free advertising as they can with ideas that will generate news stories about the picture and the people in it. Sometimes the marketing people are right in their predictions, and sometimes they are disastrously wrong, but just getting the picture into the theaters can drive all the other markets, and a picture can eventually get into the black through ancillary sales, as we will see.

If the picture does get made, after its domestic theatrical release (which includes Canada), the prints are sent into the foreign markets, sometimes with scenes added or deleted. Six months after the domestic release, the film comes out on video, sometimes with a little added advertising. Scenes may be added or deleted here also. At about this same time it goes into pay-per-view release in hotels and airplanes, and for cable subscribers with pay-per-view receiving capability.

The film is then aired on the pay channels such as HBO, then finally on network TV. When the film gets to network TV, it is chopped down to ninety-six minutes, and twenty-four minutes of commercials are added to round out the two-hour time slot.

Notice that with each succeeding release, a person has to make less effort to see the movie. Paying eight bucks to sit in a dark room with strangers requires the most effort. Stopping off at the video store requires less. In a hotel, a phone call gets the cost added to your bill. HBO requires that you write them a check once a month for many movies. Network TV hopes you will just turn on the set and not touch that dial.

When a picture is in development, sales to each of these markets will be considered, and often presales are possible if the upcoming film has the status of an *event*. Sometimes a film is deemed to have good potential in all markets but is still not made because other projects are deemed to have greater potential. A studio may decide to release only thirty films in an upcoming year, and thirty more films in development may sit on the shelf, die outright, or go into "turn-around," which means someone else buys what has been done so far to try his luck with it.

This kind of thing is called "development hell" and is considered to be even more painful than just declaring bankruptcy after a picture bombs. That's show biz, and so it's actually a wonder that entertainment is as good as it is.

The Green Light

So one morning a development type looked at his cute reader's log-lines and liked one of the ideas. He pitched the idea to Samantha, who clicked down the hall to pitch the idea to a couple of agents who handle a couple of stars. Tom's agent thought that the story was cool and especially liked the part where Tom gets badly hurt but perseveres anyway. This physical affliction would maybe get Tom nominated for Best

> Everybody in this business goes through constant rejection. It's not only an actor's problem. Hollywood is full of directors, producers, and writers who cannot get their projects off the ground. We casting directors have to go and tap dance for our jobs too. You can either get really depressed about rejection and allow it to run your life, or you insist on running your life yourself.
>
> —Gary M. Zuckerbrod, Casting Society of America

Actor. And Julia could be the one who inspires Tom to get up out of that wheelchair. If an extra scene is written in, where she could agree to look physically ugly for just a brief part of the movie and then get pretty again, she might get nominated for Best Actress. (Most of the people who vote for the Academy Awards are from Los Angeles, after all.)

Tom and Julia, to everyone's great joy, like the story and agree to do the picture. The original screenwriter is paid to go away, and he starts drinking too much. Another screenwriter, who has secretly been drinking too much for years, is then paid to turn the story into a better vehicle for the stars involved.

So a superagent and a studio head have lunch, and the studio takes the package. The studio doesn't have to haggle with the stars over salaries because the superagent has already gotten numbers from the stars and presents an "above-the-line" number to the studio head over lunch. The number includes star salaries, script cost, director salaries, packaging fee, etc. Above-the-line personages will usually get an opening credit at the beginning of the film. One of these personages will be the producer, who may be having lunch as well, and his fee will be one of the above-the-line costs.

Below-the-line costs are what it will actually cost to make the movie, including crew salaries, hotels, catering, location rentals, equipment rentals, props, etc. The producer will offset some of these costs with product placement fees charged to companies to use their products in the movie. If Paul Newman drinks a Budweiser in a scene, you can bet that Bud paid handsomely for that. (The makers of M&Ms passed on the chance to have E.T. eat their product and quite regretted it when a competitor took the deal and had their sales go up dramatically because of the success of the movie.) Besides product placement deals, a hotel might agree to provide space for the cast and crew in return for some prominent shots of the hotel in a scene or two. And so on.

Below-the-line costs can be calculated once a shooting schedule is arrived at, and the responsibility for scheduling, budgeting, and keeping the project on schedule and within the budget finally lies with the producer, who is the assembler of all the talents that become the small army that makes a Hollywood movie.

Once the project has the green light, the lawyers are brought in to do their meaningful work, after which the above-the-line costs must usually be paid whether or not the film ever gets into production. The film will become a paper corporation with assets and liabilities. It will continue to exist on paper for as long as there is any money coming in or fees and royalties are going out. This corporation, with all its assets, can of course be bought by another corporation that will take over responsibility for these things.

When the project goes into preproduction, the producer's company, which has usually been hired as a unit as part of the deal, goes into action, and the producer begins hiring the other talents necessary to make the picture. One of the people hired will get an opening credit, but is still not eligible for any Academy Awards, even though he or she can win an Emmy for work in TV. This person is the casting director.

Let us look, actors, at this life-form that will have such an impact on your careers.

Casting Directors

Casting directors neither cast nor direct. They don't even direct the casting. Casting directors direct the auditioning and to my mind should be called "audition directors," but never mind. The work they perform takes a load off the director and allows him to see only a few people for the roles being cast instead of a few hundred.

The casting director rarely has the authority to hire anyone for a role, although sometimes the producer and director will accept the recommendation of the casting director and hire an actor for a small role without ever seeing the actor. This usually happens if the director is busy, and the producer and director both have faith in the casting director's professional judgment. There are some heavyweight casting directors like Mike Fenton and Lyn Stalmaster to whom everyone listens—stars and producers alike—but they are rare.

Casting directors have a lot in common with purchasing agents, such as buyers for department stores. One way to look at what casting directors do for a living is to compare them to someone whom you might pay to go shopping for you. You give them a shopping list, and tell them to visit all the stores and report back to you on where the best buys are. This may be too much work for one person to do, so the shopper-for-hire may hire an assistant to help her. After working on a few projects, the assistant often feels perfectly qualified to open her own business, and often does so as soon as she can steal a gig from her boss. There is a professional association in Hollywood known as the Casting Society of America, and the casting directors who belong to it have been certified as good persons by the other casting directors who belong to it. (You've been seeing quotes from some of them in the sidebars in this book.)

Casting directors rely heavily on the agents they have developed relationships with, just as shoppers usually have favorite stores. They know they will get good, honest, personal service there and have come to trust those stores' products. It's now time for a look at how these "retail stores" do business.

> When you walk into an audition, you have to understand that you're there to help us with our problem. We're the ones in trouble.
> —Barry Moss, Casting Society of America

Agents

There is probably more misunderstanding about agents and what agents do for a living than there is about any other single group of people associated with the film industry. This misunderstanding is especially prevalent among actors, who naively believe that an agent's first loyalty is to them and that it is an agent's job to get them work. Most actors believe that the best way to get work is to get a good agent, who presumably will behave like their door-to-door salesman and be willing to take an actor's phone calls at home when she is having an emotional crisis. Folks, violated expectations caused by false assumptions probably account for more human pain than anything else in life, so let us look at some of these false assumptions in order to head some of these disappointments off at the pass.

Remember that we are *not* talking about agents who work for movie stars. There are less than one hundred movie stars at any given time, and because of their status, movie stars can get all kinds of people to do all kinds of strange things, like taking phone calls at 2:00 a.m. An agent's 10 percent commission on a $1 million fee is $100,000 as recompense, but because for every movie star there are about 1,200 professional union actors who do not get treated as nicely, it behooves us to consider a typical agent's relationship to a typical actor.

First of all, an agent does not really work for actors. An agent works more for her real customers, the hired representatives of producers known as casting directors. An agent works with casting directors to furnish actors to producers as the need arises.

The person who rents the product is called a producer. The person who shops for the product is called a casting director. The product is an actor who can play a character. An agency is a retail store that keeps actors on the shelf until a producer wants to rent one. Actors willing to accept agents as retailers rather than expecting them to be door-to-door salesmen will get along more effectively with their agents because they will understand that a retailer's first loyalty must be to the customer in order to stay in business.

If a certain product—an actor— gets huffy and difficult, the retailer can usually fill the space on the shelf by the end of the morning. If an agent behaved like most actors wanted her to behave, she would be out of business by the end of the month.

Look at it this way. Suppose you went into a store to buy some perfume for your sweet-sixteen-year-old niece, and the store owner tried to talk you into buying talcum powder instead. You don't want talcum powder. You want to buy your niece her first bottle of good perfume and you tell the retailer that, but she continues to argue with you. Finally, she brings out some perfume and instead of letting you consider each one, she tries to hard-sell you a certain brand. You would probably leave that store without buying anything and never go back there again.

Yet, strangely enough, most actors think this is how an agent should behave when representing them. An actor hungers to say, "Look at me! Look at me! Look at me!" and an actor wants his agent to say, "Look at him! Look at him! Look at him!" Sorry, folks, that's not the way it works.

It is quite odd, despite the fact that things don't work that way, that agents and the Screen Actors Guild maintain a kind of legal fiction that they do. Agents will look an actor right in the eye and say, "I'll work very hard for you." This means that the agent believes the actor can be fairly successful at auditions and would be nice to have on the shelf in case a customer asks for that type. Also, the Screen Actors Guild stipulates that an actor may break a contract with an agent if the agent has not gotten her fifteen days of work in any ninety-day period, as if it were the agent rather than auditions who got the actor work!

Here's what an agent really does for an actor. An agent provides an actor space on the shelf in the store so that customers can see the actor while shopping. A customer can call the Screen Actors Guild and find out which agent represents an actor to learn which store to go to in order to rent that particular actor. If asked, the agent will recommend certain "products" to the customer. This will be done privately as a service to the customer. A retailer will tell her products (actors) that she recommends them to customers all the time. This isn't true, but the products are placated and continue to sit on the shelf where the retailer wants them. A customer just might want to buy one, perhaps because a better-selling product is temporarily out of stock, i.e., unavailable due to other commitments.

> The actor has to think of himself as running his own business. If you owned a clothing store you would not just sit there and wait for the phone to ring; you'd wake up every morning and think of ways to advertise and improve sales. The actor has to take charge of his career in the very same way. You have to ask yourself, how many people did you meet today? Did you make a note of your meetings? Do you remember their names? How can you follow up in a positive way.
> —Donna Issacson, casting director

So an agent provides a place for buyers to go to buy an actor's product. HARRY HUNK. NOW AVAILABLE AT SHARK TALENT.

An agent also gets the best price possible for people she represents, because the more she can get for a product, the higher her commission. A union actor cannot make below scale, but if the agent can get double or triple scale for him, her own commission is doubled or tripled.

> The agent gets 10 percent. Are you doing the remaining 90 percent? I know very few actors who can honestly say "Yes."
> —Donna Ekhold, Casting Society of America

Agents are good at negotiating contracts. They are good at looking after the small details that actors might not think of, and agents are good at pushing for more perks in the contract as well as for more money.

Producers and casting directors usually prefer to haggle with agents rather than with actors over contracts in order to avoid hurting the actor's feelings. With an agent, it's straight business, with no egos or sensibilities muddying the waters. Producers and casting directors also have more confidence in a product represented by an agent, just as we all have more confidence in a watch bought in a store rather than off the street.

An agent is ultimately a necessity to a professional actor in order to enhance her credibility as a professional—both to have a place where shoppers can find the actor and to ensure that the actor is given the best possible deal in a contract. But an agent does not really sell the actor nor get the actor work. The actor does that herself.

The Casting Process

In many an actor's daydreams, the casting process goes something like this: the actor, having found an agent who really believes in him, concentrates on the aesthetics of his art while his agent handles the business end of

> Often when actors have agents, they think the agent will do all the work. In fact, what they should actually assume is that they themselves have to do most of the work.
> —Nancy Nayor, Casting Society of America

things. The agent begins beating the bushes for something that is just right for the actor. She learns of a role in a major motion picture that the studio execs have pictured in one way but that the agent knows would be even better if her client were given the part, or so the daydream goes. She calls the casting director and praises her client's talents and qualities and sends over the actor's headshot.

The casting director looks at the headshot and sees those wonderful qualities in the actor's face and looks at his résumé and is extremely impressed with his university and regional theater credits. She calls the agent and asks to see the actor at 10:00 the next morning. The casting director then calls the director and the producer and with breathless excitement implores them to take a look at someone really special. She goes to bed wondering if perhaps she has discovered the next Tom Cruise.

The following morning the actor arrives, delivers his monologues, and knocks everybody out with his passion. They sign him on the spot. He goes out and buys a sports car, then calls up his mother and his drama teacher to tell them the great news.

This kind of ridiculous dream pervades the acting community. So do assumptions like, if it's meant to happen it will, and "it" will fall into your lap if you just believe in yourself. Nothing could be farther from the truth. Let's look at how the casting process actually works.

When a motion picture or a television show begins crewing up, one of the people hired is the casting director. The director may request a particular casting director for the job, or he may tell the producer that he has no preference, and the producer will then pick one. Remember that the lead roles were probably cast even before the director was hired. Most or all of the costarring roles may also be in place as part of a package assembled either by the studio backing the film or by one of the big agencies that brought the project to the studio. The casting director's job at this point will be to present the director and producer with a few qualified possibilities for each of the smaller roles.

The casting director is given a copy of the script and a list of the roles that have already been cast. She goes through the script, and as each character to be cast is introduced into the story, she notes the character's name and description. Screenwriters have learned not to give lengthy descriptions of these characters because such descriptions are very often ignored. Character descriptions are only suggestions that give a "good read" to the script. The casting director duly notes what is in the script and may ask the director or producer for a meeting.

The director or producer may take the meeting or may simply return the phone call. The casting director goes over the description of each of these minor characters and asks for any preferences about casting. Preferences duly noted, the casting director writes up a casting notice describing the roles being cast and either mails it or phones it in to *The Breakdown Services*. If a movie is being cast somewhere other than L.A., the character descriptions are faxed either to a casting director hired to help with the regional casting or sometimes directly to the agents located in that geographical region, as people in these areas probably do not subscribe to this very expensive publication that is largely about the L.A. scene.

Before I go into how *The Breakdown Services* works, I want to give actors what may well be the most important piece of information of their careers. Even though the descriptions of roles being cast may include some adjectives, like friendly or jealous, or may classify the character as a

Actors have to spec-
ify in the submission
that they can be local
hires. Otherwise I
have no way of
knowing. On a film I
just completed, for
example, we hired
some Los Angeles ac-
tors who we couldn't
have hired if they
didn't have family in
New York.
—Robi Reed-Humes,
casting director

"Gabby Hayes type," in nine out of ten descriptions there will be four criteria used to define the
character. Those four criteria are the character's
gender, age, ethnic origin, and occupation. The
reasons for this will be covered later in the section on how to determine type. Keep that in the
back of your mind for now, and I'll explain it
later. Back to the casting process.

The Breakdown Services is a publication
that comes out at 5:00 a.m., five days a week,
and lists who is casting what projects. Some
hungry Hollywood and New York agents actually get up at 5:00 a.m. to see what is being
cast. Most, however, read the "Breaks" in their
offices with their morning coffee at about 9:00
a.m. Often the stars and the film's genre, such as
romantic comedy or thriller, are mentioned with
the title of the project, followed by the descrip-
tion of the roles being cast. Casting notices from bona fide producers are
accepted free by *The Breakdown Services,* which makes its money through
advertising and subscription revenue. Supposedly only bona fide agents and
managers are allowed to subscribe to this costly publication, though groups
of actors have been known to pool their money and have one of their number pose as a manager in order to submit themselves, usually to no avail. If
they were worth submitting, an agent probably would have done so.

The agent looks at the name of the project and the name of the casting
director. If the agent has a good relationship with the casting director, her
pulse quickens. The agent reads the character descriptions and then goes
over to the shelves where the headshots are kept.

Agents have their own systems for organizing actors. All agents separate
males and females, although kids are sometimes stored together rather than
as boys and girls if an agent doesn't do a lot of kid business. Some agents
have separate shelves for different ages or ethnic origins. If the role
described in the Breaks calls for a black male, mid-twenties, to play an
engineer, the agent is going to look among the black males in their twenties
whom she represents and decide which ones look most like engineers. She
is not going to say to herself something like, *Tom is a fine repertory actor
with many credits in regional theater who could easily stretch to do this
role.* If Tom doesn't look like an engineer, she doesn't send his picture out
unless, and this is important, Tom has achieved some status in the film
industry. If Tom has such status, both his agent and the casting director
might pause long enough to consider a small stretch for him. The agent
might send his picture and also telephone the casting director that she is
doing so, and the casting director may or may not be responsive to the idea.

The way actors achieve status in the industry is covered in a later chapter. For probably 95 percent of the actors in Hollywood or anywhere else, however, it is not a realistic hope to be submitted for anything that they do not look right for. Neither a nice personality nor heavy academic theater credits count for as much as your "type" in this kind of an audition situation.

In considering which actors to submit for each role listed in the Breaks, type is initially more important than talent, and what really determines type is the gender, age, ethnic origin, and occupation of the character.

In addition to type, an actor's status in the industry is also important because status is equated with quality—a false assumption perhaps—but that's how the game is played in show biz and in most other businesses as well, like it or not. Something to remember about status is that it is most often the result of survival— of sticking it out—rather than arriving on glorious clouds from heaven.

The agent assembles the headshots she is submitting to a casting director, puts them in an envelope, and goes on to the next casting notice. When she has finished going through the notices, she has a messenger service deliver the envelopes. This is a daily ritual. During the day, the agent may also get phone calls from people she has done business with in the past who want to use her services again, mainly because she did not waste their time by sending over actors who didn't look the part. She may send headshots to these clients or may get the okay just to send over the actors. If the agent has a personal relationship with the casting director and can do business on the phone, she sometimes will tell the casting director that the actor is on a certain page of *Players' Guide*.

> If I put in a request for ten characters in the breakdowns, and each of the one hundred or so agencies sends two submissions in for each role, I end up with over two thousand pictures. What would you do if you were faced with over two thousand pictures for only ten parts and a severe time crunch?
> —Joey Paul, Casting Society of America

By 11:00 a.m. submissions begin to be delivered to the casting director's office, and the office is soon inundated with them. The casting director takes the envelopes from agents with whom she has a good working relationship and gives the rest of the submissions to her assistants. The assistants are usually instructed to pick out any name actors they recognize, as well as actors who look like the types being cast. As there may be hundreds of submissions to go through, there simply is not time to give much consideration to any of them. Imagine someone dealing cards in a poker game, and you will have an idea of how quickly the headshots are looked at, comrades. Don't plan on being discovered for stardom this way.

Actors' headshots are picked out because the actors look the part. Those to be given a second look are put into piles according to roles being cast, after which the casting director continues the culling process until perhaps six actors will be called in to read for each role. The final choices are arranged so that one phone call can be made to each agent, who is told to "Send over Tom, Dick, and Harry tomorrow afternoon at 5:30. Sides (parts of the script) will be ready at the receptionist's desk today at 4:00."

> Create your own back story, so that it is a complete person saying those few lines.
>
> —Alice Cassidy, Casting Society of America

The agent phones each actor requested and may say something like, "Harry, sweetheart, I got you an audition, so pick up the sides at the Big Orange casting office after 4:00 today. I'm counting on you, dear." The actor, with visions of Porsches that dance in his head, goes over and picks up the sides. Sides are a couple of pages of the script containing some (probably all) the lines the actor will be reading the next day. Perhaps when he sees that the part is tiny he tells himself that they are just testing him for bigger and better things later. That night he may spend hours rehearsing all four of the lines he will be saying the next day, and this is fine and professional, but perhaps not for the reasons he imagines.

In L.A., as well as in most regional markets, the actors called in to audition usually show up dressed to suggest the character, though some try to suggest with their Gucci loafers that they are actors worthy of future stardom. In New York they audition a little less dressed up, maybe jeans and a sport jacket for guys. Women can imagine the female equivalent.

> Simply come in, do the scene, and leave quickly when you've finished. If you just do it and leave gracefully, you leave a much better impression. You leave them with the memory of what you just did and not with the awkward feeling of your lingering.
>
> —June Lowry-Johnson, Casting Society of America

The actors are called in one by one to read. The casting director may be alone or with the director or producer. In what is called a preread, where the casting director reads alone with an actor, she may or may not do some real acting herself with the actor. If she calls an actor back to read for the director or producer, she will read the other parts in the scene as neutrally as possible so as not to steal focus. Each actor will be thanked politely after reading, and the next actor will be called in to read.

Often a decision is made immediately after all the actors have been seen once, and the decision may be based on something as superficial as the actor's height or hair color. Competence rather than real talent may be all that is required. Remember that we may be talking about four lines that move the story along a bit. Nevertheless, some real skill will certainly be noticed.

If the part is larger than that, there will usually be callbacks. Two or three of the actors who auditioned for the role will be given another appointment and perhaps a different scene to read. But again the final choice may be based on something like, "He's better-looking than the star. Let's go with the other guy."

When a decision is made, the agent is notified by phone that her client is being booked and that the contract is being sent over. The agent calls the actor and may say something like, "You got the part, and I want you to know that I really fought for you. The producer wanted to go with another actor, but I convinced him you were perfect for this, so don't let me down." Then again, the agent may be more honest and businesslike and just say, "Mary, they're booking you. Good job." Many honest agents do, in fact, exist!

It should be apparent that an actor who tries to look like every type in his headshot looks like no type and gets no auditions. Because the romantic leads have already been cast, actors whose headshots make them look like romantic leads may be completely ignored, while a guy who looks like a plumber in his headshot will be picked out of the shuffle when the script has a plumber in it.

To give you an idea of how many headshots are sent out as submissions for these casting notices, I should mention that there is an entrepreneur in Hollywood that sells actors back their own headshots. He collects discarded headshots from casting offices, sorts them out, and sells them back to the actors for future use. Now there is a guy who discovers actors!

> Actors need to remember that even if they don't get the part, a good audition ripples out. The casting director likes you, the producers remember you. A good reading itself is a nice goal.
> —Janet Hirshenson, Casting Society of America

> There are so many reasons for not getting a role that have absolutely nothing to do with the audition. You might look like the girl who jilted the producer on his prom night.
> —Barry Moss, Casting Society of America

Television

Let's take a look at the business of television. The three major networks—ABC, CBS, and NBC—began full tilt operations after World War II by convincing radio stations to become television stations as well. Radio stations already had much of the needed equipment, such as existing antennae, that could also be used for transmitting television signals. They also had an existing corporate infrastructure that could easily accommodate this new business. A salesman selling radio advertising could call on the same clients to sell TV advertising, for example. The business of both radio and television is to sell airtime to advertisers. What makes that airtime valuable is having a lot of potential buyers tuned in to it. In these days of cable, even though most American households no longer get their TV via broadcasts across the airwaves, we still use the term *airtime*.

Based on a market survey and also perhaps on the educated hunch of a TV executive, a TV network tells a client, called a sponsor, that a certain number of people are expected to watch a given television program at a given time. The sponsor is offered airtime during the program to broadcast its advertising at the rate of so many dollars per thousand people watching. The Nielson Company is in business to calculate how many people actually watch which shows on television, and the contract between a sponsor and a network usually stipulates that the Nielson ratings will be used to decide how much money the sponsor owes the network based on the number of people who actually watched the show. One rating point equals something close to a million people watching. (The numbers change periodically.) If the number of people who actually watched the show was less than what the network estimated, the sponsor gets a partial refund. If more watched than estimated, the amount owed stays the same, hence the networks always overestimate and give back refunds when necessary.

You can see why ratings are important. They directly affect the income of the networks, and now the cable channels as well.

When a feature film is finally shown on television, it has undergone a metamorphosis of sorts. The network rents the right to show the film on TV from whoever owns the film rights and then alters the movie for television. This not only means that the nudity is cut and the cussing erased for the networks and some cable channels but also that a two-hour movie is cut to ninety-six minutes in order to insert twenty-four minutes of commercials into that two-hour time slot. I'm sure you've noticed that the commercial breaks get longer and longer as the movie progresses. This is because the audience becomes more and more hooked into finding out what happens, until finally the merciful

> Auditioning for TV is different from film. TV producers tend to be looking more for performance, more for a result, and if you can't produce it in the room they're less likely to hire you than film producers would be. In episodic television, they shoot eight pages in a day and they're looking for something pretty close to what they're going to get on the set because they don't have time for anything less. In film, there's rehearsal and a little more time. You may get to do twenty takes. You don't ever get to do twenty takes in television.
>
> —Debi Manwiller, Casting Society of America

announcement comes that "there will be no further commercial interruptions," and one watches the last five minutes of the movie in relative peace.

If a movie is produced especially for television, it is written in six acts with five cliff-hangers that wantonly await commercial insertions like a camel in heat.

Episodes for a TV series are written in much the same way, though the material is predictable enough to warrant some other term besides *cliffhangers*. People who watch certain TV shows regularly often also read the funny papers regularly. They seem to like to watch characters they have come to know, and to see what they will do in various situations, hence the name *situation comedy* or *sitcoms*, which are comedies where familiar characters find themselves in different situations. These TV shows usually begin with a teaser of some kind, a small event that reminds the audience of why they like the characters on the show, and then this week's situation is introduced. The situation is never the same in a situation comedy, although the characters and the locale usually don't change. In a family show the situation, or problem, might be something as simple as the goldfish died or Raymond wants to cook barbeque. Sometimes a secondary problem will also be introduced, such as that a kid has a test the next day in a subject she doesn't like, which Raymond will be required to deal with while he tries not to burn the steaks.

In a drama, the problem might be that someone got killed and an innocent person got framed, but the cop who is so cool that he has never been required to wear a uniform somehow knows the accused is innocent and proves it. TV shows end with the problem solved and the audience reassured that they too will survive even though their lives are less interesting than those of the characters they have seen on the tube.

At a seminar I coproduced in Los Angeles once, I listened to a TV producer praise the talents of TV writers. I asked her why it was necessary then, if the writers were so good, for canned laughter to be added to the show. She replied that when she goes to the movies, she likes to laugh with the audience and so do people watching TV at home alone, even if the laughter is fake. Is this true? Perhaps she's right. You make the call.

Know what you're auditioning for. A good hint on that is that on the page, television sitcoms are double spaced, dramas are single spaced. If you're auditioning for a show you've never seen, call your friends and ask if they've seen it.
—Patrick Rush,
Casting Society
of America

On a more positive note, let me say that in my opinion the writing on certain shows such as *West Wing*, *The Sopranos*, and *The Guardian* is excellent, and so is the acting.

Comedy acting for television is about delivering the joke. Dramas are about bringing who you are to the reality of the role.

—Patrick Rush, Casting Society of America

Television commercials finance TV shows and they are tailored to the show's audience. For example, a sitcom about a widower aired on Saturday night, when a lot of widows are sitting at home alone watching TV, and the sponsor of the show, not surprisingly, was a brand of cat food because lots of widows have cats.

Most commercials urge us to spend money we don't really have to buy things we don't really need to impress people we don't really like. (This is America, friends, where at least we know we're free!) Television and television commercials, however, are where most actors make most of their money, and despite my not-too-subtle mockery of the medium, I will say honestly that there have been very few TV jobs or TV commercials that I wasn't delighted to do because of the money involved. I remember one job I had on a TV show where the hero had nothing else to do in life but ride around in a red Mercedes convertible and help good-looking women get out of trouble. I never did understand where the character's money was supposed to come from, but I sure didn't complain about where my money came from when I took the acting job.

Commercials

Even though most TV stations have production as well as broadcast capabilities, sponsors usually hire independent production companies to produce their commercials and then simply rent airtime from the stations to broadcast them. Independent production companies can specialize in the kind of commercial the sponsor wants, whereas TV stations often are not really set up for specialty productions.

Commercials—at least those intended for national release—cost more money to make minute for minute than anything else in show business including feature films. The sound will be perfect, the lighting will be perfect—everything will be perfect except the message, which is usually that the key to human happiness can be found in the use of the sponsor's product. Most actors don't seem to mind the fact that the message is a raft of hype because actors also make more money minute for minute from commercials than from any other medium in this business. A national commercial that shoots in one day and runs for a year pays an actor more money than a year of good Shakespeare on the stage, eight shows a week. The commercial may be the financial supplement that allows the actor the luxury to do stage work at all. There are separate, as well as joint, SAG and AFTRA contracts for commercials, and just as a sponsor pays advertising rates that are dependent upon the number of people who see the ad, so actors are paid residuals largely according to the number of people who will see them in the commercial.

If you go into this business, you probably will be very glad to do television and TV commercials. There are workshops about auditioning and acting in commercials that teach it better than I can, so I won't get into those skills very much here. Think of the commercial as a thirty-second story about someone with a problem, with the hero of the story being the product that solves the problem. Two things to remember are: first, mentally put the name of the product advertised into a radiant cloud when you speak its name, and second, act like you believe that the use of the product will solve one of life's most important problems. You can do that, can't you? You're an actor, right? Hey look, whatever job you have in life, you like some of what you do and you don't like some of what you do, at least this side of paradise.

> For practice doing commercial acting, go to the grocery store and write down the copy from the back of the product labels. They are often worded very similarly to commercials. Go home and practice using the copy from the labels. Get friends to tape you and do your own self criticism.
> —Melissa Martin, casting director

Don't confuse commercials with print work. There is no union that covers work actors do in newspaper and magazine ads, and as a result, individual actors have little power in negotiations with those who produce such ads. I was in a print ad for Cannon copiers with Jack Klugman that was in *Time, Life, U.S. News and World Report, The New Yorker,* and *Scientific American,* and received a total of $385. (I somehow suspect that Klugman got more, though.) It also took me months of bitching to get paid at all. My friends back home who saw the ad thought I had hit the big time. Tell you what folks, when I got that check, all I hit was the bar.

> Commercials are using a much more subtle acting style than they used to.
> —Melissa Martin, casting director

It is often suggested for actors to have a separate headshot for commercials, one that looks like the actor is full of exuberant enthusiasm for everything, and that is probably good advice. Also, they usually don't want facial hair in commercials. As a rule they like a clean-cut, all-American look, as I mentioned in the last chapter. All-American has finally come to include blacks, Hispanics, and Asians, provided the actor looks like he or she shares middle-class American values. This is also true for industrials, or corporates as they are now being called, which will be covered in the next section.

Industrials or Corporates

Corporates are training films. They are made all over the United States and are usually commissioned by corporations to teach something to a specific audience, usually the corporation's employees. Examples are films that teach employees how to operate equipment or teach salesmen how to deal with different sales situations. Various branches of government also commission this kind of film, and because U.S. government training films are still called industrials or corporates, Washington, D.C. is the third largest producer of them after New York and Los Angeles.

Companies have found that it pays to hire professional actors instead of company employees for these films. Using employees as actors produces about the same result as using warehouse clerks to model clothes. "It somehow just don't look right." Industrials are a good source of bread-and-butter work for actors, even though union rates for training films are lower than for features, commercials, or television.

There is also a good deal of nonunion production work done by the independent production companies that make industrials, and they are a good place for actors to get started. Usually the atmosphere is informal and friendly, and sometimes the people who run these companies are as young and inexperienced as the actors they are working with. Video production companies are in most yellow pages. In New York or Los Angeles there are hundreds of independent companies, many of whom keep their own files of pleasant, cooperative actors whom they call directly for work without going through agents or casting directors.

Feature film, television, commercials, and industrials are the parts of show business where most actors earn the most money for their acting. I have tried in this book to look at each from the point of view of what things are like from behind the camera. Actors and those thinking about making acting a career instead of a hobby need to remember this other point of view and see where they, as actors, fit into the larger scheme of things. Actors must also remember that in each of these media, an actor's job remains the same: to advance the story without causing distractions.

The Stage

Here's where you have to do it more for love than for money, but if you can do stage work, the emotional rewards are far greater, and it is where you truly learn the craft of acting. I'll cover stage work again in the next chapter on the unions, but before we look at these unions, let us pause to reflect on what casting directors have to say about theater.

"Theater is where you learn to create a subtext for your character, and it's where you learn how to use your body and voice." (Ronnie Yeskel, Casting Society of America)

"I look at the picture. I look at the eyes and what's going on inside them. Then when I am looking at the résumé, the first thing I look for is its theater credits: where you have worked, what roles you've done, what regional credits you have, who you studied with. *Then* I look at the film and television credits." (Ronnie Yeskel, Casting Society of America)

"It's important for actors to pay their dues in the theater, to try to get some respectable credits under their belts." (Patrick Rush, Casting Society of America)

"I have great appreciation for those actors who juggle three jobs in order to afford to do a play for free." (Kim Orchen)

"The way to stay at peak level is to do theater. When you study the master actors, you find that they all have a solid background in the theater. I am always impressed when I ask an actor about current projects they are doing and they mention not the recent film or television work, but a theater piece." (Reuben Cannon, Casting Society of America)

"In my opinion, theater is the basis for becoming a real actor." (Phyllis Huffman, Casting Society of America)

"I always respond to people who have good training and have done a lot of theater." (Dawn Steinberg, Casting Society of America)

"When I read a résumé, I read from the bottom up so I can start with the theater. I want to know where actors trained and what they did in the theater. If there isn't any theater on a résumé, I lose interest quickly. That's your schooling; it tells me how dedicated an actor is to the job of acting. People say to me, 'Look at all those headshots.' I say, 'Don't worry, we'll weed through and find the actors." (Sally Stiner, Casting Society of America)

"You should always be practicing your craft. Join a theater group or create one of your own." (Sally Stiner, Casting Society of America)

"Generally speaking, actors with theater experience are a big plus for *Star Trek*. The show itself has a classical feel." (Ron Surma)

"If I decided to stop casting and pursue an acting career tomorrow, knowing everything I have learned in the past twenty-five years of casting, I would do as many plays as possible. I would not allow my instrument, my craft, to become dull." (Reuben Cannon, Casting Society of America)

Chapter 3

The State of the Unions

Before describing the three actors' unions, I want to talk about the term *right-to-work*, because there are many misconceptions about what the term means. One such misconception is that unions have no power in right-to-work states. Another is that a union actor can do nonunion work in a right-to-work state. Both these notions are false.

The term *right-to-work* refers to Provision 14(b) of the Taft-Hartley Act. This provision leaves it up to each individual state either to permit or prohibit what are known as *closed-shop contracts* in that state. The big union states such as New York and California permit closed-shop contracts, which stipulate that only union people may work on a certain job, whereas in most states such contracts are not permitted. The latter are the right-to-work states, and the *right* in right-to-work refers to an individual's right to work whether or not he or she wishes to join a union. One effect this law has is that in Los Angeles or New York, for example, if a producer signs a contract with SAG and then hires a non-SAG actor to do a SAG actor's work, he can be fined by the union and will probably have other hassles as well. In Florida, which is a right-to-work state, the producer can hire union or nonunion actors even after signing a union contract, provided the nonunion actors are deemed professionals by the union and given the same benefits as union actors.

Many actors get their union cards this way in right-to-work states. Once an actor joins any of the three unions to be discussed in this chapter, however, he or she may not do nonunion work even in a right-to-work state. *Get that straight now please.* He or she can be kicked out of the union for doing so. Unions have jurisdiction over their membership in all fifty states and U.S. territories, and recently SAG has adopted a policy called Global Rule

One that stipulates that a union actor may not work except under a SAG contract in France or Zimbabwe, etc. (This is SAG's rather crude reaction to all the production leaving for Canada. It also supposedly means that a SAG actor cannot teach a class in the third world and allow it to be videotaped for use by future students, which is patently absurd and which I intend to do something about in the months to come. I'm a Democrat, sure, but I'm not a National Socialist.)

Craig Fincannon of Fincannon and Associates, casting directors located in Wilmington, North Carolina, which is a right-to-work state, puts it very well indeed when he says that film actors in a right-to-work state, even though they have no legal obligation to join the unions, still have an ethical obligation to join because it was the unions that got actors such good professional treatment. You'll see what we mean in the chapters to follow.

There is another widespread misconception that might as well be addressed here and now, although it doesn't directly relate to the right-to-work laws, and that is the misconception that an actor can enroll in some school, declare that he is on "academic leave" from the union, and then do nonunion work.

While it is true that a union actor can act in a nonunion production that is a formal part of his training, he may not act in a nonunion production that is not a part of his training, even though he is enrolled in school. The burden of proof is on the actor to prove any such work is a formal part of his training. If you have any questions about any of this, talk to a union representative. Notice that I said a representative and not a secretary. Would you ask the sheriff's secretary about what's legal?

Actor's Equity Association

AEA, commonly known as Equity, is the oldest of the three actors' unions because the stage is an older medium than film or television. The conditions under which stage actors had been working prior to 1912, when the union was founded, resembled the deplorable working conditions that workers everywhere faced. It wasn't until 1933 that a minimum wage for actors was even established. Equity has jurisdiction only over actors working on the stage, and like the stage, it is not doing extremely well financially. It pains me to say this because I personally believe that the only place an actor can learn the craft of acting is on the stage. Nevertheless, actors do not go on the stage to earn a living. They do it for other, often nobler reasons and make a living in the media of film and TV. An actor who loves the craft, however, hears the call of the boards for as long as that love of the craft is alive. Many dedicated stage actors spend years maintaining a toehold in New York as a means of auditioning for regional theater, living out of suitcases while working in the regions and then returning to New York when the gig is up—although most eventually tire of that kind of life.

To get into Equity you either have to get an Equity contract from a producer who wants to hire you instead of an available Equity actor or you have to come up through the ranks as an Equity Membership Candidate. Producers are allowed to hire a certain number of extras in many Equity productions at nonunion rates. The extras get one point for every week they rehearse or perform in these Equity productions as Equity Membership Candidates, and when they have fifty points they can join Actor's Equity Association for $1000, minus the $100 it cost to become a candidate. They can then work on and off Broadway and at regional theaters across the land, provided someone offers them Equity jobs. Another way to join is to work at least one job under either a SAG or AFTRA contract and be a member in good standing of that union for one year. This reciprocity applies to membership in SAG as well.

No more community theater for stage actors once you join. My advice is to wait until the Equity contract comes to you and then decide if you want to join. Meantime, stay on the boards as much as you can because it's where you truly learn to act.

Some AEA locals permit their members to work virtually for free in certain showcase productions. Some do not. Several years ago, the members of the L.A. local of AEA, most of whom had come out to L.A. to do film and TV, forced the union to allow them to work virtually for free in those dingy little rat-hole theaters located throughout the city. These actors wanted to showcase themselves for agents and casting directors, and from what I saw on those L.A. stages, it seemed that, for the most part, actors who worked in these productions would rather showcase themselves than do good work that cleanly advances the story. This not only makes for pretty poor theater in L.A. but is probably also a waste of time. Stage acting should be done for love—paid or unpaid—to keep the tool sharp and to network with other actors. Besides, even if there should happen to be an agent or casting director in the audience, you always do better work when you check your ego at the door.

> People with stage experience are the ones who are ready for any situation. They are good at improvisation, comfortable working with other actors. I always read the résumé to see if they have studied and whether they have done any work onstage.
> —Cathy Henderson, Casting Society of America

AFTRA

The American Federation of Television and Radio Artists is the youngest of the three actor's unions, television being the newest medium, and some of its members are neither actors nor artists. A weatherman might claim to be an artist, but a newsman had better not—yet both may be members of

AFTRA. AFTRA supposedly has jurisdiction over live broadcasting and recordings put on video- or audiotape, although exceptions to this (that are also within SAG's jurisdiction) are covered in the next chapter. Merger with the Screen Actor's Guild has been discussed for years now between the leadership of the two unions, but not much has come of it so far. In the last election held, merger was defeated largely by SAG actors from L.A. who felt like they were protecting their self-interest in voting against it.

> Do theater because you want to improve your craft, not because you want casting directors to come see you.
> —Brian Chavanne, Casting Society of America

An actor can join AFTRA by paying a membership fee that varies depending on the local—$1,300 in New York or Los Angeles, for instance, and a good deal less in some smaller locals such as Atlanta. Actors who change jurisdictions pay the increase if they work in the new jurisdiction within three years after joining, but not after three years. All new members also pay the first six months, dues of $60.90 and a biannual assessment of $50 currently necessary to keep this union in the black.

AFTRA does not recommend that an actor join the union until the second AFTRA job he or she works. Some other considerations about when to join any of the unions will be covered in the next chapter of this book, "An Actor Prepares." For now let us just say that because most TV and radio work in regional markets is still nonunion, actors working in those markets usually postpone joining until they have a pretty solid résumé.

AFTRA membership can be helpful to someone moving to a new market. Many regional offices are shared with SAG and can provide signatory lists and other useful information to members. Also, if an actor works an AFTRA job and remains a member in good standing for one year, she becomes eligible to join SAG, and SAG is where the money is.

The Screen Actors Guild

This one is your moneymaker in the bigger markets in the U.S.

Expensive TV shows and TV commercials are often shot on film and then transferred to tape or CD, and actors as a rule make more money on expensive projects than on cheaper ones, making SAG actors' earnings the highest in the industry.

SAG benefits are also the best in the industry. In any year that a SAG actor makes $13,000, she gets free medical and life insurance; $26,000 gets dental and other benefits. Any year that she makes at least $15,000 in film is counted as a vested year. Ten vested years will get a SAG actor a retirement pension as well as reduced earnings requirements for health insurance prior to retirement.

The working conditions for SAG actors are also the best in the industry. Film crews fly tourist class to locations. SAG actors fly first class. Extras swelter or freeze outside on the set, while SAG actors relax in their trailers. There are even rules that extras may not eat off the same tables as SAG actors nor ride in the same vehicles with them. Personally I find this to be a rather silly exercise in vanity that upsets my democratic sensibilities. What was that Orwellian phrase? "All animals are equal, but some animals are more equal than others"?

The Screen Actor's Guild is the most powerful union in Hollywood and its president one of Hollywood's most powerful people. It is said that if the electricians go on strike, you can shoot out of town, and if the teamsters go on strike you can shoot out of state, but if SAG goes on strike you are shoot out of luck. SAG can shut down a production anywhere in the U.S. while its representatives make the producer jump through hoops, holding his wallet in one hand and his ulcer in the other. Even in right-to-work states Hollywood producers hire SAG actors whenever possible, both to keep the union happy and because it is usually more cost effective to pay a SAG actor $678 a day (as of this writing) than to work with someone with little or no experience. An actor who needs ten takes to get the line right uses up a lot of crew time, and that winds up costing more than paying a SAG actor. Often low-budget pictures using a nonunion director and a nonunion crew will still sign a SAG contract so they can use SAG actors, even though they are not using any stars. Any picture using stars will have to sign a contract with SAG, as all stars are members of the Screen Actors Guild and prefer to work with experienced, union actors.

SAG's jurisdiction covers all acting work done on film. SAG for a long time also insisted on jurisdiction over industrials because it negotiated industrial contracts before AFTRA existed, and this was true even for training films shot on videotape. Now there are joint contracts. SAG also has video and audio recording contracts, which AFTRA

> A SAG modified film pays about half what a SAG low-budget would pay. The entire budget has to be under $250,000, so they're difficult films to cast. SAG realized that they had too many members who weren't working, so they created new categories to open up work. First it was SAG scale, then SAG low-budget. That classification means that SAG cuts its rates depending on the budget of the film. It allows a lot more actors to get work and a lot more films to be made. Then there's SAG deferred where actors are paid nothing up front, but should the film ever get exhibited for pay, the actors get paid before anyone else. And there's SAG experimental, where there is no pay at all.
> —Donald Paul Pemrick casting director

claimed were raids into its jurisdiction but which AFTRA was powerless to prevent. SAG contracts are negotiated with producers' representatives every three years and then imposed on everyone else.

Speaking a single word such as "hello" turns an extra into an actor, and the speaker must be given a SAG contract if the producer is a signatory. In states such as California that permit closed-shop contracts, a union actor must be hired to say that word. If a producer wants to hire his daughter to say the line, a bonus of $1,000 must be paid to the union. The union calls it a fine. The producer calls it a bribe. Under certain circumstances a producer may hire a nonunion actor without penalty in a closed-shop state. If there is not an available union actor meeting the description of a character in the script, an albino midget, for instance, the producer can hire a nonunion albino midget, and the midget gets to join the guild. In a right-to-work state, there is no penalty legally permitted for hiring a nonunion actor, provided that actor can be called a professional, but such activity is kept to a minimum. The union can charge the producer that penalty for hiring a nonprofessional, and it will be the union that decides on what a professional is. Also, an extra in a closed-shop state may be upgraded and given a line if he or she is established in a previous shot and the director decides the actor needs to say a nonscripted line. Reshooting the whole scene in order to use a union actor might cost the producer $100,000, and SAG concedes this is not reasonable. Once an actor speaks a line in a union picture, he or she may join the guild. The cost is two days' pay plus the first six months' dues, or $1,406. Yup.

As of this writing there is still another way to get into the guild. After SAG took over jurisdiction of extras when the Screen Extras Guild went belly-up in 1989, anyone who worked three days as an extra on a union contract was then eligible to join the guild. There are modifications about to be made on this rule, which will probably be in effect when this book comes out. Here's what the guild has to say:

"The new system will provide two separate routes to guild membership via background work: 1) Union (Covered) or 2) Non-Union (Non-covered) work on SAG Signatory projects. A performer may also be able to achieve points towards membership by participating in other designated activities that raise professional standards and support the basic aims of the guild. Please call our hotline at: 800/807-4188 for questions regarding the changes in Background Actors eligibility rules."

Anyone who has been a member in good standing of another performer's union such as AEA or AFTRA for one year, and has worked at least one union job during that time, is also eligible to join SAG.

This card is your moneymaker, and you can't get an agent in L.A. without it. The time to join will be discussed in chapter four.

Chapter 4

An Actor Prepares

When you go into business, any business, you must clearly identify two things: exactly what it is that you are selling and who might want to buy it. A professional actor sells a service, like a doctor or a professor (notice the *or* at the end of the word, which signifies a professional occupation), and an actor must find someone willing to pay him for that service. This chapter is about deciding what you are going to sell. Let us all remember that no one gets a 100 percent market share. We must each first find our niche somewhere in the marketplace.

Remember that an actor's job is to advance the story without causing distractions. An actor may have the skill to make the words in a role sound wonderful, but if he doesn't *look* believable in the part, that's a distraction, and this includes being too pretty for the part. Acting is a form of communication, and an actor's physical appearance and persona communicate as much information as the way the actor delivers the text. I personally believe that acting skill is more important in stage work than appearance but that the reverse is true for film and TV, and I think most people in the business share my opinion.

> You need to go to a place where you are strong, good, and marketable, a place where you can compete and win. That's where you want to be.
>
> —Jeff Gerrard, casting director

Determining Your Type

Let's look now at what we mean by type. In the past, actors were classified as leading men, leading ladies, ingénues, and character actors. Some people still use these terms, but agents and casting directors rarely do now because the terms are virtually worthless. What does it tell you if someone is described as a leading man? That he's handsome, like Dustin Hoffman? Does a leading lady have to be beautiful, like Meryl Streep? Take a look at casting notices, and you will almost always be able to discern four main criteria for the person to be cast in the role: gender, age, ethnic (which includes cultural) origin, and the character's occupation.

> This is going to sound horrible but, in a way, the more easily typecast you are, the more you'll work. When an Italian mama comes on with her two lines, she needs to be cast so that her look says everything. The more quickly we can assess something, the more castable you are. That's where actors make mistakes. They want to play everything.
> —Fern Orenstein, Casting Society of America

The criteria of sex, age, ethnic origin, and occupation are primary in determining type, precisely because these are the four things most influential in forming any person's character. They affect the way the world treats a person and the way a person responds to life.

Think about this for a moment. Men and women see life differently, whether the causes be from heredity or from environment, and the world treats the genders differently. Moreover, whether you are male or female, you will think differently at forty than you did at twenty, and the world treats you differently. Your ethnic and cultural background gives you certain assumptions about life whether you like it or not, and even though you may have disavowed those assumptions, you have been treated at least in some small degree as a person from that ethnic or cultural group.

These first three factors in a person's character, however, are not as important as the fourth, which is occupation. When you meet someone at a party and begin to have a conversation that makes you think that you would perhaps like to get to know the person better, you usually don't ask his age, or if he is of Italian or Greek origin, though you may have a kind of passive curiosity about those questions. Usually you first ask, "So what do you do?"

In his novel *You Can't Go Home Again,* Thomas Wolfe observed that a person's occupation is by far the most important thing in determining how he views life, more important than nationality or cultural background. A French cop and a German cop, for example, have far more in common than a French cop and a French doctor.

> People are going to hire you for what you, specifically, bring to the role.
> —Darlene Kaplan, Casting Society of America

What you "do" means what you do for a living, and when asked the question, "What do you do?" we answer with "I am a teacher" or whatever one's occupation happens to be. It shouldn't surprise us, then, that characters in movie and TV scripts almost always do certain things for a living. Rarely is a character in a script described as "a passerby." He will be described as a cab driver, or a hot dog vendor, or a cop on the beat. The actor cast in that little role may be male or female, black or white, but he or she will look like he or she does that for a living.

Some handsome actor walking the streets of Studio City, hungry and broke, may curse the industry for not letting him say the cab driver's line in a movie he saw, when he could have said the line just as well as the guy who got the part *(and could have gotten his beautiful mug on the screen and possibly have been discovered, damn it!)*. He didn't get the part because he didn't *look* the part and would have been a distraction to the story rather than advancing it. See?

> There are many actors who come late into the game. I know of a doctor who became an actor after he retired and he books all the time.
> —Andrea Cohen, Casting Society of America

So how do you determine your type? Well, you do a market survey before you put your product on the market, just like Ford or Disney does.

Ford does not survey car salesmen before introducing a new model; they survey potential car buyers, the end users of their product, and they hire Gallup and Harris to do it professionally and crunch the numbers. (This is how Gallup and Harris make most of their money, by the way, not through political polls.) When a studio previews a movie before its release, it doesn't ask the opinions of critics or cinematographers. In fact, those in charge of the preview will not let people connected in any way with the film industry into the screening. The studio gets the opinions of the end users of the product, just like Ford Motor Company does, but in the case of movies the end users of

> Ninety percent is knowing what you can't do. Try to be objective.
> —Patrick Rush, Casting Society of America

the product are the moviegoing audience, those who buy the tickets. These are the same people you should survey to determine your type. For this market survey, do not ask your drama teacher what type you are, or a director at your community theater, or other actors. Ask John Q. Public.

Here's how to do it: in the first edition of this book I advised doing the market survey using one hundred 3x5 note cards, but in this edition I have supplied you with a clever form that you may photocopy and enlarge, and place on a clipboard, thus giving yourself a certain aura of professionalism as you do your survey. You can simply flip pages on your clipboard and fill in the blanks, and I'll explain all of this presently.

First let's take a look at who you will survey. Because about half of the people who go to movies are between the ages of sixteen and twenty-four,

> I recommend that actors figure out what character types they do best—the type they can sell. And you're gonna want to ask as many people as you can for an objective opinion. Market yourself that way.
> —Donna Ekhold,
> Casting Society
> of America

begin with that age group. If you are a student, you might as well get most of your sixteen to twenty-four age group answers on the campus where you go to school. If you do this survey on a campus where you are not a student, you may be asked to leave the campus, and you should do so politely, but you may have filled out a lot of blanks before you are asked to go. Another good place to find this age group is, of course, in the lines of people waiting to see a movie at a shopping mall. When you approach a person, guess his or her age (and gender, which is sometimes necessary these days) so you know which blanks to fill in, then simply smile and say "Excuse me. I'm doing some market research for a project. Would you please guess my age? Your first impression, whatever it is, please."

That's all you have to say. Most people will usually go along with answering one question. After you have filled in the age he or she has guessed, keep smiling and now ask the really important question: "Just looking at my face, what does it look like I might do for a living? Anything that comes to mind is fine." You will find that most people will give you friendly answers. Some may brush you off, but that in itself will be good training for the industry, so learn to take a deep breath, smile, and go on to the next one. Yes, this means a lot of smiling. So does the business. Obviously, when doing this survey you should be dressed as neutrally as possible so that your clothes don't lead the witness. Wear something that either a white-collar worker or a blue-collar worker might wear to the mall. Let your persona ask the questions. If you are a student and people say you look like a student, ask them what it looks like you are majoring in, so you can narrow things down. A student majoring in chemistry might also be able to play a young chemist.

As an example of how your dress can lead the witness, let me tell you a story. Just after finishing my M.F.A. in theater and then working a year doing Shakespeare at the Folger in Washington, I went out to L.A. I got some new headshots done out there wearing a black turtleneck because I wanted to show everyone that I was a serious actor, you see. Well, I did get one job with that headshot. I was cast as a choreographer on an episode of *Divorce Court*. Comrades, that headshot would have been fine if I had decided to concentrate on marketing myself to the dozens of Shakespeare festivals around the country, but the only job I got with it in L.A. was that episode on *Divorce Court*. Eventually I concluded that I needed new headshots. Again, for your survey, dress as neutrally as possible, and later when you get your headshots done, dress to look like what you are selling, as I'll explain presently.

The next group you should survey are those between thirty-one and fifty-five years old. I didn't make this suggestion in the first edition of this book because that age group doesn't go to the movies as much as they did when they were younger. They're usually married by this time and not dating anymore. They've also got kids, and the price and hassle of babysitters are deterrents to moviegoing. By the time their kids don't need baby sitters, these folks are living their own regular lives, and the movies are not about people doing that, so they don't relate, especially when they can watch the same kinds of things in the comfort of their own living rooms. The reason to survey this group is not to see how they would imagine you in film or TV but rather to see how they would imagine you in corporates and commercials. These are the economic movers and shakers. They have enormous buying power, and many commercials are aimed at them. They are also the people who will be watching corporate training films. Most professional actors around the country make far more money in corporates and commercials than they ever do in film or TV. An excellent place to do this part of the survey is among the downtown lunch crowd, between noon and 2:00 p.m. Twenty responses from this age group should be fine, and it will be interesting to compare their perceptions with those of the moviegoing crowd. This second age group will probably be more astute.

Finally, you should also go to a place that has a lot of pedestrian traffic, like a shopping mall or a supermarket, to get a more complete audience cross section. Older folks won't be found very often on school campuses or even in movie lines, but they do watch TV, and a shopping mall or a supermarket parking lot is a good place to find them. The same goes for younger teenagers. If a mall guard hassles you about no solicitation, tell him that you are not soliciting but are doing a research assignment for a class at the university and are almost finished. You might as well smile and ask his opinion of your mug while you've got him there. It might even mollify him. If they run you off from there, go someplace else, perhaps just out to the parking lot. The more completely you do this survey, the clearer picture you will have about how a moviegoing or TV audience sees you, as well as a commercial or corporate audience. Remember, the idea behind this survey is not to limit you but rather to tell you where the door to the acting market opens easiest for you, so that you can get into the professional game. Once people in the industry know you and your work, they will be more open to casting you in a wider range of roles, but that comes later, folks.

Once you have tallied and analyzed your survey, as I'll explain in a moment, you have the information you need. With respect to the other two pillars of type, you can probably decide them yourself. You already know your gender, so presumably you won't have to ask people if you look like a man or a woman. (If you do have to ask that, I regret to say that you are going to have just as hard a time in the business as you already have in life. My suggestion would be to get professional counseling first and then make a strong, brave choice.)

If you really have questions as to how people see you in terms of ethnic origin, save that question for last, because it is more important to get answers to the other two questions. If you want to know how Hispanic or Jewish you look, ask them to guess your ethnic origin after they have guessed your age and occupation. If everyone says you look Jewish, you will probably never get cast as a lumberjack, at least not in a paying job. But there are comparatively few roles that are rigid about a character's ethnic origin these days. It doesn't hurt to know it, but you can probably determine it yourself without asking.

> Wouldn't it be interesting if this role were played by an Asian or an African-American, or maybe by a woman, instead of whatever they might have originally conceived?
>
> —Joy Todd, Casting Society of America

The two basic Caucasian subgroups are Northern European (the Germanic types, including Irish and English) and Mediterranean types, with Jewish and Hispanic falling into the Mediterranean category. Al Pacino can play a Cuban or a Greek, and Andy Garcia can play an Italian without distracting anyone. Either one could be cast as ethnically Jewish if the part required it, whereas Robert Redford would be distracting in a Jewish role. His persona would continually be making a statement that might not have anything to do with the story. Paul Newman, by the way, is Jewish, and in the movie *Exodus* his persona—that is to say, the fact that he didn't look Jewish—was actually used in the story. Peter Lawford's character, a prejudiced British army officer, made the statement that he could always identify a Jew by his looks. As Paul Newman was an active Zionist Jew posing as a British officer himself, the fact that Paul fooled Peter made a statement that fit nicely into the story.

If you are Caucasian and time permits, you may want to ask them to guess your ethnic origin. If you are black or Asian, you probably don't need to ask. The American eye is not sophisticated enough to differentiate between Chinese and Japanese, nor between East or West African. Now that I've mentioned foreign markets, though, you might want to consider them. Hong Kong has a dynamic film industry, mostly kung foolish pictures, but other things get made there too. That audience can tell the difference between Japanese and Chinese, and it matters there.

As we're talking about ethnic origins in casting roles, we should mention that the way the public perceives type was the reason behind the de facto racism that pervaded the entertainment industry until affirmative action began to change things in the 1960s. A black actor would show up at a casting call and be politely told that there were "no colored parts" in the project. He might say that he hadn't come to audition for a "colored part."

"I'd like to read for the school teacher. My father's a school teacher. I can do that role. I've been around teachers my whole life!"

"I'm sorry," the casting person would say. "That's not a colored part."

The reason for this kind of thing was not racial hatred on the part of the producers, who were probably Jewish liberal Democrats for heaven's sake, but rather because it was assumed that a black actor in such a role would distract from the story. Beginning in the sixties, the producers and the unions began to take some action to change things. Negative stereotypes were not quickly eliminated by any means, but small roles that could serve as positive role models for minorities started to be given to minorities. A favorite such role was a character of color who gave some helpful information to the protagonist, perhaps the role of a forensic expert—hmm, let's make him an Asian—who said, "The cause of death was strangling, not drowning." This kind of affirmative action both reflected a changing society and also encouraged the change, thereby bringing American realities a little closer to America's professed ideals, "the way it sposed to be," as an eloquent little black child from Alabama once said. These days, movies and television have come much closer to reflecting our ethnic diversity. Where once Sidney Poitier was the only A-list black movie star, we now have movie stars of every ethnicity all over the movie and TV screens. The reason is economic as much as anything else. Black folks have some bucks to spend these days, and so do Hispanics and Asians, and the movie studios and TV networks are now competing for those box office bucks.

> It's always ultimately who's best for the part, but if you can go with a minority then why not try to make it happen?
> —Patrick Rush, Casting Society of America

But back to the survey. The forms included in this book give you space for answers from:

- fifty people from sixteen to twenty-four years old
- twenty people from thirty-one to fifty-five years old
- ten people from ten to fifteen years old
- ten people from twenty-five to thirty years old
- ten people fifty-six and up.

This author obviously feels that the first two groups are the most important. The more thorough the survey the better, though.

This market survey to determine your type may take as much as ten hours to complete, depending on how many people you choose to question, but if you skimp on this survey, you may do yourself a great deal of harm. You may waste time clinging to your affectations, which is a form of ego that just gets in the way of the work. Take a look at the forms. The way to tally the results is covered next.

16 - 24 Age Group

	FEMALE		MALE	
	Age	Occupation	Age	Occupation
1.	___	_____	___	_____
2.	___	_____	___	_____
3.	___	_____	___	_____
4.	___	_____	___	_____
5.	___	_____	___	_____
6.	___	_____	___	_____
7.	___	_____	___	_____
8.	___	_____	___	_____
9.	___	_____	___	_____
10.	___	_____	___	_____
11.	___	_____	___	_____
12.	___	_____	___	_____
13.	___	_____	___	_____
14.	___	_____	___	_____
15.	___	_____	___	_____
16.	___	_____	___	_____
17.	___	_____	___	_____
18.	___	_____	___	_____
19.	___	_____	___	_____
20.	___	_____	___	_____
21.	___	_____	___	_____
22.	___	_____	___	_____
23.	___	_____	___	_____
24.	___	_____	___	_____
25.	___	_____	___	_____
26.	___	_____	___	_____
27.	___	_____	___	_____
28.	___	_____	___	_____

	FEMALE		MALE	
	Age	Occupation	Age	Occupation
29.	____	_____	____	_____
30.	____	_____	____	_____
31.	____	_____	____	_____
32.	____	_____	____	_____
33.	____	_____	____	_____
34.	____	_____	____	_____
35.	____	_____	____	_____
36.	____	_____	____	_____
37.	____	_____	____	_____
38.	____	_____	____	_____
39.	____	_____	____	_____
40.	____	_____	____	_____
41.	____	_____	____	_____
42.	____	_____	____	_____
43.	____	_____	____	_____
44.	____	_____	____	_____
45.	____	_____	____	_____
46.	____	_____	____	_____
47.	____	_____	____	_____
48.	____	_____	____	_____
49.	____	_____	____	_____
50.	____	_____	____	_____

Mean age _____   Average above _____   Average below_____

White-collar occupations _____   Blue-collar occupations _____

Most guessed occupation _____

Related occupations _____

31 - 55 Age Group

	FEMALE		MALE	
	Age	Occupation	Age	Occupation
1.	____	_____	____	_____
2.	____	_____	____	_____
3.	____	_____	____	_____
4.	____	_____	____	_____
5.	____	_____	____	_____
6.	____	_____	____	_____
7.	____	_____	____	_____
8.	____	_____	____	_____
9.	____	_____	____	_____
10.	____	_____	____	_____
11.	____	_____	____	_____
12.	____	_____	____	_____
13.	____	_____	____	_____
14.	____	_____	____	_____
15.	____	_____	____	_____
16.	____	_____	____	_____
17.	____	_____	____	_____
18.	____	_____	____	_____
19.	____	_____	____	_____
20.	____	_____	____	_____

Mean age _____   Average above _____   Average below_____

White-collar occupations _____   Blue-collar occupations _____

Most guessed occupation _____

Related occupations _____

10 - 15 Age Group

	FEMALE		MALE	
	Age	Occupation	Age	Occupation
1.	____	_____	____	_____
2.	____	_____	____	_____
3.	____	_____	____	_____
4.	____	_____	____	_____
5.	____	_____	____	_____
6.	____	_____	____	_____
7.	____	_____	____	_____
8.	____	_____	____	_____
9.	____	_____	____	_____
10.	____	_____	____	_____

Mean age _____   Average above _____   Average below_____

White-collar occupations _____   Blue-collar occupations _____

Most guessed occupation _____

Related occupations _____

25 - 30 Age Group

	FEMALE		MALE	
	Age	Occupation	Age	Occupation
1.				
2.				
3.				
4.				
5.				
6.				
7.				
8.				
9.				
10.				

Mean age _____ Average above _____ Average below_____

White-collar occupations _____ Blue-collar occupations _____

Most guessed occupation _____

Related occupations _____

Over 56 Age Group

	FEMALE		MALE	
	Age	Occupation	Age	Occupation
1.	____	_____	____	_____
2.	____	_____	____	_____
3.	____	_____	____	_____
4.	____	_____	____	_____
5.	____	_____	____	_____
6.	____	_____	____	_____
7.	____	_____	____	_____
8.	____	_____	____	_____
9.	____	_____	____	_____
10.	____	_____	____	_____

Mean age _____   Average above _____   Average below _____

White-collar occupations _____   Blue-collar occupations _____

Most guessed occupation _____

Related occupations _____

Deciding What to Sell

When your survey is complete, tally the results. Here's how. First, average all the ages that people from each group guessed. This will give you the average or median age that you look to each group, and the average of all these groups will give you the final median age of how you look to Mr. and Mrs. John Q. Public. Then tally the results for those who guessed above the median age for each group, and also for those who guessed below the median age. (Those who guessed exactly the median age should not be included in tallying results from either of these groups.) The average of those who guessed below the median age and those who guessed above the median age will give you your believable age range. There are probably many wonderful roles within that age range. The median age itself tells you how old you should look in your headshot.

> Don't force yourself into things you are not right for. It ruins your credibility.
> —Alice Cassidy, Casting Society of America

Now that you have your age range, go back and look at the occupations guessed and mark either a WC or a BC beside each occupation, which stand for white-collar or blue-collar occupations. The labeling criteria should be whether or not you need a college degree to get the job. Count the number of each, and whichever number is the larger will indicate whether the public sees you as a white-collar or a blue-collar type. Within whichever group is larger, list the number of times each occupation is mentioned. One occupation will probably be guessed more than others, and in addition to the occupation that was guessed the most, there will probably be other similar jobs that also get a number of votes. These other occupations will suggest your line of characters.

For headshot purposes, go with the occupation that was mentioned the most, for that is your strongest suit and that will be the easiest way for you to penetrate the market. When you get your pictures done, dress for your headshot as though you were going to a job interview to try to get that job. You can always ask someone with that occupation what would be most appropriate to wear.

In the first survey I did to determine my type, I came out with a median age of forty and an age range of thirty-seven to forty-five. (I've since aged, of course, but my persona hasn't changed much.) The occupation mentioned the most was a professor, but jobs like psychiatrist, scientist, and architect were also mentioned a lot. My headshot looked like a forty-year-old professor in a tweed coat. My line of characters consisted of educated professionals. This was the product I sold, and still sell, though my age range has gone up. I still wear a beard, and as fashion norms have evolved a bit, I can now also play a CEO—though probably not a banker, as banks still don't like facial hair very much.

Do I feel limited? No, I don't. I feel like I'm saving my energy. General Motors will happily sell a sports car to a single mother with five kids but will not spend any advertising dollars trying to do that, and I will happily play a mechanic if asked, but I'm not going to try to promote myself that way.

If people tell you that you look like a mechanic and you've always wanted to play aristocratic gentlemen of leisure, then you need to do some serious soul-searching. Do you really want to spend the next five years hustling the kind of roles you are likely to get? Don't kid yourself that they are going to pay you to stretch. If you look like a mechanic but have this emotional need to play aristocratic gentlemen of leisure, you might consider either doing some politicking in your community theater or try producing projects yourself—starring yourself, paying for it yourself, and, I hate to say it, probably losing your investment.

> Overnight success is really an illusion. It often comes after ten years of hard work.
> —Kim Orchen, casting director

If, however, you are quite happy to practice your craft playing roles that your market analysis suggests you can get, you are now in a better position to succeed than most actors are, especially if you look like a mechanic or something else not very glamorous. Most actors want to compete for the glamorous roles, and most will fail. By playing nonglamorous roles, you might get into the game, earn a small but well-deserved reputation within the industry, and in a few years be given a role, glamorous or not, that makes you an overnight success after those years of hard work. Or, you might just have a satisfying thirty-year career as a working actor who plays certain kinds of roles and retires with a nest egg and a pension.

> We are always craving eighteen-year-olds who can play younger, or kids who are emancipated and have their high school equivalency.
> —Meliss Skoff, Casting Society of America

Remember that the basic difference between an amateur and a professional is that a professional does it for money. In deciding whether an attitude or a certain kind of behavior is professional or not, ask yourself not "Can I do this?" but rather "Would anyone pay me to do this?"

If your market survey tells you that you look like a certain type, and you have put in enough caring hours to turn your talent into skill and can play the type you look like, you have the ability to get paid to act. You've got something you can sell.

You may be a bit disappointed about the product you have the best chance of marketing. Welcome to the real world. A restaurateur may love his quiche but make his living selling hamburgers. Without his hamburger business he would never sell any quiche at all.

Think of your market survey type this way: if Steven Spielberg called you up and asked you to play a plumber or a waitress in his next movie, would you take the job? If you wouldn't, then the luxury of remaining an amateur is yours.

Chapter 5

Packaging Your Product

I've mentioned headshots a couple of times. A headshot is an 8x10 black-and-white picture, traditionally from the collar-bone up, although this fluctuates. Find out from professionals in the market where you intend to work, specifically agents and casting directors if at all possible, what kind of headshots seem most professional in that particular market—whether bleed-cut, letter box, three-quarter, or whatever happens to be cool at the time. Your headshot will become the package for your product, and as an actor you must never leave home without one.

When you are shopping for a product, you are often able to find it on the shelf because of the box it is in, a box that is specifically designed to tell you what's inside. That's exactly what your headshot should accomplish.

In a store, sometimes you pick up the box and read the printed information in order to reassure yourself of the product's quality. That's what your résumé should accomplish.

Remember to think of a casting director as someone who is paid to go shopping and to think of a talent agent as someone who helps a shopper in her owner-operated retail store. This should help you to make clear decisions about how to package yourself. You are going into business to sell something specific, and your first marketing goal is for your headshot to change hands between the retailer and the buyer so the buyer will look at it with interest.

> Make sure your picture represents what you're selling. If your picture doesn't represent you, you're not gonna get called in for something you could conceivably get, and you'll get called in for things you're not right for and won't get.
> —Donna Ekhold, Casting Society of America

> Remember, your agent is not responsible for packaging you—you're responsible for packaging you.
> —Donna Ekhold, Casting Society of America

Later, once you have succeeded in getting into the market and doing some business, you may be able to diversify and expand your product line, but your headshot and résumé should tell perspective buyers what you can bring to the table right now, with little or no preparation. That is the other half of what availability is about, that not only can you come to work right now but also that you can deliver something specific right now. This is what your packaging should tell them.

Headshots That Sell

Here is an area where most actors commit professional suicide, aided and abetted in this by photographers who think that it is their job to make an actor look as young and as pretty as possible, like a romantic lead who just arrived from heaven. This is precisely the segment of the market where there are the fewest roles, and because of the affectations of so many "actors" who want to get into this business, the segment of the market where there is overwhelmingly the most competition. I can give you no better advice than to try to avoid competing in this part of the market if possible.

Take charge of your own headshot session and make sure the photographer understands that the session is about your career, not his. If the photographer's attitude is not amenable to working this way, hold up one of your fingers in front of his face—you know which one—and leave. Actually, a phone call beforehand can save you both some time. Tell the photographer that you want to sell something very specific with your headshot—the specific type that was determined by your market survey—and that you want the headshot to look so much like you that if you held it next to your face, it would represent you exactly. There is nothing that makes a casting director more angry than discovering that an actor called in for an audition does not look like his headshot, and one of these days photographers will understand this. Find out what the photographer charges for seventy-two shots, a contact sheet, and two different 8x10s. Compare prices in your area, remembering that there is no need to spend a fortune on headshots. A good headshot is one that looks like you.

> It's not important if a picture has a shiny or matte finish, or if it's three-quarter or head-on, as long as it's a true representation of the person walking in that door. It makes us crazy when it's not.
> —Barbara Disek, casting director

You hear a lot of nonsense in this business, like there should be two lovely points of light in each eye or your career is over and blah, blah, blah. Nonsense. Remember the casting process and the poker player dealing cards? Your headshot should look like an honest representation of what you can bring to the table, and that should be an actor who is easy to work with and who is believable as a certain type. No more, no less.

Before you go to your session with the photographer, decide what you are going to wear. A headshot is actually at least a head and shoulders shot, and the collar of the shirt you are wearing in your headshot is going to have an effect on the casting director or the casting director's assistants who will see the picture. Remember me in the black turtleneck as the choreographer? For your own benefit, in order to convince yourself of this, try putting on a couple of contrasting outfits, one in a necktie and the other in a T-shirt for instance. Then take a couple of home photos and compare the two looks. Quite different, aren't they? Let your collar suggest your occupation and get opinions on your choice of collar from people in that occupation before your photo shoot.

Now rehearse for the shoot. Look in the mirror and practice giving good news with your eyes. Your eyes are the most important reflection of what is inside you. Mary Lyn Henry, author of *How to Be a Working Actor,* says to consider the eyes an extended handshake, and that is excellent advice. Remember it both for your headshot and for auditions.

Michael Shurtleff, author of *Audition,* likes to see a bit of mischief in the eyes, which tells him the actor would be fun to work with. My advice is, if you are a doctor type, mentally say something with your eyes like "Your child is going to be just fine. She'll be able to go home tomorrow." If you are a mechanic, you might

> Have a picture that is an actual representation of what you look like today, not three years ago. If I respond to something in your picture, I want that person to walk into my office.
> —Lisa Miller Katz, Casting Society of America

mentally say something like "It was only a loose connection." Look in the mirror and send this information with your eyes. You know your face better than any photographer ever will, and this is another reason to take charge of your shoot. You might even suggest to your photographer to set up a mirror behind the camera so that for the first few shots you can look in the mirror and snap your fingers when you want him to take the shot. This can give the photographer an idea of what you want to accomplish and help him to make professional suggestions of his own. You'll get a lot of good shots this way. When I had my headshot done by David Nations for the back cover of this book, we talked a lot first about what I wanted to accomplish, and then he went to work. I'm not surprised that he works in Los Angeles as well as Orlando.

You do not need to pay a professional makeup artist to do you up before the shoot. Are you going to hire a makeup artist before every audition? Do your own makeup and keep it light. If your wrinkles and lines will show when you are interviewed, they should show in your headshot. Those wrinkles could well be what actually gets you the part. Tell the photographer this so he doesn't take them out with too much shiny light on the face.

A few days after the shoot the photographer will give you a contact sheet, which he makes by putting the negatives on top of an 8x10 sheet of photo paper and exposing it. You will need a good magnifying glass to see the results. They sell a thing called a "loupe" in photography stores for a couple of bucks that is designed for this purpose. Again, get several opinions about which two shots best sell your type—not which ones make you the sexiest—and then order those two from the photographer. Get several opinions again about which of these two photos best sells your type and choose that one to be reproduced. In these digital days the photographer may give you the contact sheet right after the shoot and give you your shots on a disc when you decide on them.

Photographers and actors have different self-interests. He may try to sell you 3x5s at an exorbitant rate instead of a contact sheet. He will probably insist on keeping the negatives and may try to sell you several 8x10s at prices ranging from five to fifteen bucks each or tell you that you haven't a chance of success unless you hire him to shoot an expensive composite for you. Don't buy any of it. Get a good price on seventy-two shots, taken as per your instructions, with a contact sheet and two 8x10s included. Then pick one 8x10 and have it duplicated yourself. You do this by sending the 8x10 to one of the photo duplicating companies listed in the index. Personally, I recommend Photoscan in Orlando, Florida. As of this writing, you get two hundred 8x10s for $69.

As I mentioned earlier, headshot styles change. For a time, professionalism dictated that your headshot be cropped from your collarbone to just over the top of your head and also that it be borderless, or bleed-cut. In other words, it should have no white frame around it. Then in some markets the horizontal "letter box" was in, which makes an actor seem as if he is looking at you through a window. Then three-quarter shots with a wide white frame were in. Whatever style you wind up choosing, your headshot should have your name printed on the front, in letters big enough to be seen from across the room. A white strip along the very bottom with your name printed on it works just fine and is sometimes easier to have done than having your name printed across your shoulder in contrasting letters. Many actors have their union affiliations printed under their names. I am not convinced this is absolutely necessary, but perhaps it does make the actor seem more professional and may save everyone

> You're fine as long as your picture looks like you and is current. This is more important than the style or pose chosen.
>
> —Kim Orchen, casting director

some time in deciding if you should audition for a particular job. (You will definitely put union membership on your résumé.)

Folks, you cannot seriously go into this business without an 8x10 headshot that tells people what you are selling. Until you have headshots, you are an amateur, period. To get started in this business, first do your market survey, then get your headshot taken, and then have one shot duplicated. While you are waiting to get your prints back, put your résumé together.

The Résumé

Your résumé will be stapled to the back of your headshot, one staple on the top and one on the bottom. Your photo describes your product with a picture, and your résumé describes your product with words. A résumé should be factual and businesslike and say that you are capable of delivering a useful product. If you stick to the format recommended by the Casting Society of America, your résumé will seem more professional. I have included a copy of my own résumé at the end of this section for you to refer to. Remember, mine is the résumé of a working stiff, not a movie star. That's why it's relevant to your own career.

> A reasonable résumé is one that doesn't have too many little white lies on it.
> —Mike Fenton, Casting Society of America

Across the top, again in letters big enough to be seen from across the room, put your name. Keep it simple and write it the way you would introduce yourself. Would you introduce yourself to a casting director as Hatcher Thatcher Baxter the third? If you think the casting director would not be greatly impressed by this introduction and you would introduce yourself to her in your usual way as Hatch Baxter, then print that on your résumé. When you sign a contract you can specify that Hatcher Thatcher Baxter III be put in the credits if you want, but you'll probably get over that after a while and reserve that name for your signature. While we are on the subject of names, you should know that you may not be able to use your own name if someone else in the union under whose jurisdiction you will be working is already using that name. A phone call to the appropriate union will tell you if your name is still available.

Under your name, put your union affiliations. This information must go on your résumé whether or not you print such information on your headshot. If you don't list a union it is assumed you are not a member, and it is very rare for an agent to bother sending a nonunion actor to audition for a union job. If you are a union member there is no point in auditioning for nonunion jobs any more.

On the left side of the résumé, underneath your name and union affiliations, put your vital statistics of height, weight, hair color, and eye color. That's all. You don't need to put your age. Your headshot should reveal your age range, and clothes sizes are for modeling composites.

On the right side of the résumé, until you get an agent, put either your phone number or beeper number. There is no need to put your address and some reasons not to, especially if you are a female. You'll be sending out a lot of these photos and résumés, and most of them will wind up in the dumpster. Somebody sleeping in the dumpster one night might find your headshot, fall in love with you, and decide to come over to tell you so!

As soon as you get an agent, the agent will give you a sticker with his or her address and phone number. Paste this over your own phone number on your résumé, make photocopies, and attach these copies to your headshots.

Next, list your acting experience. Some actors stretch the truth, but I think this is a bad idea. The longer you stay in the business, the smaller the business becomes. If you get caught in a lie, your believability suffers, and an actor needs above all to be believable. Some actors have two résumés, one to make stage folks think that the stage is their main interest and another to make film and TV folks think you have only been doing stage work to practice for film. In other words, they have one résumé that lists stage credits first and another résumé that lists either film or TV credits first. If they have more TV credits than film, they list TV first and vice versa. This is easily done on your computer these days. I'm not sure how much this actually matters, really. I list TV, then film, and then stage, even though I've done a lot more stage.

> I often read a résumé from the bottom up—that is, I look for actors with as much stage training as possible.
>
> —Paul Weber, Casting Society of America

For stage credits list the name of the play in the first column, then the name of the character you played, then the name of the theater where the play was done or the name of the director. To have worked at the same theater twice says something good about you.

Film and TV credits list the name of the film or TV show, but not the character's name. The thinking here is that casting directors cannot be expected to have seen everything that has been produced or to remember every character's name. They want to know how big the role was. "Featured" means a day player. A weekly contract usually gets you "costar" status. "Recurring role," "guest star," and "starring role" are the other categories. Do not list extra work at all, not even to fill up all that dreadful space. It only makes you look like a beginner who doesn't know any better.

You never list your commercial credits. You put "Lists and conflicts available upon request." If you put down that you did a Coke commercial, it can prevent you from getting one for Pepsi, even if the Coke commercial is no longer running. (If it is running, or if any commercials you have done are still running, you are not permitted to do any conflicting commercials. To do so will get you fined by the union and sued by the sponsor.)

Industrials are also called corporates or training films and may be listed if they are all you have for the moment. The first column should list the name of the company that commissioned the film, the second the occupation rather than the name of the character you played, and the third column the name of the production company that made the film. Eventually under corporates you will put "Lists upon request," like you do for commercials.

It's a bad idea to list your commercials on your résumé. Just add "Commercials upon request" to your theatrical résumé. Don't let something you did regionally five years ago stand in your way of getting a job today.

—Sheila Manning, casting director

Next you list the training you have had that is relevant to the acting profession. A course in tantric yoga is not relevant, while a B.A. in theater is relevant, though not as relevant as the workshops you take with professionals. The proliferation of theater degrees has watered down their meaning unless the degree is from someplace like Juilliard. The purpose of training is to reassure people in the business that you have at least some idea about what you are doing, and the very fact that you continue to take workshops gives them confidence in you.

Next you list any special skills you have. Do not list things like "Good with children and animals." List all sports you look good at while you're playing them, as well as any kind of mechanical equipment you can operate. These things can get you a lot of work in commercials and training films. If you list a skill, make sure it is something you can do well, right now, not something you think you'd like to learn. Learn how to do them on your own time and then list them.

Remember that your résumé is a professional declaration of your abilities. If you are not a fly-by-night scam operation, if you plan to be in business for years, it is easier and much more practical to be honest every step of the way. Growth takes time. Eventually all that empty space on your résumé will be covered with your real achievements. If you don't have much to put on the résumé yet, say so honestly in a short biography of yourself and let the bio suggest your type and professional attitude. Remember that everyone you have ever heard of has had a blank résumé at one time.

ANDREW REILLY
SAG, AFTRA, AEA

Height: 5'8"
Weight: 180
Eyes: Brown
Hair: Silver Brown

Email: anreilly@yahoo.com
Cell phone: 555-555-5555

ACTING

TELEVISION

Pointman	Guest Star	Warner Bros.
Divorce Court	Starring	Blair Entertainment
Moonlighting	Costar	ABC
Roanoak	Guest Star	PBS miniseries
A Special Friendship	Featured	CBS M.O.W.
Crime to Court	Recurring	SCETV

FILM

Three Men and a Little Lady	Featured	Touchstone; Dir E. Ardolino
Chances Are	Featured	Tri Star: Dir E. Ardolino
Why Me?	Featured	Trans World Entertainment
Likewise	Featured	Warner Bros.
From the Hip	Featured	De Laurentiis Ent. Group

STAGE (Partial List)

Richard III	Norfolk	The Globe (L.A.)
Second in the Realm	Innocent III	National Archives
Chekhov in Yalta	Chekhov	Washington Stage Guild
The Winter's Tale	Antigonus	The Folger
Romeo and Juliet	Montague	The Folger
Skin of Our Teeth	Antrobus	Southern Arena Theater
Medea	Creon	Southern Arena Theater
Inspector General	Mayor	Southern Arena Theater
Caucasian Chalk Circle	Azdak	U.S.C.
King Lear	Cornwall	U.S.C.
Midsummer Night's Dream	Theseus	U.S.C.
Henry IV	Worster	U.S.C.
Tribute	Scottie	Riyadh Players
Three Sisters	Vershinan	Workshop Theater
Anastasia	Bounin	Town Theater
Julius Caesar	Julius Caesar	Town Theater, etc.

Corporates / Commercials / Voiceovers (Lists upon request)

TRAINING

Fellowship to Folger Conservatory
Acting: Michael Kahn, Director, Juilliard Acting Program
Voice: Liz Smith, Juilliard Vocal Coach
Movement and Dance: Francine Tacker, A.C.T.
Master of Fine Arts in Acting, University of South Carolina 1987
Teaching Fellowship, Florida State, Ph.D. coursework complete 1993
Jose Quintero Directing Workshop, Spring 1992
Rotary International Fellowship, Sorbonne Nouvelle, Paris 1992–1993
Michael Shurtleff Acting Workshop, Miami, February 1995

SPECIAL SKILLS

Fluent French; conversant German, Italian, Spanish. Many accents,
narration, horseback riding, ballroom dancing, fencing

Promotional Materials

Promotional materials are advertisements for yourself. If you believe that your small acting business doesn't need to advertise, that if "it" is meant to happen for you then "it" will, your business is almost certainly going to fail. Instead, take charge of what happens for you by taking charge of your own career.

Again, most actors would rather hold on to their affectations even if to do so means not working, and many of you will read the above paragraph, feel vaguely troubled by it for a while, and then ignore it. Your business will go under, probably within three years, while those of you who pay heed will struggle and stay afloat. The choice is yours.

Advertising has one purpose, and one purpose only, and that is to increase sales. When you advertise, you want to get the most bang for the buck. There is no point in spending money to advertise your product to people who will never buy it. Thus an ad in your hometown paper is largely a waste of money, whereas an ad in one of the trade papers is more focused and a better investment. Still, I don't recommend spending money on those ads either. It is not cost effective and actually seems a bit tacky. Perhaps some actors have gotten work by printing their mugs in *Variety,* but I have never met one. Up-and-coming stars sometimes have their pictures in there, and if you get to be one of those, then consult with your agent or manager about what the best course of action is. For the beginning actor there is no substitute for legwork and direct-mail advertising. In spite of the fact that casting directors are bombarded with them, postcards with your picture give you the most bang for the buck. The same places that duplicate headshots, like Photoscan in Orlando, will also print postcards for you, usually in lots of a thousand.

Casting directors are divided in their opinions as to the usefulness of postcards. Some say they ignore them, but most appreciate them. The bottom line is that they never hurt and they

> Get in the trenches and create the opportunity to be seen. Your career is about creating your own chances rather than waiting for them.
> —Mark Teschner, Casting Society of America

> Some actors mail a postcard with their picture on it and ask you to respond by checking one of the options they have printed on it:
> 1. Would you like to see me for an interview?
> 2. Would you like to see a tape of my work?
> 3. Would you like me to check back in two or three months?
> The casting director then mails the stamped, self addressed card with the option that suits them. I think this is a very good business approach.
> —Victoria Burrows, casting director

> Actors should definitely send cards to casting directors to remind them what they're up to. Often we may forget actors whose work we admire and who may be just perfect for a role we are casting.
> —Natalie Hart, Casting Society of America

can often help. I advise using them, definitely in local markets, and also in the big time. A postcard once a month to anyone who can give you a job will eventually pay off simply because of the percentages, and postcards will cost less than a third as much postage as mailing out headshots all the time.

You can also use postcards in other ways. You can use them as oversized business cards, as a kind of personalized stationary for thank-you notes after auditions, or as personal notes for use with a flyer about a play you are in or with a photocopied review of your work in that play. While it is true that some casting directors throw postcards away without reading them, most cards will get seen and read. How many people you know can resist unopened mail? Well, casting directors are people too.

Composites are used mainly for print work, and they can help you get that kind of work if you mail them to ad agencies. You don't necessarily model clothes in this kind of work. Sometimes you just hold a product and smile. Sometimes you are a character doing something. A composite usually consists of three or four pictures of you in various outfits doing various things: working, playing with a kid or a dog, being at leisure, or using a product. I'd suggest four—business, family, leisure, and repairing something.

For an actor, remember that a composite is not a substitute for a headshot; it is a supplement to a headshot. Although composites are used primarily in getting you print work, they sometimes can also be useful in getting you auditions for commercials. Rather than spending what will turn out to be a lot of money to hire a photographer to shoot the composite, I recommend getting together with some other actors with a couple of cameras and several rolls of color film. Take lots of shots of yourself, perhaps over a few sessions, and then pick out four shots of you in action. If you shoot one thirty-six-print roll of film for each situation, you will get at least one good one that you really like. Get 8x10s made of these shots and send them to the same photo shop where you got your headshot duplicated. A composite with four equal-sized photos on it can be cut into four postcards, turning five hundred composites into two thousand cards with four different poses for some variety. The shots can be of yourself exhibiting the kind of special skills listed on your résumé or imitations of print ads you see in the newspaper. You can also scan them yourself and then create your own composite on your computer, then pay to have them printed a few at a time at someplace like Kinko's or print them yourself if you've got a good printer.

To get voice-over work, you use audio cassettes pretty much the same way an actor uses headshots. You can have a tape made at a recording studio, and usually they can keep the master tape for you and duplicate cassettes at a reasonable rate upon request. Call a few studios and compare prices for the recording session and for duplication costs. Pick the cheapest. The quality is not going to vary that much for your purposes. Before you record, practice at home, perhaps on your boom box. Find a bit of straight narration that you can read with a bit of color and texture in your voice, as well as a public-service announcement. Then find a couple of magazine ads and read them as though you were doing them as a radio commercial. One thing to remember when you are recording is always to keep a clear image in your mind of what you are talking about.

Your choice of material should depend on your vocal quality, and sometimes a good indication of what that vocal quality is will be found in the results of your market survey. After all, you talked to all those people who collectively determined your type. If they thought you were a doctor, find some doctor ads. You can go to your library and find magazines that appeal to doctors, businessmen, housewives, etc. and then photocopy the ads you want to practice with. (Don't tear the ads out of the magazines. That is inconsiderate of others and unnecessary bad karma.) As you get work, make sure to get copies from the studio of what you have recorded. This is not a big deal for a recording studio, and they are usually happy to oblige after you have done a good job for them. Their final product will not only have better audio quality than your home-recorded stuff, it may also have music or other enhancements in the background.

> You don't want to include a picture of yourself on your voice-over demo because you don't want perceptions about your appearance to influence the response to your voice. It doesn't matter what your age is or what you look like.
>
> —Terry Berland, casting director

Eventually you will want to make a video demo reel of your acting work on VHS or DVD. (Eventually it will all be DVD.) Don't waste money having a demo reel shot. It will cost too much and will just look hokey. Instead, put one together from work you actually do. Each time you get a job, speak to the director as soon as you meet him and ask who you should see about getting a copy of your film or video takes. The director will give you someone's name, mainly because he doesn't want to be bothered with such things. Once you have the name, find that person and tell him honestly that the director said to see him about getting a copy of your takes. Ask him what you can do to make things most convenient for everyone. Should you call the lab yourself and arrange to pay them directly? Do not take "no" for an answer about getting copies of your work. Bug them without being rude. These technicians won't want to be bothered with you, but they don't hire

> Get me tape. I'm not saying I'm going to be able to look at it the second I get it, but I do look at everything. I don't like those amateur scenes or monologues on tape. They look stagy and they're usually not done very well.
> —Valerie McCaffrey, Casting Society of America

actors. If they are bugged, that is too bad. It is your career and you will eventually need tape on yourself, especially in L.A.

When you have some film and tape on yourself, have it transferred onto a 3/4-inch videotape and then make copies on 1/2-inch VHS tapes. Stuff copied directly on DVD doesn't lose quality with subsequent copying the way tape does. A five- or six-minute demo will be sufficient to interest those who will be interested at all. Shop and compare prices from production studios if you're going to have them do this. Perhaps a friend has a DVD burner, and you can do it yourself. I would not have advised this in the past, but technology has changed things. When you've got a demo, give copies to your agent and carry one around with you along with your headshots. You just might have a chance to use them.

When getting started in the business, the promotional materials you will need, in order of importance, are 8x10 black-and-white headshots with résumés attached to the back, postcards with your picture, and then perhaps composites, voice cassettes, and VHS cassettes or their equivalent on DVD. As soon as you get your headshots, you will also need an office to work from.

Setting Up a Place of Business

> I look at every piece of mail that comes my way. I'll also watch all the tapes that are sent to me. If you're interesting and I don't have a role for you in the project I am currently casting, I'll hang on to the photo and remember it for a later project.
> —Debra Zane, Casting Society of America

What do you think of someone who does business out of the backseat of his car? Do you trust him? Think he'll stay in business?

You *need* an office to do any kind of business. Even novelists find that they work better when they go to a room that is reserved only for work. As an actor, the marketing part of your work, which is to say the great majority of your work, will be clearer and more efficient if you do it in a room reserved for business. As you will not be receiving clients in your office but will be operating a mail-order and outside sales business that takes orders over the phone and then calls on clients, you don't need anything fancy. The room you use for an office should be as pleasant a place as possible for you to do your work, and you need a room where you can close the door. You also need your own desk and your own phone with an answering machine or voicemail that you can check from an outside phone. A cell phone of course is best these days. Your office can be your bedroom, provided you do not share it. Your mate's dirty socks sitting on top of your headshots will affect both your relationship and your career. It is possible for two people to share an office if they both have their own desks and both treat the room as a place of business. But if you do that, or if you absolutely need to use the bedroom shared with your mate, I would suggest that you partition the room. Good fences make good neighbors.

You can't share a telephone that is used for business. Your partner will screw up your messages and this will ruin your relationship, and perhaps your career. What happens when you both need to make several phone calls at the same time? You will pay more for the installation of your own phone, true, but think of it as a necessary setup expense and be done with it. Local service after that is not so expensive that it needs dividing, and you will avoid hassles about who is responsible for which long-distance calls that have been made. In spite of what I have recommended about sharing a phone, you may have to be convinced the hard way. I had to. You also need call waiting. If you don't like getting interrupted, get over it. Call waiting is now such a part of this business that anybody calling you for a job who gets a busy signal might actually think your phone is out of order and just call the next person on the list. The idea that if they really want you they'll keep trying to call is an affectation, the kind that kills careers. Your own separate line for fax or email is also a good idea, especially if you spend a lot of time on the net. That fax machine will save you driving somewhere to pick up sides, as your agent can fax them to you.

You need your own desk where you can spread your paperwork around and come back later to find it in the same arrangement as you left it. You should not have to rearrange another person's things and vice versa. You just cannot share a desk (especially with your lover). You also need a readily accessible filing system. I recommend those hanging files in some sort of an arrangement where you can reach across your desk and get a file while you are talking on the phone. Important documents can be kept in a dust-free box if you like. Or you can just keep electronic files on your computer, provided you use them. You will see the importance of files in the next chapter. I would also put a map of the city (or cities) where you work on the wall next to your desk so that you can get directions on the phone and see exactly where and what the person is talking about. Also, looking at the map while you are thinking, instead of out the window where you are likely to daydream, will probably help keep you focused. Little pins stuck in the map at places where they do a lot of casting can help with this.

You should get a good stapler for attaching résumés to headshots and a small paper cutter for trimming the résumés to fit. This is your job, not your agent's. A little porcelain wheel-in-a-well from a business supply store will save you eating a lot of envelope glue. Envelopes, large and small, as well as headshots and résumés will hang quite nicely in their own file folders. Your mailings should move across your desk like an assembly line production, even if you have popped a beer at the end of the day.

Your small business will also need a reliable delivery vehicle. Because the product being hauled around for lots of inspection and occasional sale is a human—you—the vehicle can be any one of a number of standard models, provided it runs well and has good tires and seat belts.

In big cities like New York and Chicago, the public transportation system plus occasional taxis (and a good-natured attitude on your part) is sufficient. In most other places you need a car. Because almost no one who will be considering you for a job will ever see your car, it need not be pretty. The bottom line is that it gets you there on time. It needs to be safe enough to protect the cargo (almost all have seat belts these days) and reliable enough to start on a cold morning and keep going to your place of work and then home again. If you need an expensive car to feel good about yourself, then you are perhaps an actor who will soon leave this business, as your self-esteem will undoubtedly be affected by even more challenging things in the months to come.

In the first edition of this book I recommend getting a personal computer for keeping track of contacts, doing mailings, and updating your résumé. Now I cannot imagine living without a computer for those very things, as well as for others, such as that awesome Internet. You can create your own web page and print the web address on your business card and résumé, and you can access up-to-date information when you need it. Probably I am speaking now to my more mature colleagues, who sometimes still resist that "devil box," rather than to you youngbloods who are already computer literate and can see the future for what it will be.

Internet marketing has become a fact of life, and new marketing techniques bring new scams with them. I'll warn you about the scams first and then describe an Internet marketing technique that has real value.

These days an actor is bound to see offers of exposure on the Internet to "millions of producers, agents, and casting directors worldwide! And for only a few hundred dollars!" Folks, what good does having your picture on an Internet website do you if no one goes there to look at you? This kind of thing works only if you have someone actively working for you once your picture and résumé are on the web, and most of these scams don't do that.

An example of a good site, well worth the very reasonable expense to an actor, is one I'm on, called 24/7, 247cast.com. Heather Heinz, creator of that site, began as an actor, progressed to casting assistant, and is currently a casting director. In addition to traditional castings, she offers clients the ability to view her array of talent on the Internet at the 24/7 website. That way producers, corporations, and directors may still choose to do a cattle call casting or they can do it directly from the website, which saves time and money for both the actors and our clients. The important thing here is that she is still an active casting director, not just someone who created a site. The setup fee for actors listing on the site just covers the expense of setup. For the $60 setup fee, and then $20 a month, you get your own website with your photos, résumé, and a demo tape of your work on it and are cross-referenced on her site by casting criteria such as gender and age. You also get business cards with your website address listed to use in your own marketing. This is the kind of deal you want, so compare this with any other you are tempted to list with.

Your Other Job

"So, what do you do?"

"I'm an actor."

"Oh, really? What restaurant?"

You should figure that it is going to take five years for your acting business to become established enough and profitable enough to support you without you needing an auxiliary income source. Waiting tables, tending bar, and driving a cab are three of the most common other jobs that actors do. They all pay decently, and you can do them at night, leaving your days free to make rounds and audition. There is another school of thought, however, that recommends getting a daytime job when you first go to New York or Los Angeles. The rationale is that you will have an easier time renting an apartment if they don't know that you are an actor, and because it will be months before you get any auditions anyway, you will want to have your nights free to take workshops and do showcase theater productions. This will allow you to network with other actors and possibly to get seen by agents and casting directors. I agree with this thinking with respect to New York and L.A. and will make further suggestions in the chapters on working those markets.

Whatever other job you choose, it must be something that will pay your bills without killing your spirit and that will eventually allow you some flexibility to audition. Weekend work is ideal for actors. I believe that you are well advised to pay as much attention to choosing and preparing for your other job as you do preparing for your acting business, as your morale will depend on it over time.

Here are some thoughts on possible other jobs besides the three mentioned above:

- Manage and maintain apartments.
- Any kind of outside sales where you call on customers, such as real estate or insurance sales.
- Temporary secretary.
- Photocopy stores like Kinko's with day and night shifts.
- Substitute teaching.
- Teaching anything you like to do, such as aerobics.

- Arts and crafts done at home.

Another job that has a lot to be said for it is to work as an extra. In New York and other northeastern cities actors have been doing it for years. Until recently, however, extra work was considered a bad professional move for actors working in Los Angeles. It was thought that if you got known as an extra, you would never work again as an actor. After SAG took over jurisdiction of extras, that has changed somewhat, although if you do extra work in L.A., I would still advise you to stay away from the camera as much as possible. Just take the money, which won't be much but which will carry other benefits with it. If you work as a union extra, you might make enough to get your medical and dental insurance paid for by the union and perhaps make enough to get credit for a vested year at the end of the year, ten of which get you a pension at age sixty-five.

Most of an extra's day consists of sitting around (provided you have brought your own folding chair, otherwise it will be standing around). You can do a lot of your paperwork while you are waiting for that crowd scene to shoot. Try to use the time productively instead of playing cards. You might be able to send a postcard to every casting director in L.A. by doing three days of extra work. However, don't write to them that you are busy doing extra work. Something you'll notice on an L.A. set: the ones who talk the most have usually worked the least. In the Northeast the situation is somewhat different. A day's extra work is often like old home week for stage actors in the area, and you can learn a lot there.

A final word on your other job: don't expect to get discovered working in the studio gift shop or any other place like it. You will need instead to get noticed while you are actually acting, and you will need to get noticed more than once before you really begin to have a career. Don't hope for a big break. Work for a series of small ones.

Chapter 6

The Actor As a Small Business

Finding Buyers

For the moment I am going to assume that you do not live in either New York or Los Angeles. Perhaps you live in one of the regional markets that will be covered in later chapters.

If you want to do theater in your neck of the woods, write to Theater Directories in Dorset, Vermont, for their *Summer Theater Directory* and/or their *Regional Theater Directory*. The addresses are in the bibliography. Also, check out the lists of Equity theaters at the back of this book. Perhaps there is a theater near you that will give you a job. Call them and find out their procedures for auditioning. Another thing you can do is to look in your phone book for theaters and do a search on the Internet for area theaters. You'll find many such websites in the chapters on regional markets.

Perhaps you would also like to audition at one of the theater conferences that recruit performers, such as the Southeast Theater Conference. As I've said, I recommend doing theater because the stage is where you learn to act and where you keep your tool sharp. I also think it is good for the soul. A list of those regional theater conferences that hold general auditions is also in the back of this book.

When you want to make some money, begin by opening the yellow pages in your phone book and turning to the list of advertising agencies in your city or the city closest to you. (Wow, look at 'em all!) They hire people for print work, voice-overs, and sometimes for local

There are ways to get work by yourself. With some research you can find production companies who are making industrials or local radio spots.

—Terry Berland, casting director

commercials. Now flip to the video production companies. (Damn, ten of them right here in my little town!) They hire actors for training films, voice-overs, and commercials.

Before you start calling these companies, make a hundred copies of the *Account Profile Form* found below. You can either retype it or come up with a similar one of your own. You can then create one as a template and do all this on your computer. Start thinking of potential buyers as "accounts." The information you record on your account profile forms will grow steadily, and they will constitute your own professional files of contacts and resources.

Account Profile

Name _____
Company Receptionist _____
Associates _____
Address _____
Best Route _____
Personnel Descriptions _____
Personal Data _____
Telephone _____
Projects Previously Cast _____
Currently Casting _____

(Continue what follows below on more pages as necessary.)

Date _____
Transaction _____
Follow-up _____

Date _____
Transaction _____
Follow-up _____

Date _____
Transaction _____
Follow-up _____

Date _____
Transaction _____
Follow-up _____

Date _____
Transaction _____
Follow-up _____

Date _____
Transaction _____
Follow-up _____

Date _____
Transaction _____
Follow-up _____

Don't think of ad agencies, production companies, casting directors, etc. as people who will discover you and validate your life. They are just doing business, and so are you. Think of them as accounts that you are going to cultivate on a regular basis until they eventually buy something. Your attitude should be that you have a good product to deliver when they have a need for it, and you not only want to get the initial order but you also want them to reorder in the future.

You will not be able to make a living by working just one account. You will eventually need to open a hundred accounts. Yup, a hundred. After three years of keeping in regular contact with each of them, say once a month with a postcard, you can start weeding out the less profitable accounts and concentrate all your energies on the profitable ones. This holds true for whatever market you decide to work and, incidentally, for whatever product you happen to be selling if you decide to change careers.

So there you are, starting locally. You have a hundred account profile forms, and the yellow pages open. Start with the ad agencies. Call them one at a time. When the receptionist answers the phone, begin making friends with her in your own way. Tell her your name, that you are an actor, and that you are wondering if her company hires actors and models for print work or local commercials. If they do, write the company's name in your file and tell her you'd like to send them a photo and résumé. Ask her the name of the person who does the casting. Confirm the address listed in the yellow pages and get the zip code. Ask the best way to get to their agency and write that down. Ask what projects they have done that used actors and what they might have coming up. Even if you can't get all this information on your first phone call, make sure you get the receptionist's name and thank her for her help. Then as soon as you're off the phone write her a thank-you note—either a card, letter, or postcard with your face on it. Any salesman selling any product will testify to the importance of a friendly relationship with the receptionist. This is not kissing up. This is standard professional courtesy.

> We encourage our receptionist to be aware of current projects we're involved with so they can alert us if someone who might be right for something has dropped by.
> —Barry Moss, Casting Society of America

What I am now going to recommend is controversial. Nevertheless, I believe that your first headshot should be delivered in person to the receptionist, if possible, after she has had time to receive your thank-you note. (Apparently the CD Directory of Casting Directors agrees with the practice of personal deliveries, because they classify casting directors by zip code so you can make your deliveries in one area more easily.) This will give you a chance to smile and shake hands with the receptionist and personalize your relationship a bit more. Just drop off the photo and ask her to give it to the appropriate person she has told you about. Tell her you would like to come back for a general audition whenever it is convenient, smile again, and get out of there. As soon as you get back to your car, take out the file on that account and write down what happened and what you should do to follow up, so you will remember it. If you are keeping your files on a computer, carry a handheld recorder and make a spoken note of what transpired. When you get back to your computer, that very day, type what happened into that account file. The least you should indicate by way of follow-up is to send another card or headshot a month later and ask again for a general audition.

> I suggest that after you see a casting director, you write down in a journal or card file everything about the meeting.
> —Lisa Beach, Casting Society of America

On a continuing basis, before any future transactions with an account, look first at your file on them to refresh your memory of past transactions as well as to refresh your memory of the names of the people you will be dealing with and any personal information you might have learned about them. Did one of them just take part in an AIDS walk? Do they want to save the whales? Did you just see a project that they worked on? Again, this need not be kissing up but can instead be a genuine, friendly interest in them as human beings as well as a professional interest in their work. Your attitude is what makes the difference. If you don't like them as human beings, the feeling will probably be reciprocated. There won't be much reason for them to do business with you either 'cause you sure ain't the only game in town.

When you have called the ad agencies, call the video production companies and do the same thing with each of them. Start a file on each one that hires actors. (Production companies that only shoot weddings usually don't hire actors, so ask about this.)

Once you have introduced yourself to the ad agencies and video production companies in your area, go to your library and get the phone books from other towns that you are willing to drive to for an audition. As a rule of thumb, you should be willing to drive two hours each way for a training film or a local commercial and four hours each way to audition for a feature film, national commercial, or TV show. The only way around these long trips is to live in New York, Chicago, or L.A. and perhaps in some of the other cities in the regional market chapter of this book, like Boston, Washington, or Minneapolis. You will probably be able to arrange to carpool on the longer trips with other actors auditioning for the same productions. Other actors are an excellent source of information on who is buying what. Pick their brains even if it means having to pump their egos a bit. Consider this a friendly way of gathering information. And remember that God gave you two ears and one mouth.

Promoting Your Product

It is sometimes said in this business that availability is even more important than ability. To get the job, not only must you be available but the people who hire actors must know that you are available. When you are out of sight, you are also out of mind. You will need to remind them of your availability. To do this you must stay in touch in a professional way without being a pest. I can't tell you how not to be a pest without knowing your quirks. I can give you some guidelines.

> If we, the casting community, don't know you exist, how are we going to hire you? Thousands of people race through our heads, so we need a reminder.
> —Rick Pagano, Casting Society of America

In selling yourself, a hard sell will not work, but a polite and persistent sell eventually will. Even if you are sick in bed or depressed and despondent, you must spend a minimum of an hour and a half a day, five days a week, promoting your product by making a minimum of fifteen transactions every day with people who can give you a job. The transaction can be made in person, on the phone, or with postcards, but every transaction must be recorded in the appropriate client's file. Do you think that salesmen get by on their million-dollar smiles? Wrong. The salesman who works the way I have just described outstrips Mr. Personality every time. Show this paragraph to any salesman and see if he doesn't agree.

Once you have brought or sent your headshots to scores and scores of people who might one day offer you a job, you need to stay in touch on a regular basis. You are a small business that not only produces a product but must sell it as well. At this point you cannot afford a sales manager. Do not depend on an agent to do the selling. An agency, remember, is a retail store where the customer is always right. Minding that store takes up their time and energy, and they ain't going to do your selling for you.

> Leave your picture. Do it once a month. It makes you feel proactive.
> —Melissa Martin, casting director

Let's look at the numbers. If you send out fifteen postcards a day, five days a week, that's seventy-five postcards a week, or three hundred a month, which is equal to one for every casting director in Los Angeles or New York. If someone sent you a nice note once a month for a year, wouldn't you eventually be interested in meeting that person? So would many of those casting humans. And just look at the numbers again. Seventy-five postcards a week for a year, with two weeks off for vacation, equals 3,750 postcards. Marketing through direct mail usually yields a 2 percent sales return. That would be seventy-five jobs in a year's time. At union rates that would be $37K plus, not even counting residuals.

Do you know how many actors work this way? Almost none. Most pop a beer at the end of the day and bitch about the business. Ask yourself these questions: "Is my product not good enough to be competitive even with this kind of marketing effort?" "Do I truly want to succeed in this business enough to make this kind of disciplined effort?" "Will I be able to keep doing this for five years?" If you answered "no" to any of these questions, some other vocation is probably for you, and you might as well know it now. Again, acting can be a delightful hobby, but, as you can clearly see now, it is going to be a damned tough business. That's perhaps why there will be room for you in it.

> You have to be proactive. If you're sitting at home with a beer, watching TV instead of out working in a play, maybe you're not doing enough.
> —Donald Paul Pemrick, casting director

Your face cards (postcards with your mug on them) are only one kind of promotion. Christmas cards are a must. Every business in America uses them and so should you. Other cards, such as Valentines Day cards, etc. might also be appreciated. If you are in a play, enclose a flyer and a face card with a note inviting the client to come. (If they are in the industry they will probably be allowed in free with their business cards.) If you get a good review, photocopy

> There is no great mystery to becoming a successful actor. It is the investment and the time you put into it.
> —Reuben Cannon, Casting Society of America

it and send it along with the flyer. If you have a TV episode coming up, mention it in your face card, and if you ever see any of a client's work, such as a commercial or film he or she has either cast or worked on in some way, send a card mentioning this.

Working in local commercials and training films doesn't pay much, but it will be easy for you to get copies of the film or tape of such work, and this can be put together onto a five-minute demo reel that can also be used for promotion. If you move to L.A. it will be tough to get an agent without such a reel. Because they are expensive to reproduce, these reels should be used selectively until you transfer them to inexpensive DVDs.

On the question of portfolios, I believe they are for models rather than actors. Some actors carry these "brag books" around, but few casting directors look at them. Still, they don't hurt, and they make a nice scrapbook of memorabilia that can serve during the droughts as a reminder that it is indeed possible to work.

No chapter on promotion would be complete without advice on interviewing and auditioning. There are numerous books out there on auditioning techniques, and because this is not a book on acting but rather on marketing, I will mention two books that I believe to be the best available:

> There will be work. It may not be the job you thought you wanted, but there will be something. Stick with it and don't expect anything to happen overnight.
>
> —Stanley Soble,
> Casting Society
> of America

Audition, by Michael Shurtleff, and *The Perfect Monologue,* by Ginger Friedman.

Film and TV casting is usually done with cold readings rather than with monologues, but despite the fact that you will rarely be asked to deliver a monologue at an audition for a film or TV role, every actor should have five of them ready to pull out of the hat at a moment's notice. In order of commercial importance they are:

1. A one-minute monologue that sells your type more than your skill. You can use this monologue for auditioning at big theater conferences that limit you to one minute, as well as for those occasions when a film casting director agrees to see you at your request but has nothing for you to cold read. The purpose of the one-minute monologue is to create interest in yourself as a type and to get yourself called back to read for a specific role.

2. Two contrasting monologues of two or three minutes' length that should sell your talent. These contrasting monologues should still reflect your type. They should contrast vertically rather than horizontally. There is absolutely no reason to contrast a sad plumber's monologue with a happy doctor's monologue if you will never get cast as a plumber. If you are a doctor type, have an *up* doctor monologue and a *down* doctor monologue. This will sell your skill much more effectively.

3. A classical monologue in verse, again staying true to type. If you can do something in verse that not only sounds like verse but also sounds natural, you have a shot at doing some Shakespeare onstage. Even those who scoff at this are secretly impressed by it, and I believe that doing the classics constitutes the best training there is.

If you *really* want to do Shakespeare, have a second contrasting monologue that stays at least fairly true to type. There is no point in doing Romeo if you have recently retired. The two basic types in the classics are the nobility and the commoners. My advice is to pick one of those types and stay within it, at least until you have a lot of experience.

> I really advise actors to stay close to home in terms of age and type when choosing monologues for general auditions.
>
> —Meryl Lind Shaw,
> casting director

So, where do you find the right monologues for your type? An actor by the name of Ed Hooks has made that a lot easier for us with his book *The Ultimate Scene and Monologue Sourcebook.* He spent hours and hours in the Limelight Bookstore in San Francisco going through more than three hundred contemporary plays, and has listed the scenes and monologues from them in his book, cross-referenced according to gender, age, and ethnicity. There is a new edition coming out that will also include classical works. Buy the book, look up your type, list the plays, go to the library and read them, then photocopy the monologues that are right for you. This is also an excellent reference to find scenes to do for your acting classes. Check out his website too at *edhooks.com*.

> Casting directors are your best friends. We really are. Any actor who walks in this door and is good, makes us look good.
> —Barbara Miller, Casting Society of America

If you are eager to do commercials, you might substitute a comic monologue done in a broad style for the second classical monologue.

When you are called in for a general audition or interview, whether by a casting director or a prospective agent, you will be nervous. Just accept that, but remember that this is only the first meeting and that you plan to be around for five years. If you screw up, you will one day be able to make up for it if you keep a polite, positive attitude and keep getting better at your craft. Think of the interview as a first meeting with someone you are delighted to meet, not as an interrogation in the judge's chambers.

Usually no single interview is a make-or-break situation, unless you display obviously rude or sloppy work habits. Interviews are beginnings and are sometimes called *prereads* in that only those called back will be asked to read for the producer or director. One thing you can do to help yourself relax when you are introduced to the casting director is to make a silent mental decision about how you would cast her if you were doing the casting. Keep this entirely to yourself, however. It may help you feel and seem less self-conscious yourself and will also make you appear interested in the casting director as a person. You will probably be asked to sit down across from her desk, and she will glance at your headshot and résumé. Then she may say either "Tell me about yourself" or "So what have you been doing?" Answer in a way that is friendly, honest, and entirely positive. Do not make *any* negative remarks about *anything* if you can possibly help it. They are just not called for in this situation.

> Come to the office early and get focused.
> —Ellie Kanner, Casting Society of America

Tell the casting director or the agent about the roles that you have done that you liked best, about your hobbies, and about aspects of you that *suggest* your type, but don't tell her what your type is because she naturally feels that this is her job. Remember that affable is just as important as able and available. If she gives you something to cold read, ask if you can look it over for a minute, and she will almost certainly say yes. (If on the off-chance she wants you to read it stone cold, smile and say, "Okay. Here it is, stone cold," and read it the best you can.) When you read your character's lines to yourself, make an immediate decision about what your character wants and

> Treat each audition with respect, but come in as prepared as you can be and have a great time. It's an opportunity to practice your craft. The odds of getting the part are always so slim because the competition is so strong, that you have to enjoy the audition process itself. Auditions are a great opportunity to show your talent.
>
> —Nancy Nayor, Casting Society of America

what your character is doing to try to get it, and then deliver them that way. Michael Shurtleff phrases this in a stronger way: "What am I fighting for?" in order to give more energy to the read. The casting director will probably read the other character's lines in as neutral a way as possible so as not to interfere with your reading.

When you are called for an audition for a specific role, pick up the sides as soon as they are available. (Sides, remember, are the part of a script with the lines that your character will deliver.) When you get an agent, he or she may be able to fax them to you. If the sides are not available before the audition, get to the audition early enough to take the sides out to the parking lot. Make your decisions and then read your lines aloud so as to get used to the sound of your own voice saying the lines. This may seem odd, but your own voice can scare you sometimes.

When you are finally called in to read, be friendly to everyone gathered around but don't offer to shake hands unless they offer first. Remember they are seeing many people and may not wish to shake hands with everyone. Again, the casting director will probably read the other character's lines neutrally, and again you will read yours based on what you have decided your character wants and is trying to do to get it. Remember that any decision is better than no decision. If you read well, they may have you read the lines in an entirely different way. It is a kind of phenomenon that you will be able to change much more easily and do something in a different way if you have made any kind of strong choice beforehand, whereas no choice, or nothing, tends to stay nothing. Michael Shurtleff also advises an actor to add the new requirements to what you have already done if possible.

When you are done reading, smile at them and thank them for seeing you, then walk out of there as if you'd been given the job. Go back to the receptionist and confirm the casting director's address so you can send a thank-you note. It is even better to send a note to everyone who just saw you, including the receptionist. This is especially easy once you have email addresses, but remember to keep those emails friendly and short.

Record the whole transaction with as many names as possible in the appropriate file, including what you were wearing for the audition. If you are called back, wear the same outfit. It worked the first time, and they are not interested in seeing how great the rest of your wardrobe is. Your first outfit will actually help them remember why they called you back.

This is how you promote your product. If you ever get so hot that they are all coming to look for you, you can turn much of this work over to your agent, manager, and publicist. For the next five years, however, you are almost certainly going to have to do it all yourself.

Record Keeping

Omnes commerci en tres partes divisa est. I'm being a smart-ass here, paraphrasing Julius Caesar. He began his paean to his own accomplishments with the statement that "All of Gaul is divided into three parts." I have begun this section with the statement in Latin that all of business is divided into three parts. Those three parts are production, sales, and record keeping.

Actors love to produce their product. They don't like selling it very much because they don't like the accompanying rejection, and as a rule they absolutely hate record keeping. So, probably, do you. Actors think that record keeping is greedy, penny-pinching, mercantile, and boring, but for an actor record keeping also means keeping a record of information about the people who hire you. If you do what I suggest, perhaps in five years you may be able to hire someone else to do your record keeping for you. You probably cannot afford that right now, and if you don't do it yourself—starting right now—your business will probably fail just as surely as if you waited around to be discovered rather than going out to sell yourself.

The best way to keep records is with a computer. They are cheap enough now, especially used ones with less horsepower, and these days there is just no reason not to have one. Part of the cost may even be tax deductible. To keep your records you need a minimum of three things.

First, you need a set of files on the people you will be doing business with—a separate file for each one as described in the last section. The very act of making a note in the client's file each time you have a transaction, even by postcard, will give you the lovely feeling of being on top of it all. Even during those periods when you

> Remain positive and relaxed during the audition process. Remove desperation from your thoughts, and only think about what needs to happen in the scene you are reading. Auditioning should be a joyous process. There may be two thousand people who might be right for the role, but you are one of the eight people I asked to come in. So celebrate!
> —Debra Zane, Casting Society of America

> Don't change your wardrobe, hair or look unless someone asks you to. And don't change your interpretation either. You are called back for a reason, and you never know what that reason is. So stick to what worked.
> —Jeff Gerrard, casting director

can't seem to sell anything, you will feel like you are really a part of the business and knowledgeable about it.

The second item you need is a simple expandable file divided into the twelve months of the year so that you can keep receipts for everything that you might possibly be able to deduct from your taxes. At the end of the day if you take five minutes to date the receipts and paper-clip them together with the others from that month, you can do your taxes in an hour as soon as you get your W-2s back at the end of the year. You might even have your refund in time to pay off your Christmas bills. A scanner that will allow you to copy the receipt and note the amount as well will allow you to hit a button at the end of the year to tally up deductions so you can decide right then whether to itemize or use the standard tax deduction.

I am not a tax accountant, and the tax laws may have changed by the time you read this book, so I would rather not make a list of items that you can deduct from your taxes. I would rather give you a few rules of thumb. The first is when in doubt, deduct it. You will probably not make enough to make it worthwhile to audit you. If you are audited and the IRS disallows a deduction, you will have to pay the increased tax, but they will seldom penalize you for a good-faith mistake. So what do you have to lose? I have a friend who is audited every year and who positively delights in the game. He smiles and haggles and cajoles with the auditor, telling him jokes and having a fine time. Sometimes he has to pay a little bit more, and sometimes he wins every point.

The second rule of thumb is that if the expense helped you make money as an actor, but you weren't reimbursed for the expense, it is deductible. The cost of workshops is obviously deductible. So are stamps, envelopes, stationery, headshots, photocopying, and demo tapes. Parts of your phone bill and probably your answering machine. Mileage on your car spent looking for work, i.e. auditioning, making rounds, etc. is deductible. (Commuting to a job is not because the pay you get for the job supposedly also pays you to travel to it.) The three-martini lunch used to be deductible if you talked business, but this has changed. Check with your tax person. Here is some good news: all movies and plays are deductible! Keep your ticket stubs. Ask other actors what they are deducting. If the deduction sounds reasonable, deduct it yourself. Again, let's be realistic about something: you are probably not going to be making enough money in your first years to attract the attention of the IRS and probably won't be audited. When and if you become interesting to the IRS, you will probably be able to afford an accountant to do your taxes for you, and you will be in the habit by then of saving receipts.

Your third absolute necessity for record keeping is a daily appointment book with a separate page for each day. The page should be big enough to write down where you went, who you talked to, and what you spent. This, together with saved receipts, will usually satisfy the IRS if you are audited.

You also need enough space on the page to list appointments and transaction follow-ups to be done that day. If you have a file on everyone, you can simply write down the person's name or the company name on the page for that date, followed by (F), which tells you to look in the file to see what you have to do with that person on that day. It may be that it is time to send a postcard. If you have been businesslike in your file keeping, you will have noted this in the file and written down the file name in your date book on the appropriately dated page. So, over your second cup of coffee in the morning you will have pulled the appropriate files and will be able to plan your day.

Yes, this kind of record keeping is a bit boring and requires some self-discipline. But if you feel you have a good product to sell on the market, do it whether it bores you or not. Tell yourself while you are doing this paperwork that you are making money by doing it. You just might not be paid for a while. That kind of thinking works for real estate agents and insurance salespeople. It will work for actors too.

Joining the Unions

The chapter, "The State of the Unions" told you how and why to join. This short section will help you decide if and when you should join. Let me say again that once you join a union, you are not allowed to do nonunion work, even in a right-to-work state, despite what you may hear to the contrary from the misinformed. There is a list of union offices on the websites for the unions, so if you doubt this, call them up: *sag.org, aftra.com, actorsequity.org*.

AFTRA advises you not to join until you have to join, and that means on the second AFTRA job that you do thirty or more days after the first one. You can work several AFTRA jobs within that first thirty days without having to join, but an AFTRA signatory is not allowed to hire you after thirty days from your first AFTRA job unless you join the union. In right-to-work states, though, you cannot be required to join any union, though as a union member I can not really countenance taking advantage of union benefits without eventually joining.

My advice is not to join any union until you have decided to make acting a long-term career, and then you should take the ethical question into account when deciding just when you have to join. Will your conscience let you go on taking advantage of union benefits indefinitely in right-to-work states without joining? And don't you have to join to make that real commitment to professionalism once you have enough credits to do so? You pretty much have to join the unions to work in New York or Los Angeles, but my advice is not to go there anyway until you have a decent résumé of local credits, a demo tape on yourself, and then, finally, your union card, which you should get before you go to either of those cities. In other cities there is a fair amount of nonunion work, and in some cities that is all there is. In such cities as Tallahassee or Columbia, South Carolina, joining Equity or AFTRA can mean never working there again. What then? Are you going to go to New York or Los Angeles with a union card, a virtually blank résumé, and no demo reel? Please don't do that. You will not be able to compete in those markets that way.

You may well decide not to join Equity at all unless your primary objective is to be a stage actor or you get offered a great stage role that you feel you just have to do. You do not have to join Equity to do Equity-waiver showcase productions in L.A. If you want to do stage work in New York or in the regional theaters you will have to join Equity to get decent roles. If this is what you want to do, I applaud you, my heart goes out to you, but I will not lend you any money.

If you get a SAG contract in New York or L.A., you can keep doing SAG work for a month without having to join, but after that a signatory is not allowed to hire you unless you join. After your first SAG job you can put *SAG Eligible* on your résumé and seem almost as professional in local markets as if you were a member of SAG. You can also continue to do nonunion work that way, build up your credits and your demo reel, and then join SAG as you are about to leave for the big time or are firmly committed to being a professional where you are.

An actor joining a union is like Caesar crossing the Rubicon. There should be no looking back. You should not join a union for egotistical reasons, even if you are made of money and the fees to join are not important. When you join you are making the statement that you are armed and ready to compete professionally with anyone. Join when you can honestly make that statement and are ready to prove it.

Listing with an Agent

I would suggest rereading the section on agents in chapter two, "The State of the Business," at this point because your misconceptions about what to expect from an agent may have grown back. The chapters you have just read on finding buyers, promoting yourself, and keeping records may seem like too much work for a true artist, and the little child in you may be saying, "Mama, carry me!" Sorry, your mother doesn't work at the agency.

Once again, a talent agency is a retail store from which your product gets sold, but it is up to you to get the customers to go there and ask for you by name.

The first rule when listing with an agent is not to give an agent any money up front for anything—not one cent, not for expenses they say they will have in promoting you, not for classes, not for photos or duplication, not for anything. Any agent who takes money up front cannot get a franchise from the actors' unions. Such practices on the part of agents are considered unethical, and they are. Agencies who ask for money up front—and there are plenty of them—make their money by exploiting the naive dreams of would-be actors or their parents. They almost never get actors work.

Most small cities have modeling agencies, which often call themselves "model and talent" agencies. Only a tiny part of their revenue actually comes from getting models or actors work. Almost all of their money comes from giving classes to models. They make their money primarily from the mothers of young girls who want their daughters to be popular and hope that classes in style, poise, and makeup tricks will accomplish that goal. Sometimes young career women also take such classes at night, dreaming the kinds of dreams that seem to grow in the human heart.

If there is no legitimate talent agency in your city, you can list yourself with one or more of these model and talent agencies, providing they don't ask you for money. Chances are there is a legitimate talent agency within a couple hours' drive from you unless you live out west, in which case you are used to driving longer distances anyway. Send these agencies a headshot and résumé and tell them that you plan to hustle work for yourself but would like them to represent you when you do get work and would therefore like to list with them. This is good business for both of you. Having an agent, even in Podunk, makes you seem more professional and trustable to local video production companies and ad agencies. Again, most of them, like most of us, would rather shop in a store than buy things off the street. Having an agent will also ensure that you get paid the going rate for your work and, even more important, that you get paid at all. An agency can put the screws to nonpayers better than you can, and a company that does not wish to work through agents may not be trustworthy.

If you get some work yourself and see that the agency gets a commission, you will impress the agency and make them think of you the next time that a job you're right for comes along. These are the basic reasons to have an agent.

Now let's look at some of the regional markets in the United States.

Chapter 7 | # Regional Markets for Actors

With respect to Hollywood movies, let's remember that the major roles will be cast in L.A., and most of the interior scenes will be shot there. Even if it would be cheaper to shoot interiors in a sound stage somewhere else in the country, this wouldn't matter to the big names attached to the film, because it is one thing for them to live out of a suitcase for three weeks, quite another to live that way for three months. Stars and producers want to go back to their own homes after work, like most of us, to cavort with the dogs, help the kids with homework, and sleep in their own beds. So for most films and TV series it's going to be the exteriors—the shots that establish where the story is taking place—that will be shot on location. So you might be able to get a small role in a big picture being shot at a location near you, or you might be able to get a big role in a small independent picture in the same market.

> Pick some place where there is theater that pays money, where they make commercials, where they make industrials, and that gives you the quality of life you are seeking.
> —Mike Fenton, Casting Society of America

Half the film production in the United States happens in California, and the rest is divided among the other states. New York is second in terms of film starts, and Los Angeles and New York divide most of the television production between them. Los Angeles shoots more series and New York more soaps. TV series that are shot in other locations, such as *Northern Exposure*, which was shot in Seattle, and *In the Heat of the Night*, which was shot in Atlanta, are done on location for both the local color of the shooting locations and also for the regional accents of available local actors. *Ocean Drive* and *Miami Sands,* tele-novellas recently shot in Miami, are other examples. Still, shows like *CSI Miami* and *Karen Sisco,* which supposedly take place in Miami, are shot in Los Angeles, and *Dave Barry* was shot in New York, with only a few exteriors shot in Miami.

Florida, Texas, and North Carolina all claim to be third in terms of film production, depending on which film board you are talking to, and each is slowly gaining on New York every year. The films shot there tend to be lower-budget, with some exceptions like *True Lies,* a big-budget picture that was partially shot in Miami. Many of the independent films shot in any of America's regions are so low-budget that they are not even tracked and counted among U.S. film starts. Florida, Texas, and North Carolina are right-to-work states, as are South Carolina and Georgia, which are also right up there in the rankings of films produced.

Washington, D.C. ranks third after New York and L.A. in the production of training films, mostly because of the number of them commissioned by the federal government. Washington and Baltimore together are considered one market, and several feature films are shot there every year—D.C. for its monuments and Baltimore for its any-city look.

I want to reiterate my feelings against heading to the big leagues of New York and Los Angeles right out of drama school without your union cards, a demo reel, and a solid résumé. Each of those two cities is home to around fifty thousand union actors competing for available jobs, with another hundred thousand wannabees waiting in the wings. Why should employers hire you there?

Instead, consider a regional market first. After working in one of them and getting your union cards, a résumé, and a demo reel, you might want to try New York or Los Angeles for a while, and you might do well and be happy there. You might also find you were happier and worked a lot more in the regional market where you came from.

Let's look at some of these regional markets now. If you're still in high school, you might choose your future university because it's in one of these regional markets, where you can be building a career even before you graduate.

Boston

Boston, with centuries of history and more than fifty colleges and universities inside the city limits, is a city for working actors with working minds. In addition to the intellectual and cultural events, there is plenty of acting work there, and your share of it will, of course, be the result of your skill and your persistence in going after it, like anywhere. To cheer you up if you happen to be driving a cab for a while, waiting to get your share of that acting work, take a look at the guy driving the cab in the other lane. He may have a Ph.D. from Harvard but just be unwilling to live in any city other than Boston.

SAG and AFTRA share an office in Boston, and the work under those two contracts is about evenly split. Commercials intended for a national audience will be shot on film under a SAG contract, and local ones intended for the region, as well as most of the voice-over work, will be produced under AFTRA contracts.

Some films shot there include *Good Will Hunting, The Perfect Storm,* and *Mystic River.* Again, the exteriors were shot there and the interiors back in the sound stages of Los Angeles. Some TV shows that supposedly take place in Boston have many of their exterior shots done there, including *The Practice, The Brotherhood of Poland, New Hampshire,* and *Boston Public.* As you might imagine, Boston's PBS station, WGBH, is quite active with various projects. Two of their regular shows, *This Old House* and *The New Yankee Workshop,* are produced by WGBH under AFTRA contracts.

Casting in the area, which of course includes much of New England, seems to be fairly evenly divided among Boston's casting directors, though Boston Casting, Collinge Pickman, and Tighe Doyle seem to be the big hitters in town.

Boston is also a wonderful theater town. There are large LORT Equity theaters in Boston, like the American Repertory Theater at Harvard and the Huntington Theater Company, as well as fourteen smaller theaters working under the New England Association of Theaters (NEAT) contract. There are also more than two hundred, yes, two hundred, alive and kicking theater groups in the greater Boston area.

The best source for information about working as an actor in Boston is offered by a group called StageSource. They are located at 88 Tremont Street, Suite 714, Boston, MA, 02108, telephone (617) 720-6066, *stagesource.org.*

StageSource is a nonprofit service organization dedicated to professional standards and advocacy for theater artists, with a membership of more than two thousand actors, directors, designers, technicians, and playwrights. It costs $100 a year to become a member, which will get you a discounted price of $21.95 for *The Source: The Greater Boston Theater Resource Guide* ($26.95 plus $5 S&H for nonmembers) and will also get you listed in the next edition when you renew membership at a discounted price. They also have student discounts if you are planning on studying in Boston. With membership you get access to the e-hotline with notices about auditions and a members-only message board, listing of your headshot and résumé in their talent bank for directors to peruse, a quarterly calendar of theater listings, free theater tickets, group health insurance if your union insurance hasn't kicked in yet, an annual opportunity to participate in a group audition for over sixty theater companies, and last but not least, an invitation to come to their bimonthly gatherings at local restaurants, where new members can meet those who've been around for a while. They are fine folks helping a thriving theater community to keep thriving, and I heartily recommend becoming a member if you plan to work in Boston.

Philadelphia

Philadelphia, the City of Brotherly Love, site of the signing of the Declaration of Independence, capital of the Continental Congress during the American Revolution, home of the Liberty Bell and the Walnut Theater—the oldest theater in America, where productions have been continuously staged from the time it was built in 1809, and which today has the largest subscription base of any theater in the country—is also home to a fine acting community. Some other theater organizations in the area have been around even longer than the Walnut, though not in the same facility, like Hedgerow Theater, the Philadelphia Theater Company, the People's Light & Theater Company, and Wilma Theater. The Theater Alliance of Greater Philadelphia, which includes the People's Light & Theater Company in Malvern, Pennsylvania, as well as the Delaware Theater Company, has the largest number of LORT Equity contracts annually of any region outside New York. Here's a networking tip: the Stage Managers Association holds an informal SMA drink night the first Monday of the month during the theater season, which runs from September to June. That's a great time to find out what's going on.

The Theater Alliance is an umbrella organization with a website *(theateralliance.org)*, where you can click on *member theatres* for a description of each of them. A $40 annual membership fee gets you your own web page on the site for your headshot and résumé as well as other perks such as comp tickets. There are about twenty theaters that work under Equity contracts of one kind or another, mostly Small Professional Theater contracts that don't pay much, but the pay is not why we do theater. In terms of future livelihood, a contract with one of them can get you your Equity card, which will enable you to join SAG in a year and audition for those well-paying commercials and films. Pennsylvania is not a right-to-work state, so you will need to join SAG to work under its jurisdiction there.

Many SAG commercials are shot in Philadelphia, sometimes by New York production companies who want to shoot a different look and still get home at night to tuck their kids into bed. The TV show *Hack* now in its second season, is shot there under a SAG contract. As the story location for the TV show *Cold Case* is Philadelphia, exteriors are regularly shot there. Big feature films regularly shoot in the city also, *Witness* and *Philadelphia* in the past, and more recently *Signs,* which was shot in lower Bucks County outside of Philly. *Jersey Girl,* with Ben Affleck and Jennifer Lopez, was shot there and will probably have been released by the time this book is out. AFTRA, of course, covers radio and voice-over work and also covers many commercials, usually for the local market but sometimes for national broadcasts. Most political spots are also shot under AFTRA contracts.

New York City is only eighty-seven miles away, easily accessible by train or bus and relatively inexpensive, so some Philadelphia actors occasionally work in New York and some New York actors occasionally work in

Philly. Some Philadelphia actors go on to New York and make their homes there, while others who have moved to New York discover that they prefer the community spirit of Philadelphia, where they can have acting careers, raise families, and buy homes, a state of affairs that has created a very healthy and welcoming environment for actors.

Washington/Baltimore

Washington is one of the most livable cities in the United States. Unlike New York, where the subways look, smell, and feel like cockroach cocoons, Washington's subways are not only free of graffiti but actually have carpet on the floor. D.C. has monuments and museums, restaurants of every conceivable kind, concerts of music and dance that rival New York's, and the occasional homey sight of a well-known senator munching a hot dog. The summers are pretty muggy, especially in August, and a big snowfall in the winter sometimes knocks this essentially southern city for a loop, but no place is perfect.

There are usually about six feature films a year shot in D.C., usually just the exteriors—or establishing—shots, for stories that supposedly take place in the nation's capital. As with most feature films and TV shows, the interior shots are done back in the studios of Los Angeles. *The West Wing,* for example, visits quarterly to shoot their exteriors.

Nearby Baltimore, which is part of the same market, is an "Anywhere, U.S.A.," blue-collar type of town, known for its friendly bars and fine seafood restaurants. Baltimore can be used to shoot movies for just about any urban setting. The TV show *The Wire* is entirely shot in Baltimore under a SAG contract, as was *Homicide* and *Head of State. America's Most Wanted* is an AFTRA TV show based in D.C., as is *K Street,* a new HBO series. The Discovery Channel is based in the suburb of Silver Spring, Maryland, and the nation's largest employer of radio talent, National Public Radio, is based in D.C. Both Baltimore and Richmond, a hundred miles to the south, are often used as "cover" cities for period pieces because of their historic buildings.

Washington also provides an excellent backdrop for commercials, and many of them are shot there for that reason. There are more than six hundred companies in the Washington/Baltimore area who are signatories to SAG or AFTRA contracts, more than the entire state of Florida. Only about twenty companies are signed to only one of the unions. Last year there was more work under SAG than AFTRA contracts, not counting AFTRA broadcaster salaries. The big money for actors in D.C. comes from doing training films, which can be done under either SAG or AFTRA contracts. The government, which includes the armed forces, makes scores of them every year, and so do many corporations based in Washington. Clean-cut types of all races—although mostly men with no facial hair—get most of this work. During campaign season, things get pretty busy with campaign ads, again with the big portion of the work going to clean-cut, clean shaven males. (I wonder what this says about us as a culture?) Many of those soft money issue spots are also produced in D.C.

Because the federal government cannot sign a contract with the unions, the government training films made in this market are not strictly SAG films, but the union approves of them anyway because the government agrees to all the provisions of a standard union contract. Union actors can therefore do them, and because all provisions of a standard SAG contract are honored, the union will recognize such a contract for purposes of admitting a new actor into the union. This makes the Washington/Baltimore market a good place to get a SAG card and begin a career.

Most actors in the area live in D.C. and visit Baltimore. Some Washington actors make do without a car because of the city's excellent metro. Others feel they need some kind of car to reach Baltimore and northern Virginia. Rents in D.C. are higher than in Florida and quite a bit higher than in the Carolinas but lower than New York and comparable to those in Los Angeles. There is plenty of theater in D.C. and Baltimore, both Equity and non-Equity. The League of Washington Theaters, which also includes Baltimore and surrounding areas, has fifty-one members. For a description of each of them, visit their website at *lowt.org* and click on the individual theaters. The more prestigious theaters like Arena Stage and the Shakespeare Theater of Washington (formerly the Shakespeare Theatre at the Folger) recruit mostly out of New York. In the opinion of Washington actors, this is due to the prejudices of the artistic directors of these two theaters.

This market is under New York's regional jurisdiction, and in SAG films shot here the union requires that half the extras must be SAG members. Extra work done by D.C. actors on these films turns into old home week while the extras wait around to do the crowd scene, with much friendly chattering and catching up on the news and gossip.

If you like cities and feel that you would prefer New York to Los Angeles, it would really behoove you to consider going to Washington first, especially if you are a clean-cut male with no facial hair. You can be a spear carrier for minimum wage as an Equity membership candidate in D.C. theaters and get your Equity card that way in a year. You can also get your SAG card much easier in D.C. than in New York. Sometimes you can get cast in a government training film entirely through your own efforts and then be eligible to join SAG. You can live in a cosmopolitan atmosphere while you build up your résumé, and because of its proximity to New York via an affordable train ride, you can make forays into New York before you move there. There is another advantage to D.C. that I should mention: it has the most helpful union local that I have ever come across. Once a month the SAG/AFTRA office has a special orientation session with helpful advice on the Washington/Baltimore market for actors new to unions, or new to the area, complete with coffee and donuts. Actors are given an orientation briefing and a list of SAG and AFTRA signatory companies so they can start hustling. They also help actors there with a talent directory of actors that is sent to any producer who signs a union contract. Nice, huh?

The Washington/Baltimore area has several franchised talent agencies, and in the past it was customary for actors to list with them all, as these agencies also acted as de facto casting agencies as well. That changed with increased production in the area. Pat Moran & Associates, CSA, cast only film and TV and has won both Emmy and Artio awards. Carlyn Davis Casting is very active, and Taylor-Royal Casting and Central Casting are still major players. One bit of advice: Dagmar, of Central Casting, might seem like a tough cookie when you first meet her, but she's just testing you to see if you will come unglued. Continue to be professional and polite and soon she will call you "darling" in a charming accent and trust your professionalism enough to send you on auditions. (Hi, Dagmar!)

Join the Actor's Center as soon as you get to town for networking, acting, voice and movement classes, various discounts, comp tickets, a hot line, and a great website at actorscenter.org with all kinds of links to other actor-oriented sites. It's only $60 a year, $40 for students or seniors, and is prorated after July until the end of the year. As already mentioned, check out the League of Washington Theaters at lowt.org for a list and description of the more than fifty theaters in the area. Also, be sure to visit the Backstage Bookstore to shmooze, network, and of course to buy some of the books that I recommend in this one.

Georgia and the Carolinas

For someone wishing to work full-time as an actor in this area, Georgia and the Carolinas should probably be considered one market, so you will need a well-running car. The two most convenient cities in which to live are Atlanta and Charlotte. Atlanta has more local work, mostly voice-overs, commercials, and industrials. You can also fly almost anywhere in the world from its airport. Charlotte doesn't have quite as much of this kind of local work but is more centrally located in the region and is closer to that big film studio in Wilmington, North Carolina, Screen Gem Studios. In addition to your car, it will be a good idea to acquire some actor friends with whom you can carpool no matter where you live in this market. This includes living in Atlanta too, despite its subway system.

Georgia

Atlanta, capital of the New South, began to be important as a railroad hub even before the years of the Southern Confederacy. After the Civil War it remained a railroad hub and the main center of Southern commerce. After World War II, the city convinced several airlines to become a central transportation hub, as the railroads had done, and Atlanta kept abreast of the times. Georgia's highways, though, lagged behind the times, and some folks in the neighboring southern states felt that this was a deliberate effort on the part of their neighbor to retard their own development. The federal government even came close to cutting off Georgia's highway money as a result.

Atlanta was the first southern city to reach a population of one million, and the city became the cultural capital of the New South. Film and video production companies sprang up there to make local commercials and training films, and whenever a feature was slated to shoot in the South, Atlanta was usually the site picked for the production office. Yankees and Californians were just as scared of the rural South as southerners were scared of riding the New York subway, thus demonstrating that silliness is a human, rather than a regional, affliction.

The Chez Agency of Atlanta, founded by Shay Griffin, began as a modeling and talent agency and for years was the prime player in the southern talent agency scene. As the South developed, Chez continued for a time as Atlanta's main talent agency and the main agency of the region. When the TV series *In the Heat of the Night* came to town, they changed from talent agents into casting directors, and the series became the first one to be shot from start to finish in a regional market. One hears that Shay Griffin has now moved from casting to producing, and other casting directors in Atlanta now do most of the area casting.

SAG and AFTRA share an office in Atlanta and share the work about evenly. AFTRA, of course, gets most of the voice-over work, SAG more commercials. Recently a kids' show, *Animal Tails*, began under an AFTRA contract. Some recent TV projects were *Savannah*, and *I'll Fly Away*, shot under SAG contracts. *A Stroke of Genius*, *The Undertow*, and *Dumb and Dumberer* were some recent feature films shot in the area. There is enough acting work for some of the actors in Atlanta to earn their entire (modest) living through acting, just as there is in the Florida market.

Atlanta has about twelve Equity theaters though not a local Equity office. There are several union-franchised talent agencies, and actors used to list with all of them. ("Betty Beautiful is now available at all fine agencies in Atlanta!") These days actors list with all the agencies for voice-overs and training films but usually have one agency for exclusive representation in commercials and film or TV work. One more word about Atlanta's agencies: if you don't live in Atlanta, they usually won't want to bother with you.

That is not necessarily the case with Atlanta's casting directors, however, provided you are listed with an agent somewhere else. There are several casting directors in Atlanta, and one hears that the big hitters are Atlanta Casting in Jonesboro for films, Stillwell Casting for commercials, and Kris Redding.

Atlanta also has an excellent web page designed by actors for actors, *actorsphere.com*. You should definitely take a look at it.

The Carolinas

Despite the beauty of the beaches in this region, the inland city of Charlotte is the most professionally practical place to live in the Carolinas. There is a group there called First Friday, which as you might guess meets the first Friday of every month. It was formed by actors in 1985 and is still going strong. To find out more about them and the Charlotte market, visit their website at *actors-hollywoodsouth.com* or contact Melvynw@earthlink.net for more information.

Charlotte has a couple of small Equity theaters and more production companies and ad agencies than any city in the Carolinas. Most of the work is nonunion. It is located smack dab in the center of these two states and is thus accessible to all locations in them. Several features, such as *The Last of the Mohicans* and *Dirty Dancing,* have been shot around Asheville, which is about two and a half hours away in some very pretty mountains.

Atlanta is a little over four hours away, about the same distance as Miami to Orlando, and some Charlotte actors are willing to make the trip to audition. Carpools help. The agent to list with in Charlotte, if you can, is the Jan Thomson Agency. In Columbia, South Carolina, go bug my pal Charlie Peterson at Harvest Talent. (Hi, Charlie!)

Charlotte is about three and a half hours from Charleston, South Carolina, where several features have been shot, from Civil War movies to *Prince of Tides.* Charleston is a lovely, historic city, and many movie people are quite charmed by it, despite the cold shoulder they get from the old families of Charleston who don't like these movie interlopers with their vulgar T-shirts.

Charlotte is also about four hours from the film studio built by Dino De Laurentiis in Wilmington, North Carolina. There is an interesting story that goes with the studio and the two brothers that do the lion's share of the casting in the Carolinas.

De Laurentiis is one of the world's most famous independent producers. He was shooting for a while in Mexico and got tired of paying bribes every step of the way to get anything done. This custom in Mexico is known as giving someone a "little bite" of the action, called a *mordida.* De Laurentiis was looking for a location to shoot *Firestarter* when one of his lieutenants saw a picture of a southern mansion on the cover of *Southern Living* magazine. The lieutenant thought the mansion would look good for CIA headquarters in the movie and showed the picture to Dino. Dino liked it, and they learned that the location was not only available but available quite cheaply by movie standards. The mansion was located just outside of Wilmington, North Carolina, a port city that at that time still hadn't recovered economically from the pullout of a railroad that was headquartered there.

Dino couldn't believe the prices, and they had their location for the film. Meanwhile, two brothers, Craig and Mark Fincannon, who had a friend at the North Carolina film board, got word that Dino was coming to North Carolina. They wrote to him and offered to do his extras casting. De Laurentiis met them, liked them, and gave them their first big production job.

Craig and Mark, older and younger respectively, get along better than most brothers. They worked summers together at an amusement park while they were going to college, and because both of them were movie buffs, they bought a small movie theater together. They began showing *The Rocky Horror Picture Show* 'round midnight and made their theater available to distributors at other times for screenings to be shown to local exhibitors. Then they went to work for Dino. De Laurentiis was able to bring *Firestarter* in for something like $3 million under budget, and he decided to stay put in Wilmington. He took the money he'd saved, bought some land outside Wilmington, and built some sound stages. Mark and Craig Fincannon opened an office downtown near the harbor and have been the main players in the Carolinas ever since. *The Patriot* and *Cold Mountain* were two of their more recent castings, as was *Runaway Jury* shot in New Orleans but cast by Lisa Fincannon.

De Laurentiis's fortunes have always gone up and down, and the studio is now owned by his friends at Screen Gems Studios, but Mark and Craig still do the casting. They receive submissions from agents from as far away as Virginia, Tennessee, and Georgia as well as from the Carolinas, and now they're getting them from Florida. They will look at a headshot or a demo reel sent directly by an actor but will accept submissions for roles they are casting only through agents. They don't want multiple submissions, so pick one agent to represent you to the Fincannons. They will keep your headshot in that agent's talent book for referral by telephone.

If the movie they are casting will be shot in Wilmington, auditions are held there because the director will be there. If the movie is being shot elsewhere, the Fincannons will usually hold auditions in a central location, and the callbacks will be wherever the director wants them. Actors, of course, will usually be willing to drive substantial distances for callbacks.

As in most right-to-work states, there will be more nonunion than union work, but the union work will pay much better. Working the Carolinas will mean a lot of driving, but food and rent are cheaper, and union scale is the same for work there.

If you live in the Carolinas, you may also want to subscribe to *Reel Carolina Journal* as a source for what's happening in the area. They can be reached at Reelpublisher@netscape.net, or telephone 910-233-2926. Studio Perk at the Screen Gem Studios in Wilmington is a fine place to meet actors, with a bulletin board for auditions, industry books to read, and a large adjoining room for events, and you don't need a studio pass to go there.

Y'all come see us, ya heah?

Florida

People have been wintering in Florida since the railroads were built in the last century, not only because of the wonderful winter weather but also because of the beauty that the moist tropical air gives to the moonlight on the water and to the sun coming up in the morning.

Miami has also been around for a long time as a place for actors to work, mostly because of its cultural relationship with New York. When New Yorkers began retiring to Miami, they created an audience for theater here, especially with the advent of dinner theater. In time the resulting available pool of actors, both New York imports and homegrown talent, made Miami a good place for New York production companies to shoot commercials in the winter, and those companies and their offspring now shoot there year-round.

Miami has developed a solid infrastructure of actors and technicians, and this makes for practical, efficient shooting of feature films, so a number of features are shot there. Some New York companies used to operating on New York's 78 rpm pace have complained of a vacation mentality in Florida, but, on the other hand, the reverse is true. One sees bumper stickers in Florida that read *Please Hurry up! Not everyone is on vacation!* Dave Corey, a loyal Florida actor who works regularly, tells this little story:

> I've worked on some sets where the production company was responsible for the vacation mentality, like a spot for some NY telephone company where they tried to make the location look like New York! This required the masking of palm trees and the like. I also did an on-camera McDonald's commercial for Buffalo, shoveling snow in a blinding storm. We shot it on a soundstage here in the Fall. They just wanted to spend some quality time in South Florida and were extremely laid back and wasted lots of time and money.

AFTRA and SAG both have offices in Miami. In fact, because Miami is also the South Region office of SAG and handles business for Tennessee, Mississippi, Alabama, Louisiana, and the Carolinas, the membership of the Miami local of the Screen Actors Guild is now the third largest, after L.A. and New York. This has resulted in a rather bizarre situation. Miami, like New York and L.A., is one of the few cities where SAG and AFTRA do not share an office, and SAG has two offices in Atlanta, despite the fact that it is closing other offices all over the country to save money. Perhaps one day I will hear a good explanation for not having one regional SAG office in Atlanta to handle regional business and one joint SAG/AFTRA office in Miami to take care of Miami's local business. Actually, I'm considering running for SAG National Board member from this region about the time this book comes out in order to insist on answers to these questions and others.

Because Florida is a right-to-work state, it is a good place to get your union cards. Producers can hire you even though you are not in the union, provided that they can justify you as a professional and not just the producer's local squeeze, and that then makes you eligible to join the union. The Professional Actors Association of Florida has been replaced since this book's first printing by the Union Conservatory in Miami, where members of AFTRA, SAG, and AEA can hone their skills on Tuesday night from 7:30 to 10:00 p.m. for $5. The money goes for video equipment, showcases, and other purposes decided on by the membership. Unfortunately, only a handful of members take advantage of this Conservatory. Those that do tend to belong to the rather small core of Miami actors who get most of the work, so it seems like the place to go if you want to learn from the winners.

Until you get in the union you might want to subscribe to *The Florida Bluesheet* in order to stay abreast of what's happening in the state. Many auditions of all kinds are listed in it. (Hi, Kooge!)

There are about a dozen union-franchised agents in the Miami area and an equal number of casting directors. You'll find lists of them in the appendix of this book.

Central Florida is the other main Florida market. Universal Studios and an MGM/Disney partnership each built movie studios in Orlando as adjuncts to Orlando's theme parks, mostly to take advantage of the tremendous East Coast tourist traffic that goes through there. So, after visiting Epcot Center and Disney World, tourists can now thrill to seeing actual movies being made! Rather than make their own movies, these studios more often rent studio space to independent moviemakers and TV producers, usually for productions on the low-budget side. Then if a movie that is made there turns out to be pretty good, the distribution arm of the studio may agree to market and distribute it. If not, the studio still gets its rent and the tourist dollars. Postproduction for *The Blair Witch Project* was done there.

An actor trying to make a full-time living in Florida will probably have to work both south and central Florida. The central Florida market consists of Orlando, Tampa, and Sarasota. Because it is only about an hour-and-a-half drive between Orlando and Tampa, actors living in central Florida can easily work in both these central Florida cities, and there are a respectable number of commercials and training films shot in this area, as well as some features, but these days central Florida work is mostly commercials. All the unions once had offices in that area, but the economic slump has caused them to close, and the SAG rep works out of his home now. Production of commercials dropped some after 9/11 because people were scared to travel, and the commercial strike hurt actors badly, but the market seems to be slowly recovering. Those big sound stages are still empty much of the time, but Universal has recently been bought by General Electric, which owns NBC, and this might make for some TV movie and series production again.

Florida is also attracting some European film production, and because of the bilingual nature of Miami, Spanish-language soap operas, called novellas, are shot there using Hispanic Miami actors. The novellas are then exported to South America, mostly to Argentina and Chile. One problem, I'm told, is that too many Hispanic actors in Miami have Cuban accents, so if your Spanish is of a more generic, neutral accent, you may want to check out the scene, caballero. *Miami Sands* and *Ocean Avenue* were both AFTRA shows that were done in English using a broad mix of Anglo and Hispanic actors. *Ocean Avenue* was actually cast heavily with Swedish actors because that's where it was going to show first before being syndicated all over the globe, where it has supposedly done pretty well. No doubt being able to get out of Scandinavia during those dark winter months helped green-light that particular production.

In the past, actors in both south and central Florida would often list with all the agents in their areas, and those willing to drive the four hours between the two markets list with all the agents in both markets. As a result, the same actors were often submitted by more than one agent for a certain role. The actor would write down which agent she wanted to represent her when she signed in at the casting office, and it was considered professional courtesy for the actor to credit the agent who called her first and to let the other agents know this if they call to submit her for the same audition.

A nice thing about agents in both south and central Florida is that they encourage actors to make rounds, to stop by to say hello and ask if there is anything happening for which they might be "just right." Casting directors in Florida, however, like casting directors everywhere, do not encourage personal visits, but some will see actors for general auditions during slow periods if actors request them. To find out which casting directors may be willing to see you for a general audition, send your headshot and ask for one. Or, politely drop your headshot off, smile nicely at the receptionist, and ask her to ask the casting director if you can come in for one, then thank her again with a nice smile and get out of there so you make an impression as a polite professional but not a pest. Remember to send a thank-you note to the receptionist, followed by another headshot a week later.

At these general auditions, you will probably be asked to read from a past project, but the casting director may want to see monologues, so make sure you have that well-tuned, two-minute monologue ready that will make them remember you as a type.

There isn't much action in north Florida yet, but it has potential. The TV series *Pointman* was shot in Jacksonville, and more recently *Dawson's Creek* was shot there. One advantage to Jax is that there is less local competition than in Orlando and Miami, and it is the same distance to the studios in Wilmington, North Carolina as to Miami. If you like driving, you can work a huge geographical area from there, and producers can still book you without having to pay extra for it.

There is also plenty of theater all over Florida, not just the nationally known regional theaters like Asolo, in Sarasota, and Coconut Grove, in Miami, but also dozens of small professional theaters, especially in south Florida, which work under an Equity SPT contract or letter of agreement. Once Disney signed a contract with Equity, Orlando became a potential place to get an Equity card; however, south Florida has a greater concentration of theaters. The Theater League of South Florida has a membership of more than sixty theaters of all kinds, Equity, university, and community, which are collectively known as the Stages of the Sun. Here's how they describe themselves on their web page:

> The Theater League of South Florida is a service organization whose mission is to develop, advance, strengthen and promote theater and theater education in Monroe, Miami-Dade, Broward and Palm Beach counties. Membership is open to English and non-English-speaking commercial, non-profit, community, accessible and educational theaters, regardless of Equity status, and to theater artists, including actors, directors, playwrights, technicians, designers, educators and students, and to individuals and organizations who wish to support the theatrical community.

An actor living in south Florida should definitely belong to this group to learn about area theaters and find out what shows they are planning to do and when they are having auditions. The group also sponsors annual unified auditions for area theaters, as well as other resources for other theater professionals. Go to their website at *theaterleague.net,* click on "membership and benefits," and I think you'll agree it's a group to join.

Central Florida has a similar group called the Central Florida Performing Arts Alliance, *orlandoperforms.com.* Membership is very inexpensive, and it gets you an excellent weekly email newsletter called the *Monday Memo.* All kinds of arts issues are discussed in the two-part newsletter, and area theaters place their audition announcements in the second part in plenty of time for you to get ready to audition. All arts-related jobs are also posted there in the second part.

Finally, if you are going to work the Florida market, one resource you definitely should not do without is the FAB book, put together by Annie Kidwell, a Florida actor who has been in the business for years. FAB stands for *Florida Actor's Business,* and it is updated up to eleven times a year, depending on changes in the market. It lists resources for everything you'll need to work as an actor in the state of Florida. Check out her website at *fabactor.com* for a detailed list of what it provides. You'll also want to attend her monthly networking group for theater and film professionals called

ACTion, which meets the second Monday of the month, 7:00 p.m. for networking, 7:30 for the general meeting and guest speaker. I spoke there once myself.

No need to bring sunscreen to Florida. They sell it down there.

Nashville

As home to the Grand Old Opry and focal point for the U.S. country music scene for generations, the name Nashville has long been synonymous with music for most Americans. These days Nashville is also on the global music map because of its high-tech sound studios, which are now used by recording artists worldwide for all kinds of music. On any given day there will almost certainly be a music video being made there. *Nashville Stars,* a reality TV series modeled after *American Idol,* is one of the productions shot there.

Recording contracts come under AFTRA's jurisdiction, so after establishing itself in the music business, the AFTRA office later went on to negotiate TV and commercial contracts for actors. For years the AFTRA office also took care of SAG business when a feature film came to town, but this has now changed, as in other cities that operated under similar arrangements but no longer do so because of SAG's brilliant restructuring moves. SAG commercials get made in Nashville in "flood or draught" proportions according the local SAG Council president, Steve Pippin.

Located in the middle of Tennessee and about a four-hour drive north of Atlanta, Nashville actors occasionally work that market in addition to the other main cities in Tennessee, Knoxville, and Memphis. Nashville has a strong crew base of technicians who work on the independent films shot there, and the city hosts the largest independent film festival east of the Mississippi. Two such indies were *Stuey* and *Colored Eggs,* with Olympia Dukakis. By arrangement with Regal Cinemas, the winner in the "Best Film" category gets a two-week showing in one of their Los Angeles theaters so that it can compete for Academy Awards. Check out their website at *nashvillefilmfestival.org.* The city itself was the star of the Robert Altman movie about it, and there are many good locations for filming in the area, probably the most famous of which is Nashville prison. Its gothic look made it an ideal location for such films as *The Green Mile* and more recently Robert Redford's *The Castle.*

Four of the AFTRA agents work exclusively on music contracts, the others on a variety of both SAG and AFTRA contracts. The casting directors who cast most of the film and TV commercial work are Jo Doster and Regina Moore, while Betty Clark casts most of the voice-overs. She also does all kinds of other casting and is considered the dean of Nashville's talent agents.

There is a good theater scene in Nashville. The largest theater is the Tennessee Performing Arts Center, which brings in the Broadway road shows and also provides space for other theater companies, both Equity and non-Equity. Their offerings are of the more traditional sort, as might be expected. For more cutting-edge theater, Nashville's fourteen-year-old Darkhorse Theater is an alternative theater with new works, classical theater, live music, dance, multimedia shows, and film and is also home to many of Nashville's performing arts groups, including ACT 1, Real Life Players, Actors Bridge, Dream 7, and others. Darkhorse also hosts productions from Nashville Shakespeare Festival, Mockingbird Public Theater, and Peoples Branch Theater. Check them out at *darkhorsetheater.com*.

Davis Kidd Booksellers is a good place for acting and theater books, and as a hangout, try Noshville, a Jewish Deli on music row. Also, definitely go to Bongo Java, also on music row. Many actors go there. They have a bulletin board where you might find a roommate, and upstairs they have a performance space for small productions, one-man shows, and some performance art.

Texas

Texas, lovingly called Southcoast by some of the locals, is another good place to get your union cards. The unions there make an effort to attract new members, unlike the locals in L.A. and New York, which sometimes seem to be trying to protect their current members by discouraging potential new ones. Also, the unions in Texas are willing to make some limited concessions to corporations, production companies, ad agencies, and theaters to entice them to sign union contracts, for example, allowing companies to sign union contracts on a one-production basis to encourage the hiring of union actors. Equity has an umbrella contract that makes it easier for non-Equity theaters to hire Equity actors.

Texas is a friendly state with affordable housing and an optimistic pride in itself. There is a lot of tacky new money there, which in Texas somehow doesn't seem offensive at all. Instead, the new money just seems to be a part of good ole Texas, like the cowboys who don't take their hats off in the restaurants. People from all over the country have moved to Texas and seem quite happy there, including these days some herb-tea-drinking vegetarians.

An actor working the Texas market will need a reliable car and a cellular phone because of the distances involved. Dallas used to be the most convenient place to live because there was more work in the combined Dallas/Fort Worth area than in Houston, San Antonio, or Austin, but these days Austin, the centrally located state capital, is probably most convenient.

Austin, home to the Willie Nelson/Waylon Jennings/Dixie Chicks brand of progressive country music, would seem to be a better choice of a place to locate for several reasons. Austin is about three and a half hours from Dallas and about two and a half hours from Houston, and as this is being written there are four Hollywood studio pictures being shot there, not counting Billy Bob Thornton's *The Alamo*, recently shot on a ranch outside of Austin, which has just wrapped. Other films shot in Austin include *Second Hand Lions, Where the Heart Is, Miss Congeniality, The New Guy,* and *The Rookie,* as well as the *Spy Kids* movies, I, II, and III. Sandra Bullock and Matthew McConaughey both have homes there. Austin has three fine universities with excellent film and theater departments and a very proactive film community. The Austin Film Society, a nonprofit group that promotes films in the area, negotiated a nice deal with the city to rent the hangers at their old municipal airport after the new international one was built and then turned the hangers into movie sound stages. Rick Linklater, a local director *(School of Rock, Dazed and Confused),* is a big supporter of Austin filmmaking and of independent filmmakers in Texas.

Austin has four Equity theaters and another twenty-something venues, indicating an active theater community. Their umbrella organization is called the Austin Circle of Theaters, and their website is *acotonline.org.* All the area theaters are listed with contact information. An inexpensive annual membership gets you discounted tickets and acting classes, audition notices, and a lot more. Check 'em out.

There are eight talent agencies in Austin that handle both union and nonunion talent. Some of the more active casting directors include Jo Edna Boldin, who cast the Tommy Lee Jones picture, *Cheer Up,* and Beth Sepko, who just cast the HBO series *$5.15 an Hour.*

Dallas is a million-plus city that is something like Atlanta in terms of climate and ambiance, but any city in Texas is still, and will always be, Texas. Dallas has state-of-the-art production facilities that have attracted big-name filmmakers like Kevin Costner and Oliver Stone, as well as a good deal of television production such as the *Dallas* series and *Walker, Texas Ranger.* The PBS kid show *Wishbone* is also shot there, as was the NBC movie of the week *The Saving of Jessica Lynch.* Hundreds of large corporations are located in the Dallas area, making for an excellent corporate, commercial, and voice-over market, plus lots of print work, especially for catalogs. Commercials, corporates, and digitals are shot mostly under AFTRA contracts. The Dallas AFTRA local also has an excellent website at *entertainet.com/dfwactors* with information about agents, casting directors, and FAQs for people just getting started in the business, as well as links to acting schools in the area, industry publications, and more. Also, if you move to Dallas, join S.T.A.G.E., the Society for Theatrical Artists' Guidance and Enhancement. (Yup.) The reasonable membership dues get you the monthly newsletter and access to the hotline to keep abreast of what is going on in theater, film, and TV. You will also get a chance to showcase for casting directors once a month and have access to other services to help you get started. They have a bulletin board, where you might find a roommate, and a wonderful performing arts library, where you can do research, make some contacts, and probably make some friends.

Although the Houston local of SAG handles SAG business for the state, the buzz is that this will change in the future and that the SAG office will move to the state capital of Austin, where the SAG films are getting made these days. There are still SAG commercials and corporates shot in Houston, and the union work is about evenly divided with AFTRA. Houston also has a community of independent filmmakers and a loyal group of SAG actors, but I don't get the sense that Houston is really where most of the film and TV action is in Texas these days. I'd say if you live there, be willing to drive to Austin for film work. Houston has a good theater scene, though, with about forty theaters that can be found at *houstontheater.org*.

An actor trying to work fulltime in Texas will probably need to keep his or her hand in all these Texas markets and be willing to drive all over the place. Before moving to Texas, check out the fine website created by Austin actress Mona Lee, *thebizonline.com* and then get her directory, *The BIZ Books, Actors Resources*, for a thorough guide to what's happening all over the state. It will help you get the feel of the place, and incidentally she also offers acting classes and seminars with industry professionals.

Missouri

For an actor to make his entire living as an actor in Missouri, it will probably be necessary to work the entire state, especially its two largest cities.

St. Louis

After the Civil War St. Louis came within a hair's breadth of becoming the capital of the United States. Washington, D.C. was considered by many to be a Southern city, which had only become the nation's capital upon the insistence of the Virginia slave owner, Thomas Jefferson. Moreover, after the Civil war the city was teeming with camp-following prostitutes and runaway slaves, and our national lawmakers wanted to get out of there. As the largest city of a former slave state that did not secede from the union, St. Louis seemed an ideal replacement. Situated right in the center of the country where the Mississippi and Missouri Rivers converge, it was also the gateway to the West, that vast expanse of undeveloped land waiting to be exploited. The arch of St. Louis symbolizes that gateway.

Washington, D.C. remained our capital thanks to the efforts of a local millionaire who ran those "undesirable" ladies out of town and then hired work gangs to pick up the litter and give the town a new coat of paint. The result was spiffy enough to change history.

St. Louis still made out just fine as the gateway to the West, however. It became a new city of art and culture, and to those who migrated across the Mississippi River it became "back east." St. Louis, a city of predominantly brick buildings with abundant trees that line streets and shelter homes, has now become one of the Midwest's principal industrial, commercial, educational, and cultural centers.

There is, of course, work for actors there. Most of the acting community's dollar earnings come from AFTRA contracts, both because of the earnings of AFTRA broadcasters and freelance voice-over talent, and also because most of the union contracts were first negotiated by the AFTRA local there. Producers have continued to work under those contracts for TV commercials and corporates because of a good relationship with the union and also because of the good relationship they have with the AFTRA actors, whose pension and welfare contributions go into that one union, thereby increasing health insurance and retirement benefits. There are some fifty-six AFTRA signatory producers in town, a number that makes for a healthy market where an actor can make a living. The TV show *Game of Our Lives* was produced there under an AFTRA contract. Very few SAG commercials are made there, and for out-of-town SAG work agents usually submit actors' demo tapes.

The St. Louis metropolitan area has twenty-one theaters, Equity and non-Equity, and eight dinner theaters, and this indicates a solid actor base. To check them out individually, as well as to look at other artistic and cultural events in the city, visit the St. Louis Attractions website at *stlouisattractions.com/theater.* You might also want to look at *jamesedwardashton.com* though I can't tell you much about this one.

Kansas City

The Missouri River crosses the state from west to east, and on the western end lies Kansas City, at one time the gateway to the plains of Kansas.

There has never been a SAG office or much SAG presence in Kansas City, so producers have always dealt with AFTRA there and get a fine level of service from that AFTRA office. Most of the voice-over work is freelance, performed by AFTRA members, although broadcasters do some of it, and freelancers do some broadcast-type promos. AFTRA TV commercials and corporates are also produced there.

SAG films have been few and far between in the area, although the new director of the city film commission is a SAG member, and Kansas City actors are hopeful that he will reenergize things and be a strong voice for professionalism. A few years ago, portions of *Ride with the Devil* and *Mr. and Mrs. Bridge* were shot in the area.

For theater, Kansas City has eight Equity houses, and some Kansas City actors actually make a nice living doing theater there. Don Scott, executive director of the AFTRA office, refers to the Kansas City theater scene as "an undiscovered treasure," and to me this indicates a cooperative and supportive spirit in their acting community. He also mentions that there are numerous acting classes taught by AFTRA, AEA, and SAG actors in the city, again an indication of a fine community spirit. To learn more about K.C. theater, there's a good website that describes the theater scene, *actorscraftstudio.com.*

Kansas City has four effective union-franchised talent agents but only one casting office, Wright-Laird Casting, described by a union person as "not necessarily a friend to the union actor." If you are in that market, ask locally what this means.

Finally, I think the words of Don Scott himself, executive director of the AFTRA office, sum up the Kansas City scene just fine.

> I think anyone who has ever shot in Kansas City has been pleasantly surprised. We have a wonderful talent pool, many of whom have worked in major studio films and television, and also a wealth of lesser-known talent. We have an incredible base of tech people, from directors, photographers, editors, grips, special effects (both conventional and state of the art CGI), production assistants, etc. and varied and colorful locations that can offer city skyline, country, prairie, lush, desolate, modern and period settings. Most important, the community is not jaded and burned by filmmaking, but is open and very cooperative when filmmakers choose this location.

I would certainly advise checking out the Kansas City Independent Film Coalition's website at *ifckc.com* as a way of getting familiar with that scene.

"If the American theater rejuvenates itself, it will not be in New York but in the regions." —Jose Quintero, founder, Circle in the Square Theater

"What do I tell playwrights about Broadway? I tell them to ignore it." —Edward Albee, Pulitzer Prize-winning playwright

Chicago

Someone once described theater as "people sitting in the dark watching people in the light show them what it means to be human." Chicago is probably the best theater town in America. If you believe that theater is an art that can give voice to the human soul, if you believe that theater, like poetry, should engage the mind as well as the emotions, if you feel that you must work on the stage because your heart will continue to ache unless you do, then Chicago just might be the place for you. There are other actors like you there who are committed to theater, and they will understand you.

New York theater is becoming the new Las Vegas, Off-Broadway theaters are now in New Jersey, and Chicago has become the new Off Broadway, a place where new works in theater are born. The city supports more than two hundred theaters, and the reason for that is the people of Chicago. They go to the theater, and even shows in a little hole-in-the-wall theater are often sold out.

The city government itself is so committed to theater that they will sometimes change zoning laws so that a theater can operate. Recently the city leased a historic building on the "Magnificent Mile," not to a corporation that would have paid a huge rent for it and pumped large sums of money into the economy but rather to the Lookinglass Theater, founded by *Friends* actor David Schwimmer, a Chicago actor who kept his heart there, as many Chicago actors do. John Maloney from *Fraser* is another example.

David Mamet is a Chicago playwright. Viola Spolin developed her improvisation methods for acting and teaching, and her son, Paul Sills, went on to be one of the founders of Second City, perhaps the most respected improv group in America. Tim Robbins founded his own theater company there before going to Hollywood. The Belushi brothers as well as other *Saturday Night Live* actors came out of there. Gary Sinise, John Malkovich, and Joan Allen founded Steppenwolf Theater in Chicago before becoming movie stars. John and Joan Cusack, brother and sister, are Chicago actors who still maintain residences there and go back there to work whenever possible.

The Fugitive and *Road to Perdition* are examples of big-budget Hollywood pictures shot in Chicago, but it is expensive for Hollywood to shoot there, and the movie *Chicago* was shot in Toronto. Like many cities around the U.S., the city is working on tax breaks to help redress that situation.

Although Washington, D.C. makes the third largest number of training films in the country, Chicago is third in the combined number of training films, commercials, and voice-overs made. That's the kind of work an actor can do in the daytime, leaving nights free for theater. It is also third in both SAG and AFTRA earnings after L.A. and New York. A higher percentage of actors in Chicago manage to earn their entire living from acting than in either New York or L.A., and that's something to think about if you just have to act, and especially if you just have to act on the stage. A Chicago actor can work in those little theaters, perhaps under an Equity Small Professional Theater Contract, make a couple hundred bucks a week, supplemented with a couple of day jobs a month in voice-over, print, or commercial work, and can afford an apartment, pay the bills, and do without a car due to the city's excellent transportation system.

If you move there during the summer, you might find an empty apartment, but more likely you'll have to sublet for the summer until September to sign a new lease with the landlord. Because of the city's rent regulations, leases are written October 1 and May 1. You will subscribe to *Performink*, Chicago's equivalent of New York's *Back Stage* and L.A.'s *Back Stage West*. You can subscribe directly at their website, *performink.com*. You'll also want to buy *The Book: An Actor's Guide to Chicago*. Another useful book is *Acting in Chicago: How to Break into Theater, Film and Television*, published by Act I.

Act I bookstore is now called Soliloquy, by the way, and is located at 1724 West Belmont in the Lakeview neighborhood. There will be audition notices on the bulletin boards as well as offers to sublet and share apartments.

After you have an apartment and a phone, keep submitting your headshot and résumé to agents until one of them calls you for an appointment to come in, at which time have a couple of well-tuned monologues ready. Consider taking classes at the Actor's Center, Act One Studio, and at the Audition Studio, where Ed Hooks teaches. He's the author of *The Ultimate Scene and Monologue Book* that I recommended using to find scenes and a monologue that suit your type. Start networking and hustling and keep hustling your own work even after you are listed with an agent, either with several or with one that you work with exclusively. Get information on the agents first from other actors and get several opinions on these agents and how to deal with them. Remember that no one person, especially another actor, is the last word in this business.

Something else: don't bitch about the cold when winter comes. The cold is a shared cultural experience in Chicago, where people quietly assume it is good for keeping the gene pool strong. Just get yourself a windproof down overcoat, good boots and gloves, and get with the program. Things are very cozy indoors.

The North Country Fair

As in Chicago, cold is a shared cultural experience during the winter in Michigan and Minnesota, and the rural areas of these two states make that a beautiful experience. Cross country skiing through pristine forests, ice-skating on a thousand lakes, ice-fishing with the guys while sharing whiskey and jokes, and a pleasantness in the people that has the ring of truth to it—all these things contribute to making this region a fair one indeed. Garrison Keillor tells us that "all the women are strong, all the men are good looking, and all the children are above average," and it seems he's got a point.

Both Michigan and Minnesota have beautiful location sites for films and television, and because they haven't been overused, most shots still seem new and fresh but still very American. My hunch is that in the future this area will one day provide locations for big-budget movies the way Georgia and the Carolinas do now. The state is permit-free with the exception of state parks and state roads, but location fees are very reasonable and sometimes free there as well, and the communities are film-friendly with midwestern hospitality. Independent film producers, the kind who prefer to tell stories that engage both the heart and the mind, are already taking advantage of the region. One example is an independent film by Rich Brauer called *Barn Red*, with Ernest Borgnine as an old man trying to hold on to his family farm, which housing developers are trying to acquire—not a new theme but still a very moving rendition of an old one, word has it.

With its two peninsulas reaching into the shining big sea waters of three of the Great Lakes, Michigan has over three thousand miles of coastline, while Minnesota has hundreds of miles of the Lake Superior coastline, shared with Wisconsin and Canada. The Upper Peninsula of Michigan and Minnesota's Lake Superior shoreline look like America did a century ago, and perhaps earlier. Imagine a camping trip up there, with children sitting around a fire listening to someone read Longfellow's poem of Hiawatha to them in the firelight.

The crew base in both states is very good, with plenty of depth in all key departments. I remember talking once to a best boy gaffer on a film in L.A. who was counting the days until he could get the hell out of L.A. and back to that north country, "where you can believe what people tell you," as he put it. When Jeff Daniels returned to his home state of Michigan to start his own independent film company, he chose to use Michigan crews instead of filming more cheaply across the Canadian border. Rich Brauer, mentioned above, was his director of photography on both of Daniel's pictures to date and also did the editing.

Detroit

The city in Michigan where it's easiest to make a living as an actor is, of course, Motor City, Motown, or Detroit, as you please. The major U.S. auto manufacturers are all located there. The concentration of a particular industry in one area is not unusual in the United States, nor anywhere in the world for that matter. If an area has the right geography, such as lakes for barges full of coal and iron ore, or the right climate, such as sunshine 350 days a year as in L.A., industries will begin there, labor will move there and become skilled, and support industries will sprout up. That's how 90 percent of America's tufted carpet came to be made in the little town of Dalton, Georgia, for example.

Because of its car culture, Detroit's public transportation is almost nonexistent, though I'm told you can get a great deal on a used car there. Naturally, lots of car commercials are made in Detroit, and there is a lot of work for actors in all kinds of other commercials as well. Those intended for national use are shot on film under SAG contracts. Because Michigan is a strong union state, you need to be a member of SAG to do those commercials. Some recent SAG films include 8 Mile, an Eminem film shot entirely in Detroit, In the Shadows of Motown, and part of Road to Perdition.

SAG and AFTRA share an office in Detroit, as they do in most thinking parts of the country. The radio and voice-over work, as well as TV commercials and corporates, is done under AFTRA contracts.

Detroit's union-franchised talent agencies also act as de facto casting directors, so Detroit actors consequently list with them all.

Guess what? Detroit is also a fine theater town that supports some thirty theaters. A city that can support that many theaters indicates a good theater audience as well as an actor base with real depth. Jeff Daniels opened the Purple Rose Theater in Chelsea, as well as his own independent film production company, Purple Rose Films, also located there. So far he's written and produced two feature films that were shot entirely in Michigan. This is exactly the kind of thing that ought to be happening in all the regions, and Jeff Daniels still works in Hollywood and Europe, so who's dumberer? Not Jeff Daniels. For a list of theaters in the state of Michigan, as well as other resources, check out the Theater Alliance of Michigan at *theaterallianceofmichigan.org.*

The Twin Cities

Some feel that the Twin Cities of Minneapolis and St. Paul make for an even better theater town than Chicago, but once a city becomes this good, it ceases to matter very much which one is "best." Every theater aficionado in the world has heard of the Guthrie, which has a history rivaling any theater in America, and there are many other Equity theaters in the area as well, most operating under Small Professional Theater (SPT) contracts.

SAG and AFTRA share an office in Minneapolis, run by a delightfully helpful executive director, Colleen Aho. In all, there are twenty-five local production companies signed to SAG commercial contracts. As in Michigan, there has recently been strong growth in independent films, usually shot under SAG contracts—*Detective Fiction,* for example, which was written and directed by a local actor and made it to Sundance. Both the Minnesota Film and TV Board and the cities of Minneapolis and St. Paul provide strong support services to film and TV production.

Seventy-five companies are signatories to AFTRA contracts. This includes radio and TV commercial signatories, nonbroadcast (corporate/industrial) signatories, and some others. There is also substantial radio programming work there, like Garrison Keillor's "Prairie Home Companion," which is an AFTRA show and much of which is taped in Minneapolis when they're not on the road. Digital projects are also emerging in the region, as everywhere.

Casting in the Twin Cites seems to be done mostly by four casting directors: Lynn Blumenthal, Curt Akerlind, Barbara Shelton, and Jean Rohn, though Lynn Blumenthal and Curt Akerlind are said to be bigger players in feature films, and Barbara Shelton handles more of the nonunion work.

There is an excellent resource begun by the Twin Cities Theater and Film Alliance and now run independently as a website. It is now called TC Theater and Film, and because it accepts advertising it is now free for you to peruse the lists of theaters, audition notices, etc., so do that at *tctheaterandfilm.org.* There is also a support network for new talent called the Twin Cities Actors Forum, which describes itself as "a group of local actors, directors and writers from both theater and film that share a dedication to their craft and the drive to strengthen the local arts community." You can get their newsletter for free as well as attend their weekly meetings every Tuesday at 7:30 p.m. (sharp!). Look for them at *mntalent.com.*

Colorado

Even though a large part of Colorado is as flat as Kansas, when we think of the state we think of the Rocky Mountains, and that's where the action is. At one time those mountains were home to the mountain men of legend, trapping beavers for making stovepipe hats. Then came mining, and Boulder appeared on the map along with Denver. Then the rich and famous went there to ski, and Aspen was born.

Denver is called the mile-high city, and because of the altitude and the consequent lower boiling point of water, there are no indigenous bagel bakeries there, so I'm told. It's a new city of glass and steel, with service and high-tech industries but little manufacturing. Boulder is home to a fine university as well as a spiritual center for American Buddhism and many peaceful, free, and groovy people, including my publisher. Aspen has become an American Switzerland.

There is an AFTRA/SAG office in Denver, which also handles SAG business for Nevada and which handles the fair amount of SAG work in the area. The local has some eight hundred SAG members, but as there are only about twenty local signatories to SAG and AFTRA contracts, Colorado does not seem to be a place to move just to have an acting career. Colorado should be its own reward, and an acting career is possible there, as it is anywhere. Most of the SAG work is for TV commercials, and most of the radio commercials are done under an AFTRA contract. I do know of one actress who moved from D.C. to Denver and now does very well there in voice-overs.

In the past, Westerns were shot in Colorado when they were still making them—How the West Was Won, for example—and a few years ago Dumb and Dumber was shot there, and more recently Silver City and The Laramie Project. Although the event upon which the Laramie story was based took place in Wyoming, it was more convenient to shoot the story in Colorado because of a better local film infrastructure.

There's also theater there. Denver has the Denver Center Theater Company, with four stages and four different Equity contracts depending on which stage an actor works. There is also the Bug Theater Company in Denver, and in Colorado Springs, the UCCS THEATERWORKS, a university theater that uses Equity guest artists.

If you are going to work the Colorado market it would be a good idea to join CASA, the Colorado Actors and Screenwriters Assembly. This group, as described by its founder, Cheryl Whitney, is a community of actors, writers, and filmmakers who pool their talents in order to mutually enhance their acting, writing, and filmmaking skills.

The monthly CASA General Assemblies are held as free workshops for actors and writers. Actors have an opportunity to brush up on the "cold reading" skills by performing work submitted by local screenwriters and playwrights. Actors may also present their monologues for audience critique.

Local independent filmmakers frequent the assemblies in search of new talent.

The website is *groups.msn.com/ColoradoActorsScreenwritersAssembly* (shortcut url: *devoted.to/CASA*) and is the local online hub for actors, writers, theater groups, talent agents, filmmakers, and other entertainment industry professionals and organizations. Check the boards daily for audition notices, upcoming industry-related meetings, classes, seminars, announcements, news, events, and member discussions. Actors may post headshots and bios to the site. The CASA website also contains a local resources link page.

CASA membership and all CASA-related meetings and events are free and open to the general public. Just go to the CASA website and click the "Join" button.

The Colorado SAG office also handles New Mexico and Wyoming filming. Such classic films as *Silverado, The Milagro Beanfield War,* and *Wyatt Earp* were shot in New Mexico and more recently Sean Penn's *21 Grams* and Ron Howard's *The Missing* were shot there. Some PBS shows such as *Coyote Waits* are also shot in New Mexico. In Wyoming, the sci fi film *Star Troopers* took advantage of those wide-open, undershot spaces for an otherworld kind of look. Susan Garule, executive director of the Denver SAG office, called me on her cell phone from a movie set in New Mexico to give me this information. Wouldn't it be nice if the government worked this way for us? (Thanks, Susan.) Check out her regular column for the Colorado Film and Video Association, *cfva.com,* also the site for current production news in the state.

Arizona

Once upon a time toward the beginning of the twentieth century, Hollywood was the name of a large ranch, and cattle grazed where the movie studios are now. After the movie industry blossomed in the Los Angeles area, it was still possible for some years to drive out of town to film Westerns in rural areas, but after World War II if a film producer wanted to shoot in wide-open spaces, he needed to go to Utah, Nevada, or, of course, to Arizona. In the last half of the twentieth century, Arizona was host to almost two thousand Western film and TV episodes. Starting in the 1960s the American audience lost its taste for Westerns, though there are still a few made, so now most of the movie work in Arizona tends to be low-budget features shot for under $2 million, which is cheap for a movie these days. There is also a burgeoning growth in films shot on DVD, like student films and some really low-budget experimental films shot for less than $75,000. Some technicians say a digital production can look as good as film if enough care is taken with lighting, but I'll leave that question to the behind-the-camera folks to decide.

Some big-budget features are still shot in Arizona if the story requires wide-open spaces. Examples include *Return of the Jedi* and *Tombstone,* and more recently, *Scorpion King* and *Windtalkers.* The low-budget but very popular *Bill and Ted's Excellent Adventure* was shot there, as was *Confessions of a Dangerous Mind.* The recent PBS TV special *Skinwalkers* was shot under an AFTRA contract. Phoenix and Sedona each have an annual film festival, and a fair number of Hollywood émigrés have either moved or have second homes out there in that clean air.

Most of the commercials are shot under SAG contracts, and AFTRA work is usually voice-over for radio, though there are not that many local signatories to those contracts. SAG and AFTRA share an office and also take care of Utah's business from there. The casting in Phoenix seems to be about evenly split between Darleen Wyatt, Sonny Seibel, and Gay Gilbert, who is also an active film advocate for the Arizona film community as chair of the Arizona Entertainment Alliance.

There is plenty of theater in Arizona too. Linda Durant, a local actress, teacher and host to a website *(durantcom.com)* devoted mostly to theater, reports that there are some sixty active theater companies in the Phoenix area, Equity and non-Equity. Arizona Theater, Phoenix Theater, Actors Theater, and Arizona Jewish Theater are four Equity theaters there. Southwest Shakespeare Company and the Black Theater Troupe are currently working under an Equity letter of agreement. There is also a theater company and performing arts academy in Phoenix called Theaterscape, *theaterscape.com,* that holds Equity and non-Equity general auditions once a year.

A restaurant called Durant's (no relation to Linda) with a Chicago gangland-style decor is reported to be popular with actors after a show. Techs seem to prefer to drink beer and play darts at the Georgian Dragon, and the gay glam spot is called Amsterdam. Take your pick.

In Tucson, the Arizona Theater Company and the Gaslight Theater are examples of an Equity LORT theater and a non-Equity theater, respectively. The *Arizona Republic* newspaper in Tucson reports on the theater scene and also has articles of interest to actors and film folks. Their website is *azcentral.com/ent/arts.*

So, if you like wide-open spaces, clean air, and some majestic natural scenery and are thinking about heading to Arizona, go on the web to *aroundarizona.net* and you'll find a list of eighty-eight Arizona theaters of all shapes and sizes, complete with phone numbers. Also, be sure also to check out Linda's site at *durantcom.com.*

Happy trails!

San Francisco

I asked Jean Schiffman, San Francisco actress, former editor of *Callboard* magazine, and author of *The Working Actor's Tool Kit,* what kind of actor should consider making San Francisco home, and she answered, "someone who wants the opportunity to do lots of stage work, is interested in experimental work, wants to work within a tight-knit community, doesn't expect to make a living exclusively doing film and TV, is possibly interested in video game work, and who wants to live in the most beautiful, politically liberal, arts-friendly, and expensive city in the country."

That kind of knowledgeable, articulate answer is the kind you can expect from San Francisco folks. The Bay Area is certainly lovely, and the ambiance is intellectual, artistic, and politically progressive. No place is perfect, but the only drawback I can personally think of about the Bay Area, besides the high rent, is the fact that many folks who live there seem somewhat smugly to assume that they are terrific people simply because they do live there. That said, I'll go on record as saying that I feel the quality of life in the Bay Area is among the best in the world if you can manage the rent. Oakland is less expensive than Berkeley or San Francisco, so that's probably where you should begin to look for a place. Despite a good public transportation system—BART and the buses—it's better to have a car, especially as you will probably not be living in San Francisco, at least at first. Also, that car can take you along the Pacific Coast Highway on the weekends for some of the most beautiful coastal scenery in the world.

Check out Theater Bay Area's website at *theaterbayarea.org* to start getting the feel of that market. They are a nonprofit service organization for theaters and theater professionals that has been around for twenty-five years and that publishes that monthly theater trade magazine called *Callboard*, San Francisco's equivalent of *Back Stage*, with a similar format and content including audition notices. I recommend becoming a member of Theater Bay Area so you can get half-price and comp tickets, discounts on acting classes, and also as a kind of commitment to the acting scene once you're out there. You might also hang out at Limelight Books, 1803 Market Street in San Francisco, *limelightbooks.com*. That's where Ed Hooks did the research for his book, *The Ultimate Scene and Monologue Book*, which I previously recommended for choosing your audition monologues as well as scenes for your acting class. There are frequent lectures, book signings, and other events at Limelight, and other actors hang out there a lot. You might find someone looking for a roommate or just some company for a round of beer to begin with, but it is definitely a place to hear the business buzz and get advice. Actors also hang out at Theater Bay Area, 870 Market Street.

Like New York and Chicago, San Francisco is a fine place to continue your training as an actor. The Jean Shelton Acting Studio, Full Circle Productions, Richard Seyd's classes, and the American Conservatory Theater's classes are all well known and respected. It's also a great theater town, with dozens of small Equity theaters where you can keep developing that acting muscle, meet other actors, and eventually get an agent, most of whom represent actors on an exclusive basis, so getting one will not be an immediate cakewalk. Keep at it though, and you'll eventually get one.

In terms of film work, there is some but not much, despite the fact that George Lucas lives in the area, Sean Penn and Robin Williams live there, and Francis Coppola's Zoetrope Studio (all-story.com) is still there. "It's notoriously difficult for filmmakers to shoot in San Francisco, lots of costs and obstacles and red tape involved," as Jean Schiffman adds. The reason that film permits are expensive and tough to get is because the city doesn't feel like closing things down just because someone wants to make a movie. There hasn't been a TV series shot there since *Nash Bridges* for the same reason. Still, San Francisco has always been a tolerant community, so an experimental "guerrilla" film crew, cleverly disguised as grown-ups, can usually get in and out of a neighborhood to shoot a scene for a low-budget movie without ruffling too many feathers. Oakland is somewhat more film-friendly, and these days there is more filming done there. That means a chance for extra work, which could eventually lead to a SAG card if you don't have one yet.

There is a lot of AFTRA voice-over work done in the Bay Area, with a few big hitters getting most of it, as in most places. Voicetrax, Voice One, and the Voice Factory are the places to send your demo tapes. Commercials are about evenly divided between SAG and AFTRA contracts, and most production companies are signatories to both. Nancy Hayes and Beau Boineau seem to do the lion's share of commercial casting.

The Bay Area, like the Pacific Northwest, has been hurt by runaway film production to Canada. As I write this, Congress is considering tax breaks to encourage the return of U.S. film production, and perhaps that will be taking effect by the time you read this book.

The Pacific Northwest

Portland

I haven't been to Portland yet, so I'm going to let a local actor tell you about that market just as he told it to me. Some of the things he says about getting work locally also apply to other regions, by the way.

Dear Andrew,

If you really want to work, you have a much better chance of working in Portland than you do in larger markets, which are over-run with actors. An actor in Portland can build a résumé quicker and gain valuable experience that would be difficult elsewhere. When films come to Portland, they often need and want to hire local talent in fairly big roles. I booked a lead role in a cable movie that I likely would not have gotten in the room to read for in L.A. or

New York. I also booked a big role in a Stephen King movie shooting in Seattle, which aired nationally on ABC. Even the smaller roles I have played in big movies are roles I likely would not have read for in L.A. There are just too many people in the way in L.A. There is also a healthy and growing independent scene here. In fact, Portland was voted one of the top ten cities for independent film, and I suspect will be in the top three soon. Project after project is being done here, and the quality of these projects is increasing rapidly because there are great crew people to be found here as well as actors. I did a couple of small projects in L.A., and with all that these people claimed to know, they were nowhere near the quality I am seeing in Portland. If you are good, you can star in a movie here. Not so likely in L.A., even if you are good.

Perhaps the biggest reason to stay in Portland is just flat-out quality of life. Rents are cheaper, it's easy to get around, you can have a decent little job and still get to act here. There are great restaurants, nice people, the pace is more tolerable, more great beer on tap, far fewer posers. And, get this, there are four seasons. Things change color, die, are born again, and grow. It rains, snows a little, lots of swimming holes, camping, fishing, all kinds of recreation at your fingertips, and fresh air everywhere. And being an actor is not seen as repugnant, but actually interesting. We don't have to hear that you can't throw a stick and not hit an actor, like they say about L.A.

Thanks, and best of luck with your book,

Robert Blanche
(Some of his work can be seen at
us.imdb.com/name/nm0002604)

With restructuring, SAG business is now handled out of San Francisco, but the AFTRA office in Portland is very friendly and helpful. The casting directors who do most of the casting in the area are Megann Ratzow for film, Lana Veenker for commercials, and Danny Stoltz for some of each. Check out the Oregon Media Production Association at *ompa.org*. And go down to Ashland for Shakespeare!

Seattle

When I called the Seattle local of AFTRA to get some information on this market for the first edition of this book, the lady jokingly said on the phone "Don't come here. You'll hate it. The weather is terrible! It rains all the time!" At that time there was a large migration taking place from southern California to the Pacific Northwest, and not all of it was welcome. It does rain a lot in Seattle, to be sure, but more in terms of the length of its ten-month rainy season than in the number of inches of rainfall a year. However, the weather is apparently not bad enough to prevent an ongoing migration of people from relocating to this clean, pleasant, intellectual, and cosmopolitan city. Locals came to resent this influx, complaining that Seattle was being "Californicated," especially by people from L.A. The lady at AFTRA was just good-naturedly voicing local sentiment.

Local actors and technicians in any region would prefer, of course, that film and TV production companies bring only their money to the area and hire everyone locally, but it just don't work that way. For a time there was quite a bit of film and TV production in Seattle, TV series such as *Twin Peaks, Northern Exposure,* and *The Commish,* for example. These days, however, Seattle is probably the city most affected by runaway production to Canada, with Vancouver just over three hours away to the north and about half as expensive to shoot in, both because of the currency situation as well as the tax breaks the Canadian government offers to encourage film production. This situation may change with legislation pending in the U.S. Congress. Until then, Seattle is still a wonderful place to live, especially if you want to do theater. As you have probably heard, the theater in Seattle is fine enough to put it in a league with San Francisco, the Twin Cities, and Chicago. The Seattle area has a dozen Equity theaters and has the distinction of having produced *The Kentucky Cycle,* the only play to win the Pulitzer Prize before ever playing in New York.

If you like herb tea, organic food, and intellectual conversation and quietly assume a certain superiority over people who don't, then you will probably like Seattle. If you don't much care for these things and are not a political liberal, you may not be comfortable there unless you can coexist with the peaceful, free, and groovy without talking politics. If it's any consolation, the city is also known as *the* place to get a really great cup of coffee.

Rents are not bad in Seattle, comparatively speaking, although crowding has pushed them up a bit. The public transportation system is clean and efficient; however, most of these liberals still drive cars. There is a joke among actors in the area that they belong to the "I-5 Repertory" in that many spend a lot of time on that interstate auditioning and working in Portland, Ashland, and even San Francisco—other cities where people are groovy because they live there.

Most of the paying work is AFTRA work, and SAG and AFTRA share an office. Actors list exclusively with one agent, so getting one is going to take some talking, first with other actors to do your research on the different agents, then with the agents themselves as they agree to see you. There is still a good bit of location film work shot around Seattle, *The Hunted* and *Elephant,* for example.

The Pacific Northwest is quite beautiful, and the rain is one of the reasons for that, as it's what keeps everything so green. I must confess that I like the whole area, perhaps because of my particular politics. Somehow, seeing police on mountain bikes makes me feel all warm and homey.

Before moving to Seattle, get a copy of *The Actor's Handbook: Seattle and the Pacific Northwest*, by Mark Jaroslaw. Read it to get the feel of the area, which includes Alaska and Montana, as well as Washington and Oregon, and then use the book as a resource directory once you're in the area. In Seattle there is a bookstore called The Play's the Thing Drama Bookstore, which is a good place to check the bulletin board for auditions and roommates. There is also a space there for staged readings and a lounge to sit, read, and meet other actors. The coffee there is great, and so is the herb tea.

Chapter 8

Fortress
Hollywood

A Pacific Coast Beachhead

Let me begin this chapter by saying that everything you have ever heard about Los Angeles is true—all the good and all the bad, all at once. The greater Los Angeles area is a universe where you create your own world. You may have heard a New Yorker use the expression "my New York." If you stick it out in L.A., you may one day use the expression "my Los Angeles." Rather than being a New York world, which is narrow, cramped, and intense, a Los Angeles world will usually be roomy, spread out, and laid back.

> In Los Angeles you get in your car and you drive. You can spend a whole day without really interacting with anybody.
> —Kim Orchen, casting director

And superficial, yes. The biggest complaint about Los Angeles, besides the traffic and the smog, is the lack of intellectual life. L.A. is derided for being a phony and superficial place, as New York is derided for being an aggressive, brutal place. Both descriptions are partially true and partially unfair. Rather than make judgments, my advice to you would be to bring a positive attitude to either place and then search out the things that make you happy.

Before going to L.A. I advise you to prepare for the move a year in advance. Going to either New York or Los Angeles "just to see" or "to try my luck" is like playing the lottery, which is easier and cheaper to play in your own hometown. Before you go to Los Angeles, get your SAG card, a demo reel of some of your work, and a decent résumé. Get the *Los Angeles Times* on the Internet to check out the classified ads about rents and opportunities in terms of your "other job," as well as to begin getting the feel of the city.

> You may have heard that we had an earthquake this morning in Southern California, 4.2 on the Richter scale. For those of you not familiar with earthquakes, that's strong enough to knock books off the shelves. Fortunately, in Southern California there are no books on the shelves.
> —Johnny Carson, talk show host

Then start saving your money for the move. You will need a car from the moment you arrive in Los Angeles, so you might as well bring one. As an actor you may be spending four hours a day in your car on a regular basis, so your car should be safe and comfortable. Los Angeles folks think of time spent in their cars as their private time. When you are ready to make the move, get your car in good running shape and then plan to stop in Phoenix to have it serviced by an AAA-approved mechanic before driving that last leg through the desert. Many vultures perch along that stretch of highway who claim to be mechanics and at first glance look exactly like human beings. Pack your stuff in boxes before you head west and have them shipped to you via UPS once you have a place to live in L.A. Rather than hauling furniture out there, cultivate a camp sense of humor and plan on shopping at thrift stores to furnish your domicile after you've found one, perhaps in the "late student poverty" or "post modern actor" style of decor. You might even fool someone into thinking it's the latest thing.

During that year of preparation, subscribe to *Back Stage West/Drama-Logue* to begin getting the feel of the industry from an actor's point of view. Recommended reading is M. K. Lewis's book *Your Film Acting Career*, which is almost totally L.A. oriented. Read it before you go out, and again as soon as you arrive. This book is considered one of the best around with respect to the L.A. market and you should get his viewpoint on things. Mr. Lewis likes L.A. and is a part of the Hollywood establishment. He also seems to be a nicer guy than me, judging by his book.

The *CD Directory* is something else you should subscribe to before you go, and continue to subscribe to as long as you are in the business. The addresses of all three publications just mentioned are listed in the appendix. The *CD Directory* lists the names and addresses of all the casting directors in Los Angeles. It also lists all the TV shows being shot there, as well as who is currently doing the casting.

While you're getting ready to head out there, you might list the TV shows you watch and look up the addresses of the casting directors who cast those shows. Start sending them notes, not face cards at this point but perhaps postcards of your hometown. Tell them that you enjoyed the episode and that the casting was excellent if you thought so. (Don't write if you didn't.)

Do the same when you go to the movies. The name of the casting director will be in the opening credits. Make a note of who did the casting and drop the casting director a note if you think something was well cast. Why? Put yourself in the casting director's shoes. Wouldn't you be amused and pleased to get a card from Alabama or Maine complimenting you on your work? After getting a couple of those hometown postcards, wouldn't you be somewhat curious to meet the person who sent them if he arrived in L.A., even if just to see what he looked like?

Anywhere you decide to live in Los Angeles is going to be a kind of trade-off. For auditioning, the actual city of Hollywood is probably the most central and convenient, in so far as anything is convenient in that traffic, but it is often called Hollyweird. It seems to have more than its fair share of creeps. West Hollywood is nicer and more civilized, perhaps because it has a large gay population. Studio City is also fairly convenient and is full of all kinds of movie people. It is also hot and smoggy. Culver City is definitely worth checking out for economy, convenience, and less-polluted air. Santa Monica and the beaches have clean air, longer commuting times, and higher rents, except for the rent-controlled apartments, but it is said that rent-controlled apartments in Santa Monica are usually inhabited by people who were born there.

South and East L.A. are not viable choices as places to live because you need your car, and your car will get stolen in those places. Beverly Hills, Bel-Air, Brentwood, Encino, and Pacific Palisades are probably beyond your price range. As you will presumably be a SAG member before heading out there, one thing you might do is write to SAG a month before you are planning to leave home and ask them to post on their bulletin board the note you send, which asks to rent a sublet or to share an apartment. You might get lucky. Don't send anyone any money in advance, though. You're not that lucky.

When you arrive, find a place to live, set up your desk and filing system, etc., get your own phone put in, get a California driver's license and bank account (you'll need a credit card in addition to a California driver's license to open one), get your "other job," and get your headshot done and reproduced and your résumé photocopied. Then go to Samuel French or Larry Edmund's bookstore to buy a copy of *The Agencies* and *The Pacific Coast Studio Directory*. All this may take a couple of months to do, but when it is done you will have established your beachhead and will be ready to begin your reconnaissance operations.

Reconnaissance

Once you feel settled you can start networking into the industry. In this early stage in your Hollywood career, remember once again that the Creator gave you two ears and one mouth.

Joining the SAG Conservatory is definitely a good investment. For a SAG member it costs next to nothing. They'll tell you about the benefits. Start taking acting classes to sharpen up your acting tool and perhaps take some recommended cold-reading workshops with casting directors to start meeting them and also to watch other actors working. Start auditioning for Equity-waiver plays that rehearse and perform at night. Even if you do nothing but audition for months without getting a part, it is still a good way to meet other actors. Joining the Actor's Center is another way to meet actors and take classes.

You can buy *Back Stage West* at many convenience stores Wednesday night, a day sooner than if you subscribe to it. I don't recommend subscribing once you are living in L.A. You don't save any money by subscribing, and delivery through the mail is unreliable and sometimes late. It is easier just to buy it at your local convenience store each week. Check their casting notices and start sending out headshots. The auditions listed in *Back Stage West* are usually not cast through agents. Sometimes agents, especially new ones, put notices in *Back Stage West* stating that they are accepting submissions for possible representation.

"What kind of agents?" is a question you should ask, though there is no single answer to the question of why a talent agency puts an ad in there. Sometimes an agency just happens to be short on a certain type, perhaps your own. If the notice says *union talent only,* and they are looking for your type, by all means send them a headshot. If they are looking for nonunion talent, you need to be careful because they don't have to meet union ethical and professional standards, and anyway, if you are nonunion you don't belong in Los Angeles.

Remember going through the yellow pages, phoning all the ad agencies and video production companies, and starting files on the ones who hire actors? Good. You've had practice for what you will do with *The Pacific Coast Studio Directory.* Most of the area's production companies are listed.

Don't bother sending a headshot to Steven Spielberg. He will never see it. Don't bother sending headshots to those whom the directory says make motion pictures or commercials. They cast through casting directors and agents.

Contact the ones who make educational films, corporates, or if you fancy yourself a narrator, documentaries. Call them up, see if they keep headshots on file, make friends with the receptionist—who may also be the owner and the cameraman—and start a file on the ones who could one day give you a job.

Drop off headshots if you can, send them if you can't, ask if you can have an interview or an audition, and start keeping in touch on a monthly basis. Eventually you will get some action.

The people who make these kinds of films are usually friendly, honest, and down-to-earth folks, and they're nice folks to work with. If you seem the same way to them, they will probably (eventually) be glad to hire you.

The Headshot Bombardment

There is a better way to get an agent than waiting for a notice in *Back Stage West*. Buy a copy of *The Agencies* at one of the bookstores mentioned and pick out the hundred or so agents that you think would most likely be interested in representing you. This little book describes most, if not all, the agencies in town, the kind of talent they represent, and what they specialize in, such as commercials or the representation of athletes.

Do not bother at this point in your career with submitting your headshot to the more famous agencies like ICM, CAA, or William Morris. They handle movie stars, and even if they do you a favor by taking you on, your name will stay put on the bottom of their list

> Part of marketing yourself is getting out your materials so that luck can happen.
> —Terry Berland, casting director

with no action. Stick with the smaller agencies, provided they are SAG franchised. Write each agent a cover letter and mention the same kinds of things you would say in an interview with a casting director, such as the type of roles you think you are best suited for and that you are a disciplined, reliable actor. You can either hand-address these envelopes or buy labels from the *CD Directory*, but remember that labels smack of mass mailings and therefore seem less personal. Wait a week and follow up with a phone call asking for an interview.

Gird your loins because you will be rejected by almost all of them. They will tell you that they have more talent than they can handle but to get back in touch in about six months. Nevertheless, probably before you reach number one hundred, one of them will take you on, at least for commercials. It's harder to get a theatrical agent, but one for commercials is all you need to start with.

Once you've got an agent, paste the agency sticker on your résumé, over your own address and phone number, then make a hundred copies and trim and staple them to your headshots. You are a now a professional actor, represented by an agent! Give twenty-five headshot/résumés back to your agent and telephone at least every two weeks to see if you should drop off some more. That is always a legitimate reason to call your agent, and it will remind her of your existence. Also, now that you have an agent, you can get your picture in the *Academy Players Directory*. This is useful in that your agent can tell a casting director on the phone that your picture is on a certain page, and the casting director can look you up immediately, either in the hard copy or on the Internet.

You are now ready to begin your ground assault.

The Ground Assault

Get the latest edition of the *CD Directory* and make a file on each of the two hundred plus casting directors listed in it. This is going to take hours and hours and hours, but afterward updates will only take minutes (and discipline). On the tab of the file write the name of the casting director and the name of the casting company for alphabetical placement in your filing system later. Then write the zip code of their address on the tab as well. The reason for this will be explained again shortly.

I am now going to tell you to do something that is going to make these casting directors angry with me, but as I am not a part of the Hollywood establishment, I don't care! I am going to advise you, as many casting directors will also advise you, to deliver a headshot personally to the office of each casting director and to put it in the hands of the receptionist, then to smile at her and get her name. If you try to deliver them in alphabetical order you will be driving back and forth all over town and will not finish this task for about a year. If you divide them into zip code order, however, you can plan your schedule so that you can deliver at least two and perhaps several headshots on each trip, perhaps one trip in the morning and one in the afternoon each day. Bring the files and write down the receptionist's name each time. That night, write a thank-you note to each receptionist you have met, thanking her for being so nice. Make a note in the file to send the receptionist another headshot in a week. Note the name of the casting company in your daily schedule book under the appropriate date. When that day comes, get out the file and send another headshot addressed personally to the receptionist. Write her a note asking if you can come in for a general audition.

Many, if not most, of these headshots will wind up in the trash, but a certain percentage of these receptionists will hand-carry your headshot to the casting director and ask if she wants to see you. Even if the answer is "no," the casting director will still have seen your name and face. You may not have made waves, but you have made a ripple. Keep fishing, and sooner or later you will get a bite. Ask any salesman.

At the rate of twenty-five deliveries a week it will take you three months to deliver a headshot to each casting director. At the rate of one

> If I were an actor I would go to see all the casting directors in the book and ask each one of them for a general audition. Ten of them may get angry. So, what are they going to do— yell at you? The ones who talk to you are the ones you want to do business with anyway. You'd be surprised how many people do want to see your picture and résumé. Think of yourself as a salesman. Then go and knock at a hundred doors and ninety-five will say "No" but five just might say "Yes." Most of the time you might end up talking with an assistant. But remember, in this business, this year's assistant is maybe next year's casting director.
>
> —Rick Pagano, Casting Society of America

delivery a day, five days a week, it will take you close to a year to get to them all. Despite the fact that most casting directors say "no phone calls or personal deliveries," I think that you should do it anyway. Remember Rick Pagano's question, "What are they going to do—yell at you?"

All right, all right, if you don't have the fortitude to be that "pushy," then write a generic cover letter saying that you are new in town, that you are represented by such and such an agent, and that you would like to come in for a general audition at their convenience. You can buy casting director labels from the *CD Directory*, make them yourself once and for all on your computer, or hand-address the envelopes. You will get seen by fewer casting directors this way but will also suffer fewer face-to-face rejections. And, I am sorry to tell you, you will also get fewer jobs than those who find a way to be energetic and persistent without being a pest.

> You can be the most talented actor in the world, but if you don't know how to get out there and sell yourself, nobody is going to find out what you're capable of.
>
> —Christy Dooley, casting director

Let me reiterate that casting directors are not going to come looking for you. They must know you are available for work. You have a product to sell, presumably a good one, and you have every right to make that known. Your product will be rejected ten times more than it is purchased, at least that much, but you must learn to smile and go on to the next one. Any salesman will tell you that you get a higher percentage of sales from phone calls than from mailings, and an even higher percentage of sales from personal visits. You will also get more hard knocks this way, and the best salve for such wounds is a sense of humor. If you are going to go for the higher percentages that a ground assault will give you, you must learn to take the punch and make a joke about it.

Comrades, nobody said this was going to be easy.

Showcasing and Networking

If you are acting in a play, invite as many casting directors and agents as possible. The whole cast can, and perhaps should, chip in on mailing flyers and invitations to casting directors and agents. Don't expect many people to show up, however. The theater probably looks like a rat hole. Nevertheless, doing such plays keeps your tool sharp and gets you networking with other actors.

When you get a job—a commercial, a training film, a small part on a TV show or in a feature—you have a bit of news to put on your face cards that you are sending out at the rate of fifteen a day. (Remember?) When you are not working, send casting directors and independent production companies a thought for the day or tell them all the same joke. Use your head

I think assistants can be another means for actors to get exposure to casting directors. When you mail a flyer for a play you are doing, it would be a good idea to extend the invitation to also include the assistants. If my assistant goes and sees someone wonderful, she'll let me know, and of course a lot of assistants end up as casting directors.

—Lorna Johnson, casting director

enough so that what you write will be considered both personal and professional communication and not junk mail.

Your attitude should be that you are a part of this business, that you intend to stay a part of it, and that they should be professionally interested in such information. Use your own style to stay in touch, but stay in touch.

Showcasing and networking are about getting your product seen by potential buyers and then personally showing them the reasons to buy it. You need to "just do it."

Chapter 9 | Gotham

Working in New York

Let me begin this chapter on New York in the same way that I began the chapter on Los Angeles: everything you have heard about New York is true, all the good and all the bad, all at once. Even more than in Los Angeles, you will have to create your own New York in many little ways, like walking home by a less direct route because it is safer, or perhaps because a certain block has a tree growing on it, and you like that tree. New York is a filthy, grimy city that seems at times to be dying of gangrene. It is also the most exciting place in the world. There is probably more in the plus column and more in the minus column for New York than any place on earth. In L.A. they call it Gotham. Those who know the town call it "the city that never sleeps" because more happens in a day in New York than happens in most places in a year.

Even if you are an adventurous type who loves fast-paced excitement, I would not, however, recommend going to New York alone. If you already have friends in New York, don't expect them to have much time for you once you move there. They won't, even if they had time for you on your last visit. And it is hard to make new friends in New York. Its reputation as a rude, brutal, coldhearted city did not spring full-blown from a vacuum. Looking at the faces of the people on the streets and in the subways, one gets the impression that most New Yorkers spend most of their time tuning things out. People seem to be wearing blinders. Almost anywhere is a better place to be lonesome than New York. So go with a friend or, even better, with two friends.

The rule of thumb with regard to apartments is that the closer you get to Manhattan, the smaller the space and the higher the rent. Manhattan,

> An actor who's serious should have the New York experience. There's nothing like what happens to a person, particularly an actor, on the streets of New York.
> —Marilyn Mandel, casting director

though, is where the action is, and time spent commuting to Manhattan in a crowded, filthy subway car to audition and work must be considered when choosing a place to live. When you start to see what kind of money you will have to pay to rent the smallest and nastiest of apartments, you will go from feeling disbelief to being offended and finally to the grim-faced acceptance of the situation, coupled, one hopes, with a resolve to make the dump as humanly habitable as possible. Two or three people can do that better than one. Together you can also act as each other's eyes and ears, socially and professionally. I would recommend going to New York together to find a place and then going back home for your stuff when you have someplace to put it, while being prepared to furnish the rest of the place in "early actor poverty" style from the Goodwill stores.

A car in New York will be a royal pain in the behind. Insurance might cost more than the car. There will be no place to park it. In many areas alternate sides of the street get swept on alternate nights, and if you forget and leave your car on the wrong side it will be towed and it will cost you a fortune to get it back. When you do get it back it will be damaged and will soon be further vandalized after you park it again. Driving in New York is a perpetual game of chicken and is not for the polite and patient. Most New Yorkers stoically take the subway, the bus, and taxis when they can. They also walk a lot, carrying their indoor shoes in a bag to change into once inside. In New York you must learn to keep walking without letting others crowd you off the sidewalk. This will require firmness and resolve on your part rather than hostility and is an excellent form of assertiveness training for women. A book to read on the subway, sitting or standing, is a good idea for both mental stimulation as well as for mental health.

The New York local of AEA has the largest number of Equity members in the country—far more stage actors than there are jobs. Because New York actors are generally considered the best in the country, many out-of-town companies come to New York to recruit actors. If you are willing to live a good part of the year out of suitcases, then New York is a fine place from which to audition for regional theater work.

It is also the best place in the world to train as an actor because of all the training available, but be careful of these workshops. Check them out before writing the check. I believe that the only reason to go to New York without a union card is to get this training and then to plan on going back home to get your union card. Those few who get lucky enough to get their union cards in New York may, with my blessing, stick their tongues out at me. There is also a school of thought that all time spent in the New York market is valuable time, because when you've made it in New York, you've made it. You'll have to get someone else besides me to justify that to you though.

If you have your union card and are thinking about going to New York, along with a couple of friends one hopes, one fairly good book about the New York scene is Mary Lyn Henry and Lynne Rogers's book, *How to Be a Working Actor,* which is New York oriented. Then reread the section, "An Actor's Real Work" in chapter one of this book, and chapter eight, "Fortress Hollywood." Working the New York market will be much the same as working the L.A. market in terms of your marketing method. You will read *Back Stage* instead of *Back Stage West.* You will buy *The Ross Reports* at the New York Samuel French Bookstore and send out a mass mailing to agents in the same way you would in L.A. Once you have an agent you will list in *Players Guide* instead of the *Academy Players Directory.* You will subscribe to the New York version of the *CD Directory.* And you will spend the same amount of time walking and riding the subway that L.A. actors spend in their cars in your attempt to deliver your headshots to the receptionists of casting directors.

You will continue to work the New York market in the same way you would work the L.A. market, with a file on everyone who can give you a job, fifteen transactions a day, thank-you notes, showcasing in small theaters when you can—the whole disciplined process. If you can stick it out in New York for six years using this marketing method while working a second job, taking classes, auditioning, and occasionally working as an actor, then your perseverance will probably eventually allow you to quit that second job, most of those classes, and some of the marketing as you audition and act more and more. Then you might have a twenty-year career as a working New York actor, and that sure ain't chopped liver.

Before I send you on to the lists of industry terms, talent agents, casting directors, and Equity theaters in the appendix, I want to include a story that contradicts my advice not to go to New York first—the story of a couple of young people who got their training at Southern Methodist University in Dallas and then did go directly to New York. They are not geniuses, just intelligent, talented people, and their story is included here as an example of what people can do when they take charge of their own careers.

John Clancy and Nancy Walsh met at SMU, fell in love, and got married after graduation. They went to New York where Nan signed with an agent and John toured the boroughs with a children's theater company while he continued to write the kind of plays they both wanted to do. They soon formed their own theater group called The Present Company and with other SMU friends began putting on their own productions. This led to a merger with an existing nonprofit group, after which they secured a loft on 45th Street and turned it into a performance space, where they produced John's plays and other cutting-edge theater that they had come to New York to do.

One of these productions got great reviews, and they looked into taking it to the Edinburgh Fringe Festival but found that it would cost half a year's budget, leading them to ask themselves, "Why isn't there a fringe festival in New York City?"

So they invited three hundred theater groups to a town meeting, and the New York International Fringe Festival (FringeNYC) was born. The festival was an immediate success and continues to be the cheapest way for a young theater company or artist to produce a show in New York. It also allows someone new to the city to participate in a community of performing artists and meet hundreds of potential collaborators.

They are now the principals behind Clancy Productions, a theatrical touring and producing organization "specializing in high-energy, low-budget, intellectually engaging contemporary American theater." In its first year, Clancy Productions presented work in Scotland, Ireland, England, and Canada and has been featured at the Edinburgh Fringe Festival, the Brighton Comedy Festival, and the Du Marier World Stage Festival in Toronto. Their productions have also played the Traverse in Edinburgh, the Helix in Dublin, and Riverside Studios in London. In the 2003/2004 season, their shows will play New York, Sydney, Australia, Adelaide Fringe, and Edinburgh Fringe Festival. Obviously, I'm personally proud to know them.

By the way, these folks offer professional consulting in the areas of program assessment, new program creation, and strategic growth planning, with a special emphasis on festival creation and operation. Check them out at *clancyproductions.com*.

Now, head for the appendices for a glossary of industry terms that rivals the wit of Samuel Johnson, and lists that rival the FBI's!

APPENDICES

Appendix I | # Glossary of Industry Terms

Academy Players Directory. This is a Hollywood directory of actors. It shows actors' headshots and lists how to reach them, usually via an agent or manager specified by the actor. Actors must be union or be represented by a union agent to get listed, and the actor pays for the listing, which is inexpensive and worth it. A casting director can be told by telephone that an actor is on page x of the directory. There are four volumes to this directory, which is reprinted three times a year. The volumes list the following: leading women and ingenues, leading men and younger leading men, character men and character women, and kids. My advice is to list as both character and lead and pay a year in advance for all three issues but only after moving to L.A.

Action. The director's cue to the actors to begin the scene. They don't yell "lights, camera, action" anymore. These days it goes like this: the first assistant director yells "We are rolling." The camera operator repeats "rolling," and the film begins to roll. The clapper/loader claps the slate in front of the camera, which specifies which scene is being shot, and says "marking." The clap of the slate will be used to synchronize picture and sound later. The sound man will say "speed." The director will yell "background action," and the extras will begin to move. Then the director says "action," and the actors do their stuff.

A.D. Short for assistant director. The A.D. is the first A.D., the one who coordinates the hundreds of details involved in a day's shooting, thus freeing the director to be creative. Some of the good ones might make as much as $10,000 a week. There is also a second assistant director, who is primarily an extras wrangler. On some days with big crowd scenes there may also be a "second second."

ADR. Automated dialogue replacement. A voice-over narration added to a film is an example of this.

ADTI. American Dinner Theater Institute, the dinner theater clearinghouse and central command office, located in Sarasota, Florida.

AEA. Actors Equity Association, usually called "Equity," is the actors' union for stage actors and stage managers.

AFI. American Film Institute, a conservatory-type film school located in L.A. They have an agreement with the Screen Actors Guild, which lets them use volunteer SAG actors for free in their student films, in return for giving the actors copies of the film for use as a demo tape, a good deal for actors new to the area, who might actually be working for the next George Lucas.

AFL-CIO. American Federation of Labor/Congress of Industrial Organizations, the umbrella labor organization of which SAG, AEA, and AFTRA are a part.

AFTRA. American Federation of Television and Radio Artists. The union that represents actors and other artists who work on television and radio. This union also represents nonartists, such as newsmen, who in this author's opinion belong in NABET, covered later.

Age range. The range in the ages of characters that an actor can play believably. The actor's real age is usually somewhere in this range, but not always.

AMPTP. Alliance of Motion Picture and Television Producers, whom some think of as the capitalist bad guys in the black hats. Due to their efforts, film and TV are America's third largest export.

Art director. The film equivalent of a stage technical director. He takes the production designer's concept and turns it into a plan.

ATA. Association of Talent Agents, a professional association created for establishing professional standards for talent agents, as well as for sharing information and promoting common self-interests.

Audition. Sometimes called an interview or a casting, an audition is a display of an actor's product to a potential buyer, usually a casting director.

Avail. A nonbinding term for an actor who is available (and usually eager) for a role.

Back Stage. The weekly New York show business journal that contains audition notices and other information of interest mainly to New York actors, but also to others.

Background. Human beings, also known as extras, who provide a kind of animated wallpaper as a setting for actors to do their work.

Backup. An actor held in reserve as a possible replacement for another actor.

Beauty shot. The final glamorous shot in a soap opera, over which credits are rolled, while neglected women watching at home begin to start craving chocolate.

Best boy. The one who keeps the time cards of the crew members, as well as a Rolodex of possible replacements and supplementary help, sort of like a foreman's "trusty." There is a best boy gaffer and a best boy grip.

Billing. Giving written credit where credit is supposedly due, either above the title, in opening credits as the film or TV show begins, or as the ending credits roll, in that order of an actor's preference.

Bio. A short, narrative form of a résumé, usually found in press releases or theater programs. Actors usually write their own.

Blocking. The physical movements of an actor or actors from point to point in a scene. In film and TV these points are called marks and consist of two pieces of tape on the floor in the shape of a T. An actor hits his marks when he stops at the T.

Booking. A binding agreement for an actor to play a certain role.

Boom. The overhead microphone usually held overhead on a long pole by a soundman called the boom operator.

Breakaway. A prop or part of a set that gives the appearance of being solid but actually shatters or breaks off easily for effect.

Breakdown. Not an actor's personal problem, but rather the detailed description of the roles being cast in a production.

Breakdown Services. An expensive, weekday publication to which only legitimate agents and managers are allowed to subscribe. It gives the breakdown of roles being cast in upcoming productions.

Buyout. Payment in advance in lieu of residuals, usually for commercials.

Call sheet. A list of all required personnel and the times at which they are to report to the set that is issued daily by the production staff, usually with a copy for everyone listed on the sheet.

Call time. The time at which an actor by contract must arrive on the set or designated location, or also an appointment for an audition.

Callback. A second look, a follow-up audition or interview.

Casting director. A purchasing agent, usually a woman, who is hired by the producer to go shopping for the best available deals on actors. See the section on casting directors.

Cattle call. An open audition that usually turns into a mob scene of hopefuls. No one enjoys these things.

Changes. This usually refers to different outfits. If you are asked to bring three changes, do not show up with your lines rewritten three ways. (As Michael Shurtleff once said in a workshop, "Don't change the script. Their script is precious to them, every disastrous word of it."

Client. What the actor (supposedly) is to an agent. Also, what an actor (supposedly) is to the state worker interviewing the actor in the unemployment office.

Close-up (CU). The shot an actor comes to love the best, the one of just his or her face. Actually, the camera is your friend, so don't worry. They'll make you look good.

Cold reading. The reading aloud of a script without much chance to prepare. "Cold" is how you feel inside under those circumstances. The more you read it, the warmer you get.

COLT. Chicago Off-Loop Theaters, Chicago's equivalent of New York's Off-Broadway, with similar contracts for Equity members.

Commission. The percentage of an actor's wages paid to the actor's agent or manager. A union agent may not make more than a 10 percent commission. There is no union regulation governing managers.

Composite. Several photos of an actor in different situations, used mostly for modeling and print work and sometimes for commercials.

Conflict. Something that causes an actor to be unavailable at a certain time. This can also be true after the fact. If an actor does a commercial for one product, this would become a contractual conflict for doing a commercial for a competing product while the first product is still being aired.

Copy. The words to a commercial script, as in "This copy is idiotic!"

Corporate. A film, video, or digital production commissioned by a corporation (or equivalent) for in-house use. Bread and butter employment for actors.

CORST. Council of Resident/Stock Theaters. The negotiating body for stock theaters that have a small resident company of actors. Some of these theaters are still alive and well, and Equity has a special contract for them.

COST. Council of Stock Theaters, like CORST but with no resident company. Both CORST and COST contracts are better deals for the producer than regular AEA contracts.

Cover letter. What you should write when you send a headshot to someone in order to personalize the transaction and thus reduce the chances of the headshot being circular filed.

Craft Services. The folks who fix the food on the set. Careful, it is possible to munch all day long and gain much weight.

Crane shot. Using a crane to shoot the scene from overhead, sometimes with a sweeping motion to give a real "bird's-eye view."

Crawl. The misnomer for how credits are shown at the end of a film or TV show. Credits actually scurry rather than crawl up the screen.

Credits. This term can refer either to the actual work an actor or technician has done in the past or to the written acknowledgement on the screen of the work he or she did on a particular project.

Cue. For an actor, the signal to do your stuff.

Cutaway. A shot that cuts away from a scene to show something else and then returns.

Dailies. These used to be called rushes because they were unedited film footage that was rushed to the lab so the director could see if the footage was good before moving on to other shots. Now they are called dailies, perhaps to reduce stress. They are usually watched by the director and producer first thing in the morning before beginning other shots to make sure they got what they needed the previous day. As you might imagine, actors, even movie stars, are usually not allowed to watch these because they tend to complain that their hair wasn't right, and they "just have to re-shoot that scene!"

Daily Variety. The L.A. trade publication that comes out weekdays. More for industry executives than for actors, this paper reads something like an interoffice memo of the film and TV industries. They love cute headlines like "Webs Nix Pic's Tricks," which in English means that the TV networks have said "no" to something they consider offensive in a film and will not air it.

Day player. An actor hired for less than a week and the kind of work you will get at first. On your résumé, "day player" will become "featured."

Daytime drama. Another term for soap opera, a kind of television program made with bored women in mind. The sponsors of these programs were often manufacturers of products that were once very meaningful for women, such as laundry detergent, and hence the name "soap operas." New York still has the edge on L.A. in the number of these that get made.

Dealer commercial. A commercial made and paid for by a national company, then offered to local or regional dealers, who buy their own airtime and air the commercial locally with their owns names inserted, or tagged on to the end, e.g., "Now available at Henry's Honda!"

Demo tape. Demonstration tape. Either an audio- or videotape made of portions of an actor's work and used for promotional and audition purposes.

DGA. Directors Guild of America, the union that represents directors, assistant directors, and unit production managers.

Dialect. Misnomer for an accent. A dialect is actually a branch of a language that uses different words and expressions, but you'll still hear people in this business talking about a "southern dialect" instead of a southern accent.

Dialogue. Actually, a verbal interchange between two or more people but used in show business to refer to any words spoken by an actor.

Director. In film and TV, the person whose primary job is to tell the story in pictures. The director, not the director of photography, chooses the camera angle, lens, and composition of the shot. In theater, film, and TV, the director is also the person who coordinates all artistic elements into one artistic vision, or at least is supposed to do that.

Dolly. A kind of cart, pushed by a person called a dolly grip, that carries the camera smoothly forward or backward on a track. A dolly shot brings the spectator to what is being filmed, while a zoom has the effect of seeming to bring the subject to the spectator, very effective in horror pictures.

Donut. A change that is inserted into a commercial rather than at the end of it.

Double. A performer who resembles another performer and is used in his or her place, as in "stunt double."

Downgrade. The reduction of an actor to an extra. This is not allowed by the union. Verbal downgrading of someone behind his back is a constant part of show business, however.

D.P. Director of photography, also called the cinematographer. The D.P.'s job is to light the set. Gaffers and grips, covered later, report to him.

Drama-Logue. L.A.'s former equivalent of *Back Stage*, now a West Coast edition of the latter. A weekly newspaper containing casting notices, reviews, and articles about the industry and a must-read for the L.A. actor.

Dressing the set. Adding furniture, props, and whatever else is necessary to make the set look realistic.

Drive-on pass. Written permission to drive a vehicle onto a studio lot or film set.

Drop/pickup. A type of contract that allows a film production to hire an actor, lay him off, and then rehire him again on the same film. This doesn't happen very much. Usually actors are paid for those in-between days even though they are not actually working. Go union!

Dupe. In film and TV, not a misused person but rather a duplicate of a film or tape.

Eight by ten (8x10). A photograph 8x10 inches, used for audition purposes.

Eighteen to play younger. The description of an actor who is at least eighteen years old and thus is not subject to child labor laws, but who looks younger and can convincingly play a younger character.

Electrician. The electrician on a film is called the gaffer. Electricians hang and focus lights and plug things in.

Emancipated minor. A kid who has been given permission by the courts to make his or her own decisions and for the most part has the legal status of an adult; often a teenage star who has already gotten laid and is pissed off at his parents.

Employer of record (EOR). Professional accounting organizations responsible for issuing checks and W2s to actors. Sometimes called union paymasters in situations where a production company wants to hire a union actor without having to sign a union contract.

Equity. The term by which Actors Equity Association is usually referred.

Equity waiver. As in "Equity waiver contract" or "Equity waiver theater." These are small L.A. theaters seating ninety-nine or less that do not have to comply with most provisions of regular Equity contracts. Actors usually work in these theaters to showcase themselves for film work, as discussed in the section on Fortress Hollywood.

Exclusivity. Sole rights granted by an actor to an agent or by an actor to a commercial producer with regard to not making commercials for competitive products.

Executive producer. The person who puts the financial deal together to get a film or TV program made.

Exhibit A. The part of the AFTRA Network Code that covers prime-time TV, AFTRA's equivalent of SAG's Basic Television Agreement for TV shows shot on film.

EXT. Exterior. A scene that is to be shot outside.

Extras. Human beings who are treated like cattle. Experienced extras keep their sense of humor, and bring lawn chairs and a deck of cards, something to read, or some paperwork to do.

Field rep. Someone from the AFTRA or SAG office who visits the set to ensure that producers are complying with union rules.

First refusal. A nonbinding courtesy extended to a producer with regard to an actor's availability. The actor gives the producer first refusal before accepting another job.

Five out of seven. A five-day workweek that does not necessarily begin on Monday.

Fixed cycle. A thirteen-week period for which a commercial producer pays an actor for the use of his image on tape or film.

Flipper. False teeth for kids with baby teeth. Also a dolphin rumored to be making a comeback.

Forced call. A requirement to return to the set less than fifteen hours after being dismissed. This results in an actor getting a whole day's additional pay!

Foreign replay. Reruns outside the U.S. and Canada for which actors get paid additional residuals.

Four A's. Associated Actors and Artists of America. A mini-umbrella organization inside the AFL-CIO comprised of the performers' unions.

Franchised agent. An agent that AEA, AFTRA, or SAG approves of as a certified good person. The union does a background check for a criminal record and a credit check on agents wishing to be franchised before allowing such agents to represent union talent.

Freelancing. Working without either a full-time employer or an exclusive agent, i.e., the way most actors work.

FX. The script or contract notation for effects, i.e., special effects.

Gaffer. The gaffer is the chief electrician on a film crew who reports directly to the director of photography.

General interview. An audition for a casting director, but with no specific project in mind. An actor requests this in the hope that he or she will be remembered by the casting director at a later time when something comes along for which the actor is right. Casting directors sometimes grant general interviews when they are not busy with other things.

Glossy. An 8x10 headshot with a shiny finish.

Gofer. Someone, usually attached to the production office, who runs errands and goes fer this, goes fer that, etc.

Golden time. Overtime after the sixteenth hour on the set. Big, big bucks.

Grip. A cross between a construction worker and a moving man. A grip is a crew member who moves pieces of the set around and either moves or builds things for the electricians to hang lights on. It should be noted that not all grips are Neanderthals.

Guaranteed billing. The type and position of credit given an actor for a performance, usually negotiated into an actor's contract by an agent, e.g., an opening credit with "guest star" billing.

Hand model. Someone with photogenic hands for commercials. There is money in this and also for hair, teeth, and occasionally feet.

HAT/BAT contract. Hollywood Area Theater/Bay Area Theater contracts, similar to COLT and Off-Broadway contracts.

Headshot. An 8x10, black-and-white, head and shoulders photo of an actor, without which he or she is not a professional.

Hiatus. The period in which a TV show is not in production. (To say that an actor is in hiatus is an unnecessary redundancy, as it is one of the basic assumptions of the industry.)

Hold. A binding, contractual stipulation that an actor be available for a job.

Holding fee. What an actor is paid for a hold.

Hollywood Reporter. *Daily Variety's* competitor, as *Newsweek* is to *Time*.

Honey wagon. A towed vehicle where you find the toilets.

IATSE. International Alliance of Theatrical Stage Employees. Called IA on the West Coast, and "Yatsee" on the East Coast, this is the union to which most crew members belong, such as camera crew, gaffers, grips, makeup artists, etc. Drivers belong to the Teamsters.

Industrial. A nonbroadcast film or tape used primarily for educational or training purposes. Also called training films and corporates, which is the term I prefer.

Inserts. A shot that will be inserted into other footage, perhaps of hands doing something or of an object important to the story. Directors will sometimes shoot an insert first thing in the morning so that when studio execs come to work, they will hear that a production has already gotten its first shot of the day. The director hopes that the execs will therefore not come down to the set to hassle him.

INT. Interior. Script notation for an indoor location. Every scene in a screenplay is noted DAY or NIGHT, INT or EXT, followed by a description of where the scene takes places, e.g., INT NIGHT, John's living room.

In-Time. The time an actor or crew member is due, or due back, on the set. Same as call time.

Lift. Using or "lifting" footage from one project to another. Often done with commercials.

Liquidated damages. What producers owe to actors et al. when they don't fulfill their contractual obligations. Unions usually require a bond to make sure actors get paid this money.

Long shot (LS). This doesn't refer to an actor's chance for success, which is assumed, but rather to a camera angle that shows the actor's whole body, as opposed to a close-up or a "two-shot," which shows two actors from about the waist up. This last shot, by the way, is called "an American shot" in France. Mais, qu'est-ce que je sais, moi? Je n'ai aucun idea pourquoi!

Looping. Matching sound to picture in a postproduction studio.

LORT. League of Resident Theaters. These are nonprofit theaters of various sizes located throughout the country, which, in league with one another, negotiate collectively with Equity.

Manager. With respect to actors, this person is something between a sales representative and a therapist. This person may not negotiate a contract for an actor. An agent or a lawyer must do that. Because managers are not regulated by the unions, he or she may charge more than a 10 percent commission on an actor's earnings. Nevertheless, many actors, especially stars, have managers.

Matching. This term refers to the casting of actors whose physicality harmonizes, or matches, such as casting members of a family, for instance.

Meal penalty. A monetary bonus paid by the producer to union actors or union extras for not feeding them within six hours of their call time.

Monologue. In show biz, any speech by a single actor. Playwrights write monologues for exposition purposes. Actors use them for audition purposes. Hint: think of a monologue as an outburst and know what caused it.

MOS. "Mit out sound," as imported German directors used to say back in the thirties. Also stands for "motion only shot," which amounts to the same thing.

MOW. Movie of the Week. A two-hour, made-for-TV movie comprised of six acts and five cliff-hangers into which commercials are inserted. The themes of MOWs are usually about some topical issue, a crime of the week, a disease of the week, etc.

NABET. National Association of Broadcast Employees and Technicians, the union to which all broadcasters should belong instead of to AFTRA so as not to impede AFTRA's merger with SAG. Ah well, never mind.

National commercial. A commercial that will be aired nationwide, meaning big bucks for the actor. Commercials that will be aired in New York or L.A. are automatically considered national commercials.

Network approval. The right of a network to consent to the actor being cast in a certain role, as in the case of a hit series. An actor auditioning under these circumstances is usually very nervous, as the outcome will either mean huge bucks or time in the unemployment line again.

Network code. AFTRA's contract with the networks. Among TV execs, this term might refer to their own professional standards, but actors are more concerned with the first definition.

Night premium. A 10 percent bonus paid to union actors for work performed (or for being on the clock) after 8 p.m.

Nomex. Trademark name for fireproof long underwear used by stuntmen.

Non-Equity. Actors that are not members of AEA, or theater productions that have not signed agreements with AEA. Equity actors may not work in such productions.

Off-Broadway. New York theaters of less than five hundred seats located outside the theater district.

Off-camera (OC or OS for "Off Stage"). Dialogue or sounds heard but not seen.

Off-Off-Broadway. An eclectic bunch of small, threadbare, often experimental New York theaters found throughout the city. Many hang on by operating under Equity's showcase code, where actors work for free in order to get seen. If you go to New York to work as an actor, you will become very familiar with these theaters.

Open call. Auditions open to all actors whether or not they have been submitted by agents.

Out clause. A contractual clause that lets someone get out of a deal.

Out of frame. A location that is not in view of the camera.

Out-time. The official time when an actor is no longer on the clock. This is after an actor has changed out of wardrobe and reports back to the second A.D., not when the second A.D. first says "You're wrapped." Check this out-time on the sheet as you sign out.

Overdubbing. Putting a new soundtrack over an existing one, like in a record studio for a commercial.

Overtime (OT). Usually any time on the clock over eight hours a day or forty hours a week.

P.A. Production Assistant. These people are gofers with walkie-talkies and fanny packs who take orders from assistant directors. Sometimes they actually know what they are doing.

Pages. Parts of a script, often rewritten, containing specific scenes.

Pan. A sweeping motion of the camera, like turning your head.

P&G. Proctor & Gamble. This refers to a squeaky clean, all-American, white-bread, WASP look in an actor.

Pay or play. A clause in a contract that stipulates that you get paid even if you don't work.

Paymaster. A union-approved employer of record. Sometimes a nonunion company wishing to hire a specific union actor will hire him or her through a paymaster and abide by union rules for this one actor.

Pension and health. An additional 12 percent of an actor's salary a producer is required to pay toward an actor's health insurance and retirement fund.

Per diem. Money paid by the day to actors for meals not provided by the producer on location, usually breakfast and dinner.

Photo double. An actor hired to perform in the place of another actor because he or she looks like that actor.

Pick up. A shot that is needed to catch up with the production schedule, usually a shot that needs to be redone.

Picked up. Signed up; given a contract. This applies to actors hired for a production and also to TV series that get slated or renewed for a season.

Pilot. In TV jargon, the first show of a potential series that introduces the characters and the show's setting.

Players Guide. The New York equivalent of *The Academy Players Directory.*

Plosives. The letters p,b,t,d,k,g, all of which make a popping sound when pronounced. Some actors doing voice-over work turn slightly away from the microphone when speaking these letters in order to minimize this sound.

POV shot. Point-of-view shot, sometimes called an over-the-shoulder shot because that is where the camera is placed. It tells the audience what a character is seeing.

Prime time. The hours when most people watch TV, 8:00 to 11:00 p.m. EST, 7:00 to 10:00 p.m. CST.

Principal. An actor who either speaks or performs special business to advance the story.

Producer. The person at whose desk "the buck stops." That's why this person picks up the award for Best Picture. This person's desk is also the place where the buck starts. He or she hires everyone in the production.

Product conflict. Promoting two competitive products, a situation that for various reasons an actor is contractually obligated to avoid in commercials.

Production contract. Standard Equity contract for a single Equity production. A producer must pay higher minimums under this kind of contract, and it is thus in the producer's best interest to try to get another kind of contract, such as a LORT or CORST contract.

Production designer. Sometimes called "an art director who knows the producer," this person comes up with the concept or vision of what the setting should look like. His drawings look more like artwork, whereas the art director's drawings look more like blueprints.

Prop master. The person who finds the props and keeps track of them. If you abuse a prop, this person will abuse you.

Props. Properties; objects placed on a set for use in the story that are not part of the set decor. If the object is touched or referred to in the scene, it is a prop and not a set piece.

PSA. Public-Service Announcement. Note that SAG and AFTRA actors are not permitted to do these "simply as a public service" without also being paid to do them.

Quote. The money an agent asks for an actor's services or the price anyone quotes for anything.

Ratings. The number of people watching or listening to a certain program at a certain time.

Regional commercial. A commercial that will be aired only in a certain area of the U.S. (There would be no point in airing a snowmobile commercial in Florida, for instance.) These commercials cost less to make and to air, and consequently actors are paid less to do them, but actors still get paid more for these than for a local commercial.

Release. The end of a contractual obligation. This term can refer to the end of a day's work, to a commercial being taken off the air and thus allowing the actor to do a commercial for a competitor, or to other provisions of a contract.

Release letter. A written agreement terminating a contract. Most often this refers to a letter sent by an actor to an agent telling the agent good-bye.

Rerun. The rebroadcast of a TV program.

Residual. Additional money paid to an actor when a commercial, TV show, film, or radio spot is aired again.

Résumé. Professional information that an actor attaches to the back of an 8x10 headshot, including credits, training, etc. See the section on résumés.

Reuse. Rebroadcast of a commercial.

Rewrite. Changes in the script. In a film script, these changes use color-coded paper, and by the end of the shoot the script looks like a rainbow.

Right-to-work states. States that do not permit closed-shop contracts. See the chapter on unions.

Rounds. As in "making rounds." Going from place to place, dropping off headshots while bravely trying to smile.

Running part. A recurring role in a TV series.

SAG. Screen Actors Guild.

Scale. The minimum a union actor can be paid for a job. This includes the producer's 12 percent contribution to the actor's pension and welfare fund.

Scale plus 10 (percent). The actual amount it costs the producer to hire a union actor. Because taking the 10 percent agent's commission out of the actor's pay would mean that the actor would make less than the minimum allowed, the producer must actually pay scale plus 10. This does not apply to commercials or industrials.

Screen test. These days, a videotape or DVD made to see how an actor would look in a certain role.

Script. The written form of a story that will be performed on stage, screen, television, or radio.

Script supervisor. The secretary on the set, although they don't like this description. She makes a record of everything that happens on the shoot with regard to shooting the script, including such things as the type of lens used for each take, any changes in dialogue, etc., etc.

Session fee. Initial money paid to an actor for performing in a commercial. Residuals come later.

Set. Where the action is. This can be a specially constructed indoor scene, but the term also refers to an outdoor location where something is being filmed or taped. In the middle of a field, the A.D. will still say "Quiet on the set" before the camera rolls.

Set decorator. The person working directly under the art director who finds the necessary materials to build and decorate the set and who supervises the swing gang in building it.

Set teacher. Sometimes called a studio teacher. A tutor hired to teach kids on the set. Also responsible for enforcing child labor laws. Not all states require set teachers.

SFX. Notation for sound effects, not special effects, which is FX.

Showcase. A theater performance in which actors work for free hoping to get seen.

Sides. Parts of a script that are mostly used for auditions and day players, who usually don't get the whole copy of the script.

Sight and sound. The right of the parent of a child performer to remain within sight and sound of the child, i.e., to be on the set whether you like it or not.

Signatory. A producer who signs a union contract.

Sign-in sheet. A written record of who has auditioned or who has shown up to work. Actors auditioning for AFTRA and SAG jobs should remember to sign out as well, in that they may be entitled to compensation if kept more than an hour at the audition.

Silent bit. Action performed by an extra that advances the story, such as a waiter serving something to a character. This gives the extra a little more money, called a "bump." In a union commercial, the performer must be paid as a principal for performing the same action if his face is recognizable.

Single card. A special credit in a film or TV show in which only one actor's name appears.

Sitcom. Situation comedy. See the section on television.

Slate. A little chalkboard with a black-and-white-striped clapper used to identify film or TV takes. Also, a verb, as in "slate yourself." This means the camera is rolling and you should say your name and give the name of your agent if that is appropriate.

Soap. See Daytime Drama.

Soundtrack. In film or TV, the separately recorded audio portion.

Special business. A specific action by an extra or actor that advances the story. See Silent Bit.

Spot. A commercial.

SSDC. Society of Stage Directors and Choreographers. A professional association that sets standards for, and promotes the common interests of, stage directors and choreographers. This organization is a professional association but not a union.

Stage manager. In theater, the person who takes over from the director and runs the show after it opens. In film or TV, the stage manager is a custodian/facilities manager. It is a hard, thankless job onstage or in the studio and one deserving of admiration and respect as well as appreciation.

Stage right and stage left. Looking at the audience, stage right is to your right, stage left is to your left, downstage is in front of you, and upstage is behind you.

Standard union contract. A contract, previously negotiated between the unions and the producers, that stipulates minimum acceptable pay and working conditions for union actors.

Standards and practices department. The network censors.

Stand-in. In some countries this person is called a lighting double. A stand-in is special extra, about the same size and coloring as a principal actor, who stands on an actor's marks and walks through the actors blocking while the lights are being set. This is a great job for someone just starting out. Because you are there to watch the shot rehearsed and set up, it is like being paid to go to film school. Work well with the crew, and the director will probably give you a line in the movie, thus making you eligible for your union card.

Station 12. The part of the Screen Actors Guild that assures that actors are paid-up members and clears them to work on SAG productions.

Station 15. The part of the Screen Actors Guild that assures that prospective employees of SAG talent are signatories to SAG contracts.

Storyboard. A script in comic book form.

Studio. A room, a sound stage, a whole building, or a group of buildings used for recording, taping, or filming. The plural, "the studios," refers to the seven major Hollywood motion picture studios.

Stunt coordinator. The person charged with the design, coordination, and supervision of stunts and other dangerous activities. Even though they are members of SAG, these guys are usually independent contractors with their own teams of stunt folks.

Stunt double. A stuntman or woman who resembles a principal actor and performs a dangerous activity in that actor's place.

Submission. Offering or suggesting an actor for a role, usually done by an agent to a casting director.

Syndication. The practice of selling TV shows to individual TV stations or cable companies rather than to the networks.

Taft-Hartley. As in "We can Taft-Hartley you." The practice of allowing nonunion actors to work on a union project as stipulated by certain provisions of the Taft-Hartley Act.

Tag. An announcement that is "tagged," or added, to the beginning or end of a commercial or TV show, as in "Now available at XYZ Superstore, right here in town!"

Take. The filming, or videotaping, of an action sequence as in "take a picture." The sequence may have to be reshot many times, i.e., will require many takes, before they get what they want. If there is no action occurring in what is being filmed or taped, it is usually called a shot rather than a take.

TCG. Theater Communications Group. An organization funded by the Ford Foundation that acts as an audition clearinghouse for regional theaters who have come to New York to recruit actors. They hold general auditions a couple times a year and then have callbacks for specific castings.

Teleprompter. Actually a brand name. A piece of equipment that scrolls text upward, allowing the narrator to read it while looking at the camera.

Test market. There are many business connotations for this term, which refers to trying something out in a certain, limited market first, but for an actor's purposes let us say that this term refers to airing a commercial in only one market to test its effectiveness. If successful, the commercial may then be aired in other markets, resulting in more money for the actor.

Theatrical. TV or film work rather than corporate or commercial work. Some actors have a theatrical agent and a commercial agent.

Three-quarter (3/4-inch) tape. Videotape for professional use. Something may be shot on 3/4-inch tape and then duplicated onto 1/2-inch tape for viewing on regular VCRs.

Tight shot. A close-up of something, either an actor's face or an object, etc. "Go in tight on his hand."

Trades. Publications geared for people who work in a specific industry, such as the entertainment industry trades.

Turnaround. For an actor, this term refers to the time between actual dismissal and his or her call time the next day. For a producer, this term refers to a place in "development hell" where the deal for his picture has been bought by someone else who, undoubtedly, will have a whole new set of demands.

Two-shot. A medium shot showing two characters from the waist up.

TYA. Theater for Young Audiences. An equity contract for producers of children's theater.

Type. By this author's definition, the "look" of a character as well as the actor who plays him, which I believe is a function of gender, age, ethnic/cultural origin, and occupation. See the chapter "An Actor Prepares."

Typecasting. Casting a role based on physical appearance more than on acting skill.

Under five (U-5). In an AFTRA contract, a principal role that has less than five lines.

Understudy. An actor hired to perform a role if the principal actor hired cannot do so.

Upgrade. Promotion from an extra to a principal.

Upstage. The area at the back of the stage, away from the audience. Downstage is toward the audience. Stages at one time were raked so that the back really was higher. This allowed characters upstage to be seen from the audience, which for centuries was seated in a level area. Eventually, someone got the fine idea to switch this situation around.

Use cycle. The thirteen-week period during which a commercial is actually used, or aired, as opposed to a holding cycle, which has different contractual provisions.

Voice-over (VO). An audio recording where the actor is heard but not seen.

Waivers. Board-approved exceptions to union contracts.

Walk-on. A really small role where you walk off almost as soon as you walk on.

Walla Walla. Fake background noise to simulate crowd mutterings; the words "rhubarb" and "plastic avocado" are also used.

Wardrobe. Both the costumes or clothes an actor wears, as well as the place where he goes to get them and later to turn them back in.

Wardrobe allowance. If you are a principal, money you get paid for wearing your own stuff. Extras don't get paid for this unless it's formal wear.

Wardrobe fitting. Going over to wardrobe to get your costume, then trying it on and letting them put pins in it where it needs to be altered. You get paid for this unless you are making above scale.

WGA. Writers Guild of America. The union for film and TV writers.

Wild spot. The equivalent of syndication for commercials, i.e., commercials that are aired on a station-by-station agreement rather than aired on the networks.

Wild track. An audio recording not made at the same time as a filmed sequence and not having a direct relationship to it.

Work permit. Written permission to work, usually required for children and immigrants.

Wrap. The end of a day's work and/or the end of a production, especially the latter. The expression comes from wrapping up a can of shot film for shipment.

Zed card. A modeling composite.

Zoom. A camera lens that can mechanically adjust from a close-up to a long shot and vice versa without moving the camera. "Zooming in" has the effect of making the object seem to rush to the audience, zooming out of making the audience "rocket away" from the object. The dolly shot has the opposite effect.

Appendix II | # Talent

Agents

AFTRA Agents

The symbols, which appear next to the agent's address, indicate the type of representation offered by that agent. Such things often change, however, so check with the agency for updates.

(A)	Athletes
(B)	Broadcasters
(C)	Commercials
(Ch)	Children
(CD)	CD - ROMS
(DD)	Daytime Drama
(F)	Foreign/Ethnic
(H)	Hosting
(Id)	Industrials
(If)	Infomercials
(In)	Interactive
(M)	Models
(Mu)	Musical Artists
(NB)	Non-Broadcast
(O)	Older People
(P)	Promos
(R)	Phonograph Recordings
(T)	Television Programs
(V)	Voice Over
(*)	People with Disabilities

Atlanta Agents

ATLANTA MODELS & TALENT INC.
2970 Peachtree Rd. NW # 660
Atlanta, GA 30305
(404) 261-9627
All Areas Except A, B, F, R

THE BURNS AGENCY
3800 Bretton Woods Road
Decatur, GA 30032
Attn: Carrie Miller and Rona Burns
(866) 744-5037
All Areas Except A, B, DD, M, R

GENESIS MODEL & TALENT
1465 Northside Dr. # 120
Atlanta, GA 30318
(404) 350-9212
All Areas Except A, B, DD, R

GLYN KENNEDY, INC.
16 Willow Bend Drive
Carterville, GA 30121
(678) 461-4444
All Areas Except CD, DD, Mu

THE PEOPLE STORE
2004 Rockledge Road, NE
Atlanta, GA 30324
(404) 874-6448
All Areas

ARLENE WILSON, INC.
887 West Marietta St., # N-101
Atlanta, GA 30318
(404) 876-8555
All Areas Except A, B, CD, H

Boston Agents

MAGGIE, INC.
35 Newbury Street, 5th Fl.
Boston, MA 02116-3105
(617) 536-2639
M, F,C, If, T, CD, NB, Id, P, *

MODELS GROUP
374 Congress St., #305
Boston, MA 02110
(617) 426-4711

Chicago Agents

AMBASSADOR TALENT AGENTS, INC.
333 N. Michigan Ave., # 910
Chicago, IL 60601
(312) 641-3491

ARIA MODEL & TALENT MGMT., LLC.
1017 W. Washington, Suite 2C
Chicago, IL 60607
(312) 243-9400

ARLENE WILSON TALENT, INC.
430 West Erie, Suite 210
Chicago, IL 60610
(312) 573-0200

BAKER & ROWLEY TALENT AGENCY,
INC.
1327 West Washington Boulevard,
Suite 5C
Chicago, IL 60607
(312) 850-4700
All Areas

BEST IMPRESSIONS AGENCY, INC.
477 East Butterfield Road, # 302
Lombard, IL 60148
(630) 434-2214
C, If, In, N, P, T, V

BIG MOUTH TALENT AGENCY
935 West Chestnut, Suite 415
Chicago, IL 60622
(312) 421-4400
All Areas Except *

THE EMMRICH AGENCY
18622 Brook Forest Avenue, Suite 59
Shorewood, IL 60431
(815) 577-8650
C

ENCORE TALENT AGENCY, INC.
700 North Sacramento Blvd., Suite 231
Chicago, IL 60612
(773) 638-7300
B, C, V, S, If, T, In, NB, Id, P

ETA, INC.
7558 S. Chicago Ave.
Chicago, IL 60619
(312) 752-3955

FORD TALENT GROUP
641 West Lake Street, Suite 402
Chicago, IL 60661
(312) 707-9000

GEDDES AGENCY
1633 N. Halsted, # 400
Chicago, IL 60614
(312) 787-8333

SHIRLEY HAMILTON, INC.
333 East Ontario, Suite 302
Chicago, IL 60611
(312) 787-4700

LINDA JACK TALENT
230 East Ohio, # 200
Chicago, IL 60611
(312) 587-1155

JENNIFER'S TALENT UNLIMITED, INC.
740 N. Plankinton, Suite 300
Milwaukee, Wisconsin 53203-2403
(414) 277-9440

LILY'S TALENT AGENCY
1301 West Washington, Suite B
Chicago, IL 60607
(312) 601-2345

LORI LINS LTD.
7611 West Holmes Avenue
Greenfield, WI 53220
(414) 282-3500

NAKED VOICES, INC.
865 North Sangamon, Suite 415
Chicago, IL 60622
(312) 563-0136

NORMAN SCHUCART ENTERPRISES
1417 Green Bay Rd.
Highland Park, IL 60035
(708) 433-1113

SALAZAR & NAVAS, INC.
760 North Odgen # 2200
Chicago, IL 60622
(312) 666-1677

STEWART TALENT MGMT.CORP.
58 West Huron
Chicago, IL 60610
312-943-3131

VOICES UNLIMITED, INC.
541 North Fairbanks, Suite 2735
Chicago, IL 60611
(312) 832-1113

Cleveland Agents

DOCHERTY, INC.
2044 Euclid Avenue, Suite 500
Cleveland, OH 44115
(216) 552-1300
All Areas

IMPACT MGMT. TALENT (IMI)
9700 Rockside Road, Suite 410
Cleveland, OH 44125
(216) 901-9710

THE TALENT GROUP, INC.
2530 Superior Avenue, Suite 6C
Cleveland, OH 44114
(216) 622-8011
C,V, In, NB, Id, P

Dallas-Fort Worth Agents

THE CAMPBELL AGENCY
3906 Lemmon Ave., # 200
Dallas, TX 75219
(214) 522-8991
A, C, F, M, O, T, V,*

MARY COLLINS TALENT AGENCY
2909 Cole Avenue, Suite 250
Dallas, TX 75204-1307
(214) 871-8900
C, F, O, P, T, V, *

KIM DAWSON AGENCY, INC.
2710 N. Stemmons Fwy., # 700
Tower North
Dallas, TX 75207-2208
(214) 630-5161
All Areas

THE HORNE AGENCY
4420 West Lovers Lane
Dallas, TX 75209
(214) 350-9220

PEGGY TAYLOR TALENT, INC.
437 Southfork, Suite 400
Lewisville, TX 75067
(972) 219-7362
All Areas Except B, DD, H, P

IVETT STONE AGENCY
14677 Midway Road, # 113
Addison, TX 75001
(972) 392-4951
C,F,O,R,T,V,*

THE TOMAS AGENCY
14275 Midway Rd., # 220
Dallas, TX 75244
(972) 687-9181
All Areas Except A, B

Denver Agents

DONNA BALDWIN TALENT
2237 West 30th Avenue
Denver, CO 80211
(303) 561-1199
All Areas Except A, DD, H, R

BARBIZON TALENT AGENCY
7535 E. Hampden Ave. # 108
Denver, CO 80231
(303) 337-7954
All Areas

VOICE CHOICE
6909 South Holly Circle, # 201
Englewood, CO 80111
(303) 756-9055
C, CD, Id, If, It, NB, P, R, T, V

Detroit Agents

C.L.A.S.S. MODELING & TALENT
AGENCY
2722 E. Michigan Ave., Suite 205
Lansing, MI 48912-4000
(517) 482-1833
All Areas Except A, B, DD, H, Mu

THE I GROUP, LLC
29540 Southfield Rd., # 200
Southfield, MI 48076
(810) 552-8842
All Areas Except A, DD, H, Mu

PRODUCTIONS PLUS
30600 Telegraph Rd., # 2156
Birmingham, MI 48025-4532
(810) 644-5566
All Areas Except CD

THE TALENT SHOP
30100 Telegraph Rd., # 116
Birmingham, MI 48025
(810) 644-4877
A, B, C, D, F, H, M, O, S, T, V,*

Houston Agents

ACTORS ETC., INC.
2620 Fountainview, # 210
Houston, TX 77057
(713) 785-4495
All Areas Except A, DD, H

HOLLYWOOD & BROADWAY CON-
NECTIONS
105 Holman Street
Houston, TX 77004
(713) 528-2306
All Areas

PASTORINI-BOSBY AGENCY
3013 Fountainview, # 240
Houston, TX 77057
(713) 266-4488
All Areas Except A, DD, H

WILLIAMS TALENT, INC.
13313 Southwest Freeway, Suite 194
Sugar Lane, TX 77478
(281) 240-3145
B, C, Id, If, T, NB, P, V

SHERRY YOUNG, INC.
2620 Fountainview, Suite 212
Houston TX 77057
(713) 266-5800
C, If, It, NB, R, P, T, V

Kansas City Agents

ENTERTAINMENT PLUS
114 A West 3rd Street
Kansas City, MO 64105
(816) 474-4778
All Areas Except CD, DD, F, H, IF, *

EXPOSURE, INC.
215 West 18th Street
Kansas City, MO 64108-1204
(816) 842-4494
All Areas Except A, DD, H, In

HOFFMAN INTERNATIONAL
6705 West 91st Street
Overland Park, KS 66212
(913) 642-1060
All Areas Except A, DD, H, In

I & I AGENCY
1509 Westport Road, Suite 200
Kansas City, MO 64111
(816) 410-9950

TALENT UNLIMITED
4049 Pennsylvania Ave., #300
Kansas City, MO 64111
(816) 561-9040
All Areas Except A,*

Los Angeles Agents

5 STAR TALENT AGENCY
2312 Janet Lee Dr.
La Crescenta, CA 91214
(818) 249-4241

ABRAMS ARTISTS AGENCY
9200 Sunset Blvd., #1130
Los Angeles, CA 90069
(310) 859-0625
All Areas

ACME TALENT & LITERARY
4727 Wilshire Boulevard, # 333
Los Angeles, CA 90010
(323) 954-2263
C, Ch, F, O, T

THE AGENCY
11350 Ventura Blvd. # 100
Studio City, CA 91604
(818) 754-2000
T, C, V, Ch, A, O, F

AGENCY FOR THE PERFORMING
ARTS, INC.
9200 Sunset Blvd., 9th Fl.
Los Angeles, CA 90069
(310) 273-0744
T, B

ıGENCY WEST ENTERTAINMENT
5750 Wilshire Blvd. North # 640
Los Angeles, CA 90036
(323) 857-9050

AIMEE ENTERTAINMENT ASSOC.
15840 Ventura Blvd. # 215
Encino, CA 91436
(818) 783-9115
T, O, F, Mu

AKA TALENT AGENCY
6310 San Vincente Boulevard, # 200
Los Angeles, CA 90048
(323) 965-5600

ALLEN TALENT AGENCY
15760 Ventura Blvd. # 700
Encino, CA 91436
(213) 605-1110
C, B, D, F, M

ALVARADO REY AGENCY
8455 Beverly Boulevard, Suite # 410
Los Angeles CA 90048
(213) 655-7978
C, Ch, F, Mu, O, V, T

AMSEL, EISENSTADT & FRAZIER, INC.
5757 Wilshire Blvd., Suite 510
Los Angeles, CA 90036
(323) 939-1188
A, F, Mu, O, T

ANGEL CITY TALENT
1680 Vine St. # 716
Hollywood, CA 90028
(323) 650-6885
C, Ch, F, O, T, V, *

ARTISTS AGENCY
1180 S. Beverly Drive, # 301
Los Angeles CA 90035
(310) 277-7779
T

ARTISTS GROUP, LTD.
10100 Santa Monica Blvd., # 2490
Los Angeles, CA 90067
(310) 552-1100
T, Ch, F, O, *

A.S.A.
4430 Fountain Ave., # A
Hollywood, CA 90029
(323) 662-9787
A B C, D, F, M, Mu, R, T, V

ATKINS & ASSOCIATES
303 South Crescent Heights Blvd.
Los Angeles, CA 90048
(323) 658-1025

THE AUSTIN AGENCY
6715 Hollywood Blvd. #204
Hollywood, CA 90028
(323) 957-4444

BADGLEY & CONNOR, INC.
9229 Sunset Blvd., # 311
Los Angeles, CA 90069
(310) 278-9313
F,O,T

BAIER/KLEINMAN INTERNATIONAL
3575 Cahuenga Blvd., W # 500
Los Angeles, CA 90068
(818) 761-1001
F, T

BALDWIN TALENT, INC.
8055 W. Manchester Avenue
Playa del Rey, CA 90292
(310) 827-2422
A,C, F, T, V, Mu, Ch, O, *

BOBBY BALL TALENT AGENCY
4342 Lankershim Blvd
Universal City, CA 91602
(818) 506-8188
A, C, Ch, D, F, O, M, Mu, R, T, V

BARON ENTERTAINMENT
5757 Wilshire Boulevard, Suite 659
Los Angeles, CA 90036
(323) 936-7600

BAUMAN REDANTY & SHAUL
5757 Wilshire Blvd., # 473
Los Angeles, CA 90036
(323) 857-6666
T, V

MARIAN BERZON AGENCY
336 E. 17th St.
Costa Mesa, CA 92627
(714) 631-5936
C, Ch, F, M, O, T, V,*

BONNIE BLACK TALENT AGENCY
12034 Riverside Drive, # 103
Valley Village, CA 91607
(818) 753-5424
C, Ch, F, M, O, T

THE BLAKE AGENCY
1333 Ocean Avenue, Suite J
Santa Monica, CA 90401
(310) 899-9898

BRADY, BRANNON & RICH, LLC
5670 Wilshire Blvd. # 820
Los Angeles, CA 90036
(323) 852-9559
A, C, F, M, O

BRAND MODEL & TALENT AGENCY
1520 Brookhollow Drive, # 39
Santa Ana, CA 92705
(714) 850-1158

THE BRANDT COMPANY
15250 Ventura Blvd., # 720
Sherman oaks, CA 91403
(818) 783-7747

BRESLER KELLY & ASSOCIATES
11500 W. Olympic Blvd. # 510
Los Angeles, CA 90064
(310) 479-5611
T

DON BUCHWALD & ASSOC., INC.
PACIFIC
6500 Wilshire Blvd., 22nd Floor
Los Angeles, CA 90048
(323) 655-7400
B, Ch, F,T,*

BUCHWALD TALENT GROUP, INC.
A Youth Agency
Commercial Department
6300 Wilshire Boulevard, Suite 910
Los Angeles, CA 90048
323-852-9555
Theatrical Department
6500 Wilshire Boulevard, Suite 2210
Los Angeles, CA 90048
323-852-9559

IRIS BURTON AGENCY, INC.
1450 Belfast Dr.
Los Angeles, CA 90069
(310) 288-0121
C, Ch, T, V

CAREER ARTISTS INTERNATIONAL
11030 Ventura Blvd., # 3
Studio City, CA 91604
(818) 980-1315
C, D, M

CASSELL-LEVY, INC.
843 N. Sycamore
Los Angeles, CA 90038
(323) 461-3971
A, B, C, D, F, Mu, O, R, V,*

CASTLE HILL ENTERPRISES
1101 S. Orlando Ave.
Los Angeles, CA 90035
(323) 653-3535
C, Ch, F, Mu, O, T, V ,*

CAVALERI & ASSOCIATES
178 South Victory Blvd., # 205
Burbank, CA 91506
(818) 955-9300
C, Ch, F, M, Mu, O, V,T,*

PAGNE/TROTT AGENCY
Wilshire Blvd. # 303
erly Hills, CA 90212
,0) 275-0067
, B, C, F, M, T

THE CHARLES AGENCY
11950 Ventura Bl., Ste. # 3
Studio City, CA 91604
(818) 761-2224

THE CHASIN AGENCY
8899 Beverly Blvd., # 716
Los Angeles, CA 90048
(310) 278-7505
T

CHATEAU BILLINGS TALENT AGENCY
5657 Wilshire Blvd., # 340
Los Angeles, CA 90036
(323) 965-5432

CINEMA TALENT AGENCY
2609 Wyoming Ave., Suite A
Burbank, CA 91505
(818) 845-3816
A, C, Ch, F, O, T, V

CIRCLE TALENT ASSOCIATES
433 N. Camden Dr., # 400
Beverly Hills, CA 90210
(310) 285-1585
C, Ch, F,O, T, *

CLEAR TALENT GROUP
10950 Ventura Blvd.
Studio City, CA 91604
(818) 509-0121
C, Ch, D, F, O, M, T

COLEEN CLER TALENT AGENCY
178 S. Victory Blvd. # 108
Burbank, CA 91502
(818) 841-7943
C, Ch, M

COAST TO COAST TALENT GROUP,
INC.
3350 Barham Blvd.
North Hollywood, CA 90068
(323) 845-9200
A, C, Ch, M, O, V, T

COMMERCIALS UNLIMITED
8383 Wilshire Blvd., # 850
Beverly Hills, CA 90211
(323) 655-0069
A, B, C, Ch, D, F, M, O, V

COMMERCIAL TALENT
9157 Sunset Blvd. # 215
Los Angeles, CA 90069
(310) 247-1431

CONTEMPORARY ARTISTS, LTD.
610 Santa Monica Blvd, # 203
Santa Monica, CA 90401
(310) 395-1800
Ch, F, O, T

CORALIE THEATRICAL AGENCY
4789 Vineland Ave., # 100
North Hollywood, CA 91602
(818) 766-9501
A C, Ch, D, F, O, M, Mu, T, V, *

CREATIVE ARTISTS
9830 Wilshire Blvd.
Beverly Hills, CA 90212
(310) 288-4545

THE CROFOOT GROUP, INC.
23632 Calabasas Rd., Suite 104
Calabasas, CA 91302
(818) 223-1500
B, T, V

CULBERTSON-ARGAZZI GROUP
8430 Santa Monica Blvd. # 210
W. Hollywood, CA 90069
(323) 650-9454

CUNNINGHAM, ESCOTT, DIPENE &
ASSOC., Inc.
10635 Santa Monica Blvd., # 130
Los Angeles, CA 90025
(310) 475-2111
All Areas

DIVERSE TALENT GROUP
1875 Century Park East # 2250
Los Angeles CA 90067
(310) 201-6565
(C, Ch, F O, T, V,*)

ELLE CHANTE TALENT AGENCY
231 West 75th Street
Los Angeles, CA 90003
(323) 750-9490

THE ENDEAVOR AGENCY, L.L.C
9701 Wilshire blvd., 10th Fl.
Beverly Hills, CA 90212
(310) 248-2000

EPSTEIN - WYCKOFF - CORSA - ROSS
& ASSOCIATES
280 S. Beverly Dr., # 400
Beverly Hills, CA 90212
(310) 278-7222
A, C, Ch, F, O, T, V

FERRAR MEDIA ASSOCIATES
8430 Santa Monica Blvd., # 220
Los Angeles, CA 90069
(323) 654-2601
C

FLICK EAST-WEST TALENT, INC.
9057 Nemo St.
West Hollywood, CA 90069
(310) 271-9111
C, F, M,O,T

JUDITH FONTAINE AGENCY
205 South Beverly Dr., # 212
Beverly Hills, CA 90212
(310) 471-8631
C, Ch, M, O,

GWYN FOXX TALENT AGENCY
6269 Selma Ave. # 18
Los Angeles, CA 90028
(323) 467-7711
All Areas

BARRY FREED COMPANY
468 N. Camden Drive, # 201
Beverly Hills, CA 90210
(310) 860-5627
T

ALICE FRIES AGENCY
1927 Vista Del Mar Avenue
Los Angeles, CA 90068
(323) 464-1404
A,B, C, Ch, D, F, M, Mu, O, R, T, *

GAGE GROUP, INC.
14724 Ventura Boulevard, # 505
Sherman Oaks, CA 91403
(818) 905-3800
C, F, O, T, V

DALE GARRICK INTERNATIONAL
8831 Sunset Blvd., # 402
Los Angeles, CA 90069
(310) 657-2661
B, C, Ch, F, O, T,*

GEDDES AGENCY
8430 Santa Monica Blvd., # 200
West Hollywood, CA 90069
323-848-2700
F, T, *

LAYA GELFF ASSOCIATES
16133 Ventura Blvd., # 700
Encino, CA 91436
(818) 996-3100
B, T

PHIL GERSH AGENCY INC.
232 N. Canon Dr., # 202
Beverly Hills, CA 90210
(310) 274-6611
C, T, V

GOLD-LIEDTKE & ASSOCIATES
3500 W. Olive, # 1400
Burbank, CA 91505
(818) 972-4300
A C, Ch, M, O, T, V

MICHELLE GORDON & ASSOC
260 S. Beverly Dr., # 308
Beverly Hills, CA 90212
(310) 246-9930
C, F, O, T

GRANT, SAVIC, KOPALOFF & ASSOCI-
ATES
6399 Wilshire Boulevard, Suite 414
Los Angeles, CA 90048
(323) 782-1854
C, Ch, F, M, O, R, T, V

GREENE & ASSOCIATES
7080 Hollywood Blvd. # 1017
Hollywood, CA 90028
(323) 960-1333
C, T, V

GVA TALENT AGENCY, INC.
9229 Sunset Bl. # 320
Los Angeles, CA 90069
310-278-1310
F, Mu, O, T, V

BUZZ HALLIDAY & ASSOCIATES
8899 Beverly Blvd., # 715
Los Angeles, CA 90048
(310) 275-6028
T

MITCHELL J.HAMILBURG AGENCY
8671 Wilshire Bl. # 500
Beverly Hills, CA 90211
(310) 657-1501

VAUGHN D.HART & ASSOC.
8899 Beverly Blvd., # 815
Los Angeles, CA 90048
(310) 273-7887
F, O, T

BEVERLY HECHT AGENCY
12001 Ventura Pl., # 320
Studio City, CA 91604-2626
(310) 505-1192
C, Ch, F, O, M, T

HERVEY-GRIMES TALENT AGENCY,
INC.
10561 Missouri # 1
Los Angeles, CA 90025
(323) 475-2010
C, Ch, F, M, O, T, *

HILLTOP TALENT AGENCY
27520 Hawthorne Blvd. # 133
Rolling Hills Estates, CA 90274
(310) 265-0611
B, C, Ch, D, F, O, T, V, *

DANIEL HOFF TALENT AGENCY
1800 N. Highland, # 300
Los Angeles, CA 90028
(323) 962-6643
All Areas

HOLLANDER TALENT GROUP
14011 Ventura Boulevard, # 202
Sherman Oaks, CA 91423
(818) 382-9809
C, Ch, T, V

HOUSE OF REPRESENTATIVES TALENT
400 S. Beverly , # 101
Beverly Hills, CA 90212
(310) 772-0772
F, O, T

HOWARD TALENT WEST
10657 Riverside Drive
Toluca Lake, CA 91602
(818) 766-5300
C, Ch, F, O, T,*

HWA TALENT REPRESENTATIVES
3500 W. Olive Avenue # 1400
Burbank, CA 91505
(818) 972-4310
T

IFA TALENT AGENCY
8730 Sunset Blvd. # 490
W. Hollywood, CA 90069
(310) 659-5522

IMPERIUM 7, LLC
9911 W. Pico Blvd. # 1290
Los Angeles, CA 90035
(310) 203-9009
Ch, O, F, V

INNOVATIVE ARTISTS COMMERCIAL
& VOICEOVER, INC.
1505 Tenth Street
Santa Monica, CA 90401
(310) 656-0400

INNOVATIVE ARTISTS TALENT & LIT-
ERARY AGENCY
3000 Olympic Blvd., Bldg. 4, Suite
1200
Santa Monica, CA 90404
(310) 553-5200
F, O, T

INNOVATIVE ARTISTS YOUNG TAL-
ENT DIVISION
3000 Olympic Blvd., Bldg. 4, Suite
1200
Santa Monica, CA 90404
(310) 553-5200
Ch

INTERNATIONAL CREATIVE MGMT.
(I.C.M.)
8942 Wilshire Blvd.
Beverly Hills, CA 90211
(310) 550-4000
All Except Models

J.L.A. (JACK LIPPMAN AGENCY)
9151 Sunset Blvd.
W. Hollywood, CA 90069
(310) 276-5677
A, B, C, Ch, D, M, O, R, T, V

THOMAS JENNINGS & ASSOCIATES
3400 Riverside Drive, 8th Floor Dees
Suite
Burbank CA 91505
(818) 848-0721

KAPLAN-STAHLER AGENCY
8383 Wilshire Blvd., # 923
Beverly Hills, CA 90211
(310) 653-4483
T

KAZARIAN-SPENCER & ASSOC., INC.
11365 Ventura Blvd., # 100
Studio City, 91604
(818) 769-9111
A, B, C, Ch, D, F, M, O, T, V, *

WILLIAM KERWIN AGENCY
1605 N. Cahuenga, #202
Hollywood, CA 90028
(323) 469-5155
C,T

ERIC KLASS AGENCY
139 S. Beverly Dr. #331
Beverly Hills, CA 90212
(310) 274-9169
T

KM & ASSOCIATES
4922 Vineland Avenue
N. Hollywood, CA 91601
818-766-3566

PAUL KOHNER, INC.
9300 Wilshire Blvd., # 555
Beverly Hills, CA 90212
(310) 550-1060
T

L.A. TALENT, INC.
7700 W. Sunset Blvd.
Los Angeles, CA 90046
(323) 656-3722
A, C, Ch, F, O, M, T, V

STACEY LANE AGENCY
1085 Carolyn Way
Beverly Hills, CA 90210
(818) 501-2668
C, D, Ch, O, T, V ,*

LATIN TALENT AGENCY
1112 Beachwood Dr.
Los Angeles, CA 90038
(323) 464-9400
B,C, F, M, T, V

SID LEVIN TALENT AGENCY
8484 Wilshire Blvd., # 750
Beverly Hills, CA 90211
(323) 653-7073
C, Ch, F,O, T,*

ROBERT LIGHT AGENCY
6404 Wilshire Blvd., # 900
Los Angeles, CA 90048
(323) 651-1777
Mu, R, T

KEN LINDNER & ASSOC.
2049 Century Park E., # 3050
Los Angeles, CA 90067
(310) 277-9223
B,V

LJ & ASSOCIATES
17328 Ventura Blvd. # 185
Encino, CA 91316
(818) 589-6960

LONG BEACH TALENT AGENCY
6444 E. Spring Street, # 275
(562) 498-7305
All Areas

LOVELL & ASSOC.
6730 Wedgewood Place
Los Angeles, CA 90068
(323) 876-1560
T,O

JANA LUKER AGENCY
1923 1/2 Westwood Blvd., # 3
Los Angeles, CA 90025
(310) 441-2822
C, Ch, F, O, T

LYNNE & REILLY AGENCY
10725 Vanowen Street, # 113
North Hollywood, CA 91605-6402
(213) 755-6434
C Ch, Mu, O, R, T,V

McCABE/JUSTICE, LLC
8285 Sunset Blvd. # 1
Los Angeles, CA 90046
(323) 650-3738
C, Ch, F M, O, Mu, V, T,

McDONALD/SELZNICK ASSOCIATES,
INC
1611A N. El Centro Avenue
Hollywood, CA 90028
(323) 957-6680
C, Ch, D, Mu, R, T

MALAKY INTERNATIONAL
10642 Santa Monica Blvd., # 103
Los Angeles, CA 90025
(310) 234-9114

ALESE MARSHALL MODEL & TALENT
AGENCY
23639 Hawthorne Blvd. # 200
Torrance, CA 90505
(310) 378-1223
C, Ch, F, M, O, T, V

MAXINE'S TALENT AGENCY
4830 Encino Ave
Encino, CA 91316
(818) 986-2946
C, Mu, R, T, V

MEDIA ARTISTS GROUP
6404 Wilshire Boulevard, Suite 950
Los Angeles, CA 90048
(323) 658-5050
A, B, C, Ch, F, O, M, T

MERIDIAN ARTISTS AGENCY
9229 Sunset Boulevard, # 310
Los Angeles CA 90069
(310) 246-2611

METROPOLITAN TALENT AGENCY
4526 Wilshire Blvd.
Los Angeles, CA 90010
(323) 857-4500
T

THE MORGAN AGENCY
7080 Hollywood Boulevard, # 1009
Hollywood, CA 90027
(323) 469-7100

WILLIAM MORRIS AGENCY, INC.
151 El Camino
Beverly Hills, CA 90212
(310) 274-7451
A B C, F, Mu, R, O, T, V, *

H. DAVID MOSS & ASSOC.
733 N. Seward St.
Los Angeles, CA 90038
(323) 465-1234
A, B, C, Ch, F, O, T,*

SUSAN NATHE & ASSOC. (CPC)
8281 Melrose, # 200
Los Angeles, CA 90046
(323) 653-7573
C, Ch, F, O, V,*
OMNIPOP, INC.
10700 Ventura Blvd., 2nd Fl.
Studio City, CA 91604
(818) 980-9267
C, F, Mu, R T,V,,*

THE ORANGE GROVE GROUP, INC.
12178 Ventura Blvd. # 205
Studio City, CA 91604
(818) 762-7498
Ch, D, F, M, Mu, O, R, S, T, *

ORIGIN TALENT
3393 Barham Boulevard
Los Angeles, CA 90068
(323) 845-4141

OSBRINK TALENT AGENCY, CINDY
4343 Lankershim Blvd. # 100
Universal City, CA 91602
(818) 760-2488
C, Ch, M, T, V

PAKULA/KING & ASSOCIATES
9229 Sunset Blvd., # 315
Los Angeles, CA 90069
(310) 281-4868
T

PARADIGM, A TALENT & LITERARY
AGENCY
10100 Santa Monica Blvd., # 2500
Los Angeles, CA 90067
(310) 277-4400
C, Ch, D, F, O, M, T, V

THE PARADISE GROUP
8749 Sunset Blvd., Suite B
Los Angeles, CA 90069
(310) 854-6622

PINNACLE COMMERCIAL TALENT
5757 Wilshire Boulevard, Suite 510
Los Angeles, CA 90036
(323) 939-1188
A, B, C, Ch, D, F, M, Mu, O, *

PLAYBOY MODEL AGENCY
9242 Beverly Blvd.
Beverly Hills, CA 90210
(310) 246-4000
B, C, F, M, T, V

PRIVILEGE TALENT AGENCY
14542 Ventura Boulevard, # 209
Sherman Oaks, CA 91403
(818) 386-2377

PROGRESSIVE ARTISTS
400 S. Beverly, # 216
Beverly Hills, CA 90212
(310) 553-8561
T

QUALITA DELL' ARTE
5353 Topanga Canyon Road, Suite 220
Woodland Hills, CA 91364
(818) 598-8073
All Areas

REBEL ENTERTAINMENT PARTNERS,
INC.
8075 W. Third, # 303
Los Angeles, CA 90048
(213) 935-1700
B, C, F, O, R, T, V

SARNOFF COMPANY, INC.
10 Universal City Plaza, # 2000
Universal City CA 91608
(818) 753-2377
B,M,T

SAVAGE AGENCY, INC.
6212 Banner Ave.
Los Angeles, CA 90038
(213) 461-8316
C, Ch, R, T, V

JACK SCAGNETTI AGENCY
5118 Vineland Ave., # 102
North Hollywood, CA 91601
(818) 762-3871
C, D, F, M, O, T, V, *

IRV SCHECHTER COMPANY
9300 Wilshire Blvd., # 400
Beverly Hills, CA 90212
(310) 278-8070
T

SANDIE SCHNARR TALENT, INC.
8500 Melrose Ave., # 212
W. Hollywood, Ca 90069
(310) 360-7680
C, V

JUDY SCHOEN & ASSOC.
606 N. Larchmont Blvd., # 309
Los Angeles, CA 90004
(323) 962-1950 T

SCHULTZ/CARROLL ASSOCIATES
6422 Coldwater Canyon, # 206
Valley Glen, CA 91606
(818) 760-3100
F, O, T

SCREEN ARTISTS AGENCY
4526 Sherman Oaks Avenue
Sherman Oaks, CA 91403
(818) 789-4897

SDB PARTNERS, INC.
1801 Ave. of the Stars # 902
Los Angeles, CA 90067
(310) 785-0060
T

SHAPIRA & ASSOC., INC., DAVID
15821 Ventura Blvd. # 235
Encino, CA 91436
(818) 906-0322
C, M, T, V

SHAPIRO-LICHTMAN STEIN
8827 Beverly Blvd.
Los Angeles, CA 90048
(310) 859-8877

SLESSINGER & ASSOC., MICHAEL
8730 Sunset Blvd. Suite 270
West Hollywood, CA 90069
(310) 657-7113
T

SMS TALENT, INC.
8730 Sunset Blvd. # 440
Los Angeles, CA 90069
(310) 289-0909
F, O, T

CAMILLE SORICE TALENT ANGECY
13412 Moorpark St., # C
Sherman Oaks, CA 91423
(818) 955-1775
Mu, O, T

SPECIAL ARTISTS AGENCY
345 N. Maple Dr., # 302
Beverly Hills, CA 90210
(310) 859-9688
A, C, M, V

SCOTT STANDER AGENCY
13701 Riverside Drive, Suite 201
Sherman Oaks, CA 91423
(818) 905-7000

STARCRAFT TALENT AGENCY
1516 N. Formosa Ave.
Hollywood, CA 90046
(323) 845-4784
ALL

THE STEVENS GROUP
14011 Ventura Boulevard, # 201
Sherman Oaks, CA 91423
(818) 528-3674

STONE MANNERS AGENCY
6500 Wilshire Blvd. # 550
Los Angeles, CA 90048
(323) 655-1313
T, V

PETER STRAIN & ASSOC.
5724 W. 3rd Street, # 302
Los Angeles, CA 90036
(323) 525-3391

MITCHELL K. STUBBS & ASSOCIATES
8675 W. Washington Boulevard # 203
Culver City, CA 90232
(310) 888-1200
B, C, M, Mu, R, T, V

SUPERIOR TALENT AGENCY
11425 Moorpark Street
Studio City, CA 91602
(818) 508-5627
All Areas

SUTTON-BARTH-VENNARI, INC.
145 S. Fairfax Ave., # 310
Los Angeles, CA 90036
(323) 938-6000
C,V

SWB THEATRICAL
8383 Wilshire Blvd.# 850
Beverly Hills, CA 90211
(323) 655-0069

TALENT GROUP, INC.
6300 Wilshire Blvd. # 900
Los Angeles, CA 90048
(323) 852-9559
B,C, Ch, F, M, R, T, V

HERB TANNEN & ASSOC.
10801 National Blvd. # 101
Los Angeles, CA 90064
(310) 466-5822
C, Ch, , F, O, T, V

THOMAS TALENT AGENCY
6709 LaTijera, # 915
Los Angeles, CA 90045
(310) 665-0000
C, D, F, Mu, T

THORNTON & ASSOC., ARLENE
12711 Ventura Boulevard, # 490
Studio City, CA 91604
(818) 760-6688
B, C, R, V

TISHERMAN AGENCY
6767 Forest Lawn Dr. # 101
Los Angeles, CA 90068
(323) 850-6767
B, C, F, O, V,*

TWO ANGELS AGENCY
2026 Cliff Drive, Suite 200
Santa Barbara, A 93109
(805) 957-9654

UNITED ARTISTS TALENT AGENCY
14011 Ventura Blvd. # 213
Sherman Oaks. CA 91423
(818) 788-7305

UNITED TALENT AGENCY
9560 Wilshire Boulevard
Beverly Hills, CA 90212
(310)-273-6700

THE VISSION AGENCY
1801 Century Park E., 24th floor
Los Angeles, CA 90067
(310) 553-8833

VOX, INC.
5670 Wilshire Boulevard, # 820
Los Angeles, CA 90036
(323) 852-9559
V

THE WALLIS AGENCY
4444 Riverside Drive, # 105
Burbank, CA 91505
(818) 953-4848
C, F, O, T, V

BOB WATERS AGENCY
4311 Wilshire Blvd. # 622
Los Angeles, CA 90010
(323) 965-5555
F, O, T

WAUGH AGENCY, ANN
4741 Laurel Canyon Blvd., Suite 200
North Hollywood, CA 91607
(818) 980-0141
C, Ch, F, O, T, V, *

WILSON & ASSOC., SHIRLEY
5410 Wilshire Blvd., Suite 806
Los Angeles, CA 90036
(323) 857-6977
C, Ch, F, O, T

WRITERS & ARTISTS AGENCY
8383 Wilshire Blvd., # 550
Los Angeles, CA 90211
(323) 866-0900
Ch, F, O, T

STELLA ZADEH & ASSOC.
17328 Ventura Boulevard
Encino, CA 91316
(818) 424-2226
B,T

ZANUCK, PASSON & PACE, INC.
4717 Van Nuys Boulevard, Suite 102
Sherman Oaks, CA 94103
(818) 783-4890

Florida Agents

AZUREE MODELING & TALENT
AGENCY
1115 Kentucky Avenue
Winter Park, FL 32789
(407) 629-5025
All Areas Except A, DD, H

BOCA TALENT & MODEL AGENCY
829 SE 9th Street Palm Plaza Suite 4
Deerfield Beach, FL 33441
(954) 428-4677
A, B, C, Ch, D, F, M, O, T, V, *

CENTRAL FLORIDA TALENT, INC.
2601 Wells Avenue, Suite 181
Fern Park, FL 32730
(407) 830-9226

THE DIAMOND AGENCY
204 West Bay Avenue
Longwood, FL 32750
(407) 830-4040

DIMENSIONS III TALENT AGENCY
5205 South Orange Avenue
Orlando, FL 32809
(407) 871-2575

THE GREEN AGENCY, INC.
1329 Alton Road
Miami Beach, FL 33139
(305) 532-9225
C, DD, H, Id, In, NB, T,V

IRENE MARIE, INC.
728 Ocean Dr.
Miami Beach, FL 33139-6203
Dade (305) 672-2344
Broward (954) 771-1400
All areas except B, V

MARION POLAN TALENT AGENCY
10 N.E. 11th Ave.
Ft. Lauderdale, Fl 33301
(954) 525-8351
All Areas Except DD
Agent Specializing in Spanish language

THE SHEFFIELD AGENCY
P.O. Box 101418 (mailing address only)
Fort Lauderdale, FLA 33310
(954) 523-5887
(Please call AFTRA for agency office
location)

WORLD OF KIDS, INC.
1460 Ocean Drive, Suite 205
Miami Beach, FL 33139
(305) 672-5437
C, Ch, M, D, Mu, T, V, *

Nashville Agents

ADVANTAGE MODELS & TALENT
230 Franklin Road, Suite 802
Franklin, TN 37064
(615) 790-5001

AGENCY FOR THE PERFORMING
ARTS
3017 Poston Avenue
Nashville, TN 37203
(615) 297-0100

CREATIVE ARTISTS AGENCY
3310 West End Ave., 5th Fl.
Nashville, TN 37203
(615) 383-8787

THE DAN AGENCY
209 10th Avenue South, Suite 302
Nashville, TN 37203
(615) 244-3266
All Areas

D.S. ENTERTAINMENT
4741 Trousdale Drive, Suite 2
Nashville, TN 37220
(615) 331-6264

BUDDY LEE ATTRACTIONS INC. (TN)
38 Music Square E., # 300
Nashville, TN 37203
(615) 244-4336

WILLIAM MORRIS AGENCY INC.
2100 West End Ave., Suite 1000
P.O. Box 37203
Nashville, TN 37203
(615) 385-0310

TALENT & MODEL LAND, INC.
P.O. Box 40763
Nashville, TN 37204
(615) 321-5596

TALENT TREK AGENCY (NASHVILLE)
2021 21st Avenue, South, Suite 102
Nashville, TN 37212
(615) 279-0010

TALENT TREK AGENCY (KNOXVILLE)
5401 Kingston Pike, Suite 450
Knoxville, TN 37919
(865) 977-8735

New York Agents

ABOUT ARTISTS AGENCY
1650 Broadway, Suite 1406
New York, NY 10019
(212) 490-7191
CD, Id, If, Mu, NB, V, P, R, T

ABRAMS ARTISTS & ASSOC.
275 Seventh Avenue
26th Floor
New York, NY 10001
646-486-4600
All Areas

ACCESS TALENT, INC.
37 East 28th St., Suite 500
New York, NY 10016
(212) 684-7795
B, C, F, Id, If, NB, O, P, R, T, V

ACME TALENT & LITERARY
875 Avenue of the Americas, Suite
2108
New York, NY 10001
(212) 328-0388
C, Ch, F, Mu, O, T, V, *

ATLAS TALENT AGENCY, INC.
36 West 44th Street, Suite 1000
New York, NY 10036
212-730-4500

BRET ADAMS LTD.
448 44th St.
New York, NY 10036
(212) 765-5630
D, In, Mu, O, R,T,

AGENTS FOR THE ARTS, INC.
203 West 23rd St., 3rd Fl.
New York, NY 10011
(212) 229-2562
B, C, D,Id, Mu, NB, O, P, T, V, *

AMERICAN INT'L TALENT AGENCY
303 West 42nd St., # 608
New York, NY 10036
(212) 245-8888
All Areas Except A, B, DD, H

BEVERLY ANDERSON
1501 Broadway, # 2008
New York, NY 10036
(212) 944-7773
D, Mu, O, F, V, C, R, T, In

ANDREADIS TALENT AGENCY
119 West 57th St., # 711
New York, NY 10019
(212) 315-0303
All Areas

ARCIERI & ASSOCIATES
305 Madison Ave., Suite 2315
New York, NY 10165
(212) 286-1700

THE ARTISTS GROUP EAST
1650 Broadway, Suite 711
New York, NY 10019
(212) 586-1452
Mu, O, F, T, Id

THE, RICHARD ASTOR AGENCY
250 West 57th St., # 2014
New York, NY 10107
(212) 581-1970
D, F, Mu, O, T

BARRY HAFT BROWN ARTISTS
AGENCY
165 West 46th St., # 908
New York, NY 10036
(212) 869-9310
C, DD, T

BAUMAN REDANTY & SHAUL
250 West 57th St., # 473
New York, NY 10019
(212) 757-0098
A, B, D, F, M, Mu, O, R, T,V, *

BERMAN, BOALS & FLYNN, INC.
230 West 30th Street, Suite 401
New York, NY 10001
212-868-1068

BIENSTOCK INC., N.S.
1740 Broadway, 24th Fl.
New York, NY 10019
(212) 765-3040
All Areas Except A, DD, H

DON BUCHWALD & ASSOC.
10 East 44th St.
New York, NY 10017
(212) 867-1200
All Areas Except A, DD H

CARRY COMPANY
49 West 46th Street, 4th Floor
New York, NY 10036
(212) 768-2793

CARSON-ADLER AGENCY, INC.
250 West 57th St.
New York, NY 10107
(212) 307-1882
C, Ch

THE CARSON ORGANIZATION, LTD.,
234 West 44th Street, Suite 902
New York, NY 10036
(212) 221-1517
All Areas Except B

CORNERSTONE TALENT AGENCY
37 West 20th Street, Suite 1108
New York, NY 10011
(212) 807-8344
D, C, F, Id, O, R, T, V, *

CREATIVE ARTISTS AGENCY
767 Fifth Avenue
New York, NY 10153
(212) 833-3600
All Areas

CUNNINGHAM, ESCOTT, DIPENE &
ASSOC.
257 Park Avenue South, Suite 900
New York, NY 10010
(212) 477-1666
ALL AREAS

GINGER DICCE TALENT AGENCY
1650 Broadway, # 714
New York, NY 10019
(212) 974-7455
C, ,CD, Ch, F, If, O, M, NB, Id, T, P, V

DOUGLAS, GORMAN, ROTHACKER
& WILHELM, INC.
1501 Broadway, # 703
New York, NY 10036
(212) 382-2000
F, Id, If, Mu, O, R, T

DULCINA EISEN ASSOCIATES
154 East 61st St.
New York, NY 10021
(212) 355-6617
C, D, F, Id, Mu, O, R, T, *

EASTERN TALENT ALLIANCE
1501 Broadway, Suite 404
New York, NY 10036
(212) 840-6868
In, R, N, P, T

ELECTRIC TALENT, INC.
172-13 Hillside Avenue, Suite 202
Jamaica Estates, NY 11432
(718) 883-1940
C, DD, Id, In, T, P, V

ENDEAVOR AGENCY, LLC
270 Lafayette Street, Suite 605
New York, NY 10012
(212) 625-2500
All Areas

EWCR & ASSOCIATES
311 West 43rd St., # 304
New York, NY 10036
(212) 586-9110
Ch, T, ACTORS

FLAUNT MODEL MANAGEMENT
114 East 32nd Street
New York, NY 10016
(212) 679-9011
C, CD, Id, If, In, F, MV, NB, O, P, T

FRESH FACES AGENCY, INC.
108 South Franklin Avenue, Suite 11
Valley Stream, NY 11580
(516) 223-0034
All Areas

FRONTEIR BOOKING INT'L, INC.
1560 Broadway, #1110
New York, NY 10036
(212) 221-0220
C, CD, Ch, Id, F, M, T, V

THE GAGE GROUP
315 West 57th St., # 4H
New York, NY 10019
(212) 541-5250
B,C, CD Id, In, R, NB, P, T, V

GARBER TALENT AGENCY
2 Penn Plaza
New York, NY 10121-0099
(212) 292-4910
C, D, F, Mu, O, R, T, V, *

GENERATION TV
20 West 20th Street, # 1008
New York NY 10011
(646) 230-9491

THE GERSH AGENCY NY, INC.
130 West 42nd St., # 2400
New York, NY 10036
(212) 997-1818
T

PEGGY HADLEY ENTERPRISES, LTD.
250 West 57th St., Suite 2317
New York, NY 10107
(212) 246-2166
D, F, Mu, R, T

HARDEN-CURTIS ASSOCIATES
850 Seventh Ave., # 405
New York, NY 10019
(212) 977-8502
F, Id, O, T, *

HARTIG-HILEPO AGENCY, LTD.
156 Fifth Ave., Suite 820
New York, NY 10010
(212) 929-1772
C, D, If, In, Mu, O, P, S, R, T, V

HENDERSON/HOGAN AGENCY, INC.
850 Seventh Ave., # 1003
New York, NY 10019
(212) 765-5190
C, Ch, D, Id, If, Mu, O, P, R, T, V, *

THE BARBARA HOGENSON AGENCY
165 West End Avenue, Suite 19-C
New York, NY 10023
(212) 874-8084
CD In, R, T, V

HWA TALENT REPRESENTATIVES
220 East 23rd St., # 400
New York, NY 10010
(212) 889-0800
All Areas Except A, B, Ch, H

INDEPENDENT ARTISTS AGENCY
159 West 25th Street, Suite 1011
New York, NY 10001
646-486-3332
T, DD

INGBER & ASSOCIATES
274 Madison Ave., Suite 1104
New York, NY 10016
(212) 889-9450
C, CD, F, Id, If, In, NB, O, P R V

INNOVATIVE ARTISTS TALENT &
LITERARY AGENCY
235 Park Avenue South, 7th Floor
New York, NY 10003
(212) 253-6900
Ch, F, O, T

INTERNATIONAL CREATIVE MGMT.
(I.C.M)
40 West 57th St.
New York, NY 10019
(212) 556-5600
All Except Models

JORDAN, GILL & DORNBAUM
AGENCY, INC.
1133 Broadway, Suite 623
New York, NY 10010
(212) 463-8455
C, Ch, CD, D, F, Id, In, M, NB, P, T, V

STANLEY KAPLAN TALENT
139 Fulton Street, Suite 503
New York, NY 10038
(212) 385-4400

KAZARIAN/SPENCER & ASSOC., INC
162 West 56th Street, Suite 307
New York, NY 10019
(212) 582-7572
C, If, It, N, P, T

KERIN-GOLDBERG ASSOCIATES
155 East 55th St., # 5D
New York, NY 10022
(212) 838-7373
B, Ch, CD, D, F If, In, It, Mu, O, T, *

KING, LTD., ARCHER
317 West 46th Street, Suite 3A
New York, NY 10035
(212) 765-3103
DD, Id, In, NB, P, T

KOLSTEIN TALENT AGENCY,
dba NAOMI'S WORLD OF
ENTERTAINMENT, INC.
85 C Lafayette Avenue
Suffern, NY 10901
(845) 357-8301
All Areas

THE KRASNY OFFICE, INC.
1501 Broadway, # 1303
New York, NY 10036
(212) 730-8160
A, B, C, CD, D, F, Id, If, Mu, N, O, P,
T, V

LALLY TALENT AGENCY
630 Ninth Ave., # 800
New York, NY 10036
(212) 974-8718
D, F, Mu, O, R, T, *

LANTZ OFFICE, THE
200 West 57th St., # 503
New York, NY 10019
(212) 586-0200

LEADING ARTISTS, INC.
145 West 45th Street, # 1204
New York, NY 10036
T, DD

BERNARD LIEBHABER AGENCY
352 Seventh Ave., 7th Floor
New York, NY 10001
212-631-7561
Ch, F, O, T,, V

THE LEUDTKE AGENCY
1674 Broadway, Suite. 7A
New York, NY 10019
(212) 220-3532
All Areas Except Models

BRUCE LEVY AGENCY
311 West 43rd St. # 602
New York, NY 10036,
(212) 262-6845
A, B, C, D, F, M, Mu, O, R, T, V, *

WILLIAM MORRIS AGENCY
1325 Ave. of The Americas
New York, NY 10019
(212) 586-5100
All Areas

NICOLISI & COMPANY, INC.
150 West 25th Street, Suite 1200
New York, NY 10025
(212) 633-1010
T,S

NOUVELLE TALENT INC.
20 Bethune Street, # 4A
New York, NY 10014
(212) 645- 0940
Id, F, M, P

OMNIPOP TALENT AGENCY, INC.
55 West Old Country Rd.
Hicksville, NY 11801
(516) 937- 6011
B,C, CD, Id, If, NB, P, R, T, V

FIFI OSCARD AGENCY, INC.
110 West 40th Street
New York, NY 10018
(212) 764-1100
C, CD, Ch, Id, If, It, M, NB, P, T, V

PARADIGM
500 Fifth Avenue, 37th Floor
New York, NY 10110
(212) 703-7540
C, Ch, DD, F, Id, If, M, O, P, T, V

PROFESSIONAL ARTISTS UNLIMITED
321 West 44th Street, Ste. 605
New York, NY 10036
(212) 247-8770
B, D, F, If, Mu, O, R, T

GILLA ROOS LTD.
16 West 22nd St., 3rd Floor
New York, NY 10010
(212) 727-7820

SCHIOWITZ/CLAY/ROSE
165 West 46th Street, Suite 1210
New York, NY 10036
(212) 840-6787

SCHULLER TALENT/NEW YORK KIDS
276 Fifth Ave., Suite 204
New York, NY 10001
(212) 532-6005

SILVER, MASSETTI & SZATMARY/EAST
LTD.
145 West 45th St., # 1204
New York, NY 10036
(212) 391-4545
TV Programs Only

ANN STEELE AGENCY
240 West 44th Street, Suite 1
Helen Hayes Theatre
New York, NY 10036
(212) 278-0896
C, CD, Ch, DD, F, Id, Mu, NB, O, P, T,
V,

STONE MANNERS AGENCY
900 Broadway, Suite 803
New York, NY 10003
(212) 505-1400
DD,V,H,T,P,In

PETER STRAIN & ASSOC., INC.
1501 Broadway, # 2900
New York, NY 10036
(212) 391-0380

TALENT NETWORK GROUP (TNG)
111 East 22nd Street, 3rd Floor
New York, NY 10010
(212) 995-7325
C, Id, If, T

TALENT REPRESENTATIVE, INC.
20 East 53rd St., Suite 2A
New York, NY 10022
(212) 752-1835
C, Id, If, R, T, V

TAMAR WOLBROM, INC.
130 West 42nd Street, Suite 707
New York, NY 10036
(212) 398-4595
B,C, CD, Id, If, NB, O, P, R, T, V

WRITERS & ARTISTS AGENCY
19 West 44th St., # 1000
New York, NY 10036
(212) 391-1112
C, Ch, F, If, It, O, R, T, V

Philadelphia Agents

THE CLARO AGENCY, INC.
1513 W. Passyunk Ave.
Philadelphia, PA 19145
(215) 465-7788
B, C, Ch, CD, DD, F, Id, If, It, M, NB,
O, P, R T, V

EXPRESSIONS MODELING & TALENT,
INC.
110 Church St.
Philadelphia, PA 19106
(215) 923-4420*
C, DD, Ch, F, Id, If, M, NB, O, P, T, V

GOODMAN AGENCY
605 West Rt. 70
Cherry Hill, NJ 08002
(609) 795-7979 (actors)
(609) 795-3133 (clients)

GREER LANGE TALENT AGENCY
3 Bala Plaza West, Suite 201
Bala Cynwyd, PA 19004
(610) 747-0300
C, CD, F, Id, If, In, M, NB, O, P, V, *

MCCULLOUGH ASSOC.
8 S. Hanover Avenue
Atlantic City, NJ 08402-2615
(609) 822-2222
A, D, C, F, Id, If, M, O, P, T

MODELS ON THE MOVE
1200 Route 70, Ste. 6
Barclay Towers
P.O. Box 4037
Cherry Hills, NJ 08034
(609) 667-1060
All Areas Except H, R

PLAZA 7
160 North Gulph Road
King of Prussia, PA 19406
(610) 337-2693
C, Ch, F, Id, If, M, NB, O, P, T, V, *

REINHARD AGENCY
2021 Arch St., Suite 404
Philadelphia, PA 19103
(215) 567-2008
All Areas Except MU

GAIL WILLIAMS AGENCY
525 South 4th Street, #365
Philadelphia, PA 19147
(215) 627-9533
All Areas

Phoenix Agents

ROBERT FORD/BLACK AGENCY
4300 N Miller road, #202
Scottsdale, AZ 85251
(480) 966-2537
(480) 967-5424 (fax)
All Areas Except H, R

DANI'S AGENCY
1 E. Camelback Rd. # 550
Phoenix, AZ 85012
(602) 263-1918
All Areas Except B

FOSIS MODELING & TALENT AGENCY
2777 N. Campbell Ave. # 209
Tucson, AZ 85719
(520) 795-3534

LEIGHTON AGENCY
2375 East Camelback, 5th Floor
Phoenix, AZ 85016
(602) 224-9255
All Areas Except A, B, DD, *

SIGNATURE MODELS & TALENT
AGENCY
2600 N. 44th Street, Suite 209
Phoenix, AZ 85008
(602) 966-1102
All Areas Except Mu

Pittsburgh Agents

THE TALENT GROUP
2820 Smallman St.
Pittsburgh, PA 15222
(412) 471-8011
All Areas Except A, DD, H, Mu

DOCHERTY, INC.
109 Market Street
Pittsburgh, PA 15222
412-765-1400
ALL AREAS

Portland Agents

CUSICK'S TALENT MGMT.
1009 N.W. Hoyt, #100
Portland, OR 97209
(503) 274-8555
All Areas Except *

ERHART TALENT
037 SW Hamilton Street
Portland, OR 97201
(503) 243-6362
B, C, CD, Ch, Id, If, F, M, NB, O, R, T,
V, *

MASHIA TALENT MANAGEMENT
2808 NE Martin Luther King, Jr.
Boulevard, Suite L
Portland, OR 97212
(503) 331-9293
C, Id, If, In, NB, R, T, V

RYAN ARTISTS
239 NW 13th Street, Suite 215
Portland, OR 97209
(503) 274-1005

URSA TALENT, LLC
1310 Coburg Road, Suite 10
Eugene, OR 97401
(541) 485-4495
C, If, It, N, P, T, V

San Diego Agents

ARTIST MGMT. AGENCY, INC.
835 Fifth Ave., #411
San Diego, CA 92101
(619) 233-6655

ELEGANCE MODEL & TALENT
2763 State Street
Carlsbad, CA 92008
(760) 434-3397

JET SET TALENT AGENCY
2160 Avenida de la Playa
La Jolla, CA 92037
(858) 551-9393
C, If, NB, R, T

NOUVEAU MODEL & TALENT
909 Prospect Street, # 230
San Diego, CA 92037
(858) 456-1400

SAN DIEGO MODEL MGMT.
438 Camino Del Rio North, # 116
San Diego, CA 92108
(619) 296-1018
C, CH, D, M, O, V

SHAMON FREITAS & COMPANY
9606 Tierra Grande St., # 204
San Diego, CA 92126
(858) 549-3955

San Francisco Agents

BOOM MODELS & TALENT AGENCY
2325 Third Street, # 223
San Francisco, CA 94107
(415) 626-6591
All Areas

THE ES AGENCY
6612 Pacheco Way
Citrus Heights, CA 95610
(916) 723-2794
B, C, T, V

FILM-THEATRE ACTORS EXCHANGE
3145 Geary Blvd., # 752
San Francisco, CA 94118
(415) 379-9308
C, CD, Id, NB, T, V

GENERATIONS MODEL & TALENT
AGENCY
340 Brannan Street, Suite 302
San Francisco, CA 94107
(415) 777-9099
C, Ch, F, M, O, T, V,*

J.E. TALENT, LLC
323 Geary Street, # 302
San Francisco, CA 94102
(415) 395-9475
C, Id, If, In, NB, P, R, T, V

LOOK MODEL & TALENT
166 Geary Blvd., # 1406
San Francisco, CA 94108
(415) 781-2841
All Areas Except A, DD, H, R

MARLA DELL TALENT
2124 Union Street
San Francisco, CA 94123
(415) 563-9213
All Areas Except DD, H, If

PANDA TALENT AGENCY
3721 Hoen Ave.
Santa Rosa, CA 95405
(707) 576-0711
All Areas

SHOW OFF TALENT
5050 El Camino Real, Suite 104
Los Altos, CA 94022
(800) 506-1977 (within California)
(650) 903-1710
All Areas

STARS - THE AGENCY (SF)
23 Grant Avenue, 4th Floor
San Francisco, CA 94108
(415) 421-6272
All Areas

TALENT PLUS AGENCY/LOS LATINOS
(HISPANIC DIVISION)
DYER BUILDING
2801 Moorpark Ave. # 11
San Jose, CA 95128
(408) 296-2213
All Areas Except *

TONRY TALENT
885 Bryant Street, Suite 201
San Francisco, CA 94103
(415) 543-3797
All Areas

TOP MODELS & TALENT AGENCY
The Flood Building
870 Market St., Suite 1076
San Francisco, CA 94102
(415) 391-1800
All Areas

Seattle Agents

THE ACTORS GROUP (WA),
3400 Beacon Ave S
Seattle, WA 98114
(206) 624-9465

COLLEEN BELL MODELING & TALENT
AGENCY
14205 SE 36th St, # 100
Bellevue, WA 98006
(425) 649-1111

DRAMATIC ARTISTS AGENCY
50 - 16th Avenue
Kirkland, WA 98033-4909
(206) 442-9190

ENTCO INTERNATIONAL, Inc.
7017 196TH ST SW
Lynnwood, WA 98036
(425) 670-0888

KID BIZ TALENT AGENCY
One Bellevue Center
411 108th Ave., N.E., Suite 2050
Bellevue, Washington 98004
(425) 455-8800

SEATTLE MODELS GUILD
1809 Seventh Ave., Suite 608
Seattle, WA 98101
(206) 622-1406

TOPO SWOPE TALENT AGENCY
1932 1st Ave., Suite 700
Seattle, WA 98101
(206) 443-2021

St. Louis Agents

PRIMA MODELS
522 A. S. Henley Rd.
St. Louis, MO 63105
(314) 721-1235
C, Ch, D, F, M, O,T, V, *

TALENT PLUS INC. (ST. LOUIS)
1222 Lucas, Suite 300
St. Louis, MO 63103
(314) 421-9400
C, CD, Ch, F, Id, If, O, M, NB, P, R, V,
*

Tri-State Agents

ASHLEY TALENT
10948 Reading Road
Cincinnati OH 45241
(513) 554-4836

CAM TALENT - CINCINATTI
1150 W. Eight St., # 262
Cincinnati, OH 45203
(513) 421-1795
All Areas

CAM TALENT - COLUMBUS
1350 West 5th Ave., Suite 25
Columbus, OH 43212
(614) 488-1122
All Areas

CREATIVE TALENT
5864 Nike Drive
Hilliard, OH 43026
(614) 876-7750
A, B, C, Ch, D, F, M, Mu, O,*

GOENNER TALENT, JO
2299 Miamisburg - Centerville Road
Dayton, OH 45459
(937) 312-0021 Dayton
(513) 733-3330 Cincinnati
All Areas Except A, H

HEYMAN TALENT, INC
3308 Brotherton
Cincinnati, OH 45209
(513) 533-3113
(317) 255-5702 Indianapolis
(614) 444-4494 Columbus
All Areas Except A, H

HELEN WELLS AGENCY
12811 East New Market Street
Carmel, IN 46032
(317) 843-5363
C, Ch, F, M, O, V,*

Twin Cities Agents

CARYN MODEL & TALENT
Butler Square Bldg.
100 N. 6th St., # 270B
Minneapolis, MN 55403
(612) 349-3600
All Areas

MEREDITH MODEL & TALENT
800 Washington Avenue North, Suite
511
Minneapolis, MN 55401
(612) 340-9555
All Areas

MOORE CREATIVE TALENT, INC.
(Formally Eleanor Moore Agency and
Creative Casting)
1610 West Lake Street
Minneapolis, MN 55408
(612) 827-3823
All Areas

THE WEHMANN AGENCY
1128 Harmon Place, # 205
Minneapolis, MN 55403
(612) 333-6393
All Areas

Washington, DC Agents

THE BULLOCK AGENCY
5200 Bullock Avenue, # 102
Hyattsville, MD 20781
(301) 209-9598
All Areas Except Athletes

KIDS INTERNATIONAL
938 East Swann Creek Rd., Suite 152
Ft. Washington, MD 20744
(301) 292-6094

TAYLOR-ROYALL, Inc.
6247 Falls Road
Baltimore, MD 21209
(410) 828-6900
(410) 828-1280
C, R, T,V

Wisconsin Agents

ARLENE WILSON TALENT, INC.
807 North Jefferson St., 200
Milwaukee, WI 53202
(414) 283-5600

SAG Agents

Many of these agents have previously been listed as AFTRA Agents, because they are franchised by both unions. Again, things often change with respect to the kind of services agencies provide, so check with individual agencies for more up to date information.

Arizona Agents

ROBERT BLACK AGENCY
4300 N. Miller Road # 202
Scottsdale AZ 85251
Tel: (480)966-2537
Full Service

DANI'S AGENCY
One East Camelback Road Suite 550
Phoenix AZ 85012
Tel: (602)263-1918

FOSI'S TALENT AGENCY
2777 N Campbell Avenue # 209
Tucson AZ 85719
Tel: (520)795-3534

LEIGHTON AGENCY, INC
2375 E. Camelback Road 5th Floor
Phoenix AZ 85016
Tel: (602)224-9255

SIGNATURE MODELS & TALENT
2600 N. 44th St. Suite # 209
Phoenix AZ 85008-1521
Tel: (480)966-1102

Boston Agents

MAGGIE, INC.
35 Newbury Street
Boston MA 02116
Tel: (617)536-2639

MODEL CLUB, INC.
115 Newbury St. Suite 203
Boston,MA 02116-2935
Tel: (617)247-9020
Full Service

THE MODELS GROUP
374 Congress Street Suite # 305
Boston MA 02210
Tel: (617)426-4711

Chicago Agents

AMBASSADOR TALENT AGENTS
333 N. Michigan Ave Suite 910
Chicago IL 60601
Tel: (312)641-3491

ARIA MODEL & TALENT MGMT.
1017 W Washington Street # 2C
Chicago IL 60607
Tel: (312)243-9400

BAKER & ROWLEY TALENT
AGENCY, INC.
1327 W. Washington, Suite 5-C
Chicago IL 60607-1914
Tel: (312)850-4700
Full Service

BIG MOUTH TALENT
935 W. Chestnut, Suite 415
Chicago IL 60622
Tel: (312)421-4400

ENCORE TALENT AGENCY, INC.
1532 N. Milwaukee #204-205
Chicago IL 60622
Tel: (773)384-7300

E.T.A INC
7558 S Chicago Ave
Chicago IL 60619
Tel: (773)752-3955

FORD TALENT GROUP, INC.
641 West Lake Street Suite 402
Chicago IL 60661
Tel: (312)707-9000
Full Service

GEDDES AGENCY
1633 N. Halsted Street Suite 400
Chicago IL 60614
Tel: (312)787-8333
Adults

SHIRLEY HAMILTON
333 E Ontario Suite B
Chicago IL 60611
Tel: (312)787-4700

LINDA JACK TALENT
230 East Ohio Street Suite # 200
Chicago IL 60611
Tel: (312)587-1155

LILY`S TALENT AGENCY
1301 W. Washington Suite B
Chicago IL 60607
Tel: (312)601-2345

NAKED VOICES, INC.
865 North Sangamon Avenue Suite 415
Chicago IL 60622
Tel: (312)563-0136
Type: Adults

SALAZAR & NAVAS, INC
760 N. Ogden Ave Suite 2200
Chicago IL 60622
Tel: (312)666-1677

NORMAN SCHUCART ENT.
1417 Green Bay Rd
Highland Park IL 60035-3614
Tel: (847)433-1113

STEWART TALENT MANAGEMENT
58 West Huron
Chicago IL 60610
Tel: (312)943-3131

THIRD COAST ARTISTS, INC.
641 W Lake Street Suite 402
Chicago IL 60661
Tel: (312)670-4444

VOICES UNLIMITED, INC
541 N. Fairbanks Ct. Suite 2735
Chicago IL 60611-3319
Tel: (312)832-1113

ARLENE WILSON TALENT, INC
430 W Erie Street Suite #210
Chicago IL 60610
Tel: (312)573-0200

Colorado

DONNA BALDWIN TALENT
2237 West 30th Avenue
Denver CO 80211
Tel: (303)561-1199

MATTAS TALENT AGENCY
1026 W. Colorado Avenue
Colorado Springs CO 80904
Tel: (719)577-4704
Full Service

MAXIMUM TALENT, INC.
1660 S. Albion Street Suite 1004
Denver CO 80222
Tel: (303)691-2344
Full Service

VOICE CHOICE
6909 S. Holly Circle Suite 201
Englewood CO 80112
Tel: (303)756-9055
Adults Full Service

Dallas

THE CAMPBELL AGENCY
3906 Lemmon Avenue Suite 200
Dallas TX 75219
Tel: (214)522-8991
Full Service

MARY COLLINS AGENT C. TALENT
2909 Cole Avenue Suite #250
Dallas TX 75204-1307
Tel: (214)871-8900
Type: Full Service

KIM DAWSON AGENCY
700, Tower North 2710 N. Stemmons
Freeway
Dallas TX 75207
Tel: (214)630-5161

THE HORNE AGENCY, INC
4420 West Lovers Lane
Dallas TX 75209
Tel: (214)350-9220
Type: Full Service

IVETT STONE AGENCY,
14677 Midway Road Suite 113
Addison TX 75001
Tel: (972)392-4951

PEGGY TAYLOR TALENT
437 Southfork Suite 400
Lewisville TX 75067
Tel: (214)651-7884

TOMAS AGENCY
14275 Midway Road Suite 220
Addison TX 75001
Tel: (972)687-9181
Type: Full Service

Detroit

AFFILIATED MODELS INC
1680 Crooks Road Suite # 200
Troy MI 48084
Tel: (248)244-8770

THE I GROUP, LLC
29540 Southfield Rd. Suite 200
Southfield MI 48076
Tel: (248)552-8842
Full Service

PRODUCTIONS PLUS
30600 Telegraph Road Suite 2156
Birmingham MI 48025
Tel: (248)644-5566

THE TALENT SHOP
30100 Telegraph Road Suite 116
Birmingham MI 48025
Tel: (248)644-4877
Full Service

Florida

ALEXA MODEL & TALENT
4100 W Kennedy Blvd. Suite 228
Tampa FL 33609
Tel: (813)289-8020

ALLIANCE TALENT GROUP, INC.
1940 Harrison Street Suite 300
Hollywood FL 33020
Tel: (954)727-9500
Full Service

ARTHUR ARTHUR (MIAMI) INC.
South Hillsborough Office Comp
6542 US Hwy 41
North Apollo Beach FL 33572
Tel: (813)645-9700
Full Service

ARTHUR ARTHUR (MIAMI) INC.
300 Biscayne Boulevard Way Suite 723
Miami FL 33131
Tel: (305)995-5889
Full Service

AZUREE TALENT, INC.
1115 Kentucky Avenue
Winter Park FL 32789
Tel: (407)629-5025
Full Service

SANDI BELL TALENT AGENCY
2582 S. Maguire Road Suite 171
Ocoee FL 34761
Tel: (407)445-9221

BENZ MODEL-TALENT AGENCY
1320 6th Avenue East
Tampa FL 33605
Tel: (813)242-4400
Full Service

BERG TALENT & MODEL AGENCY
15908 Eagle River Way
Tampa FL 33624
Tel: (813)877-5533

BOCA TALENT AND MODEL AGENCY
829 SE 9th Street
Deerfield Beach FL 33441
Tel: (954)428-4677
Full Service

BREVARD TALENT GROUP, INC.
906 Pinetree Drive
Indian Harbour Beach FL 32937
Tel: (321)773-1355

CENTRAL FLORIDA TALENT, INC.
2601 Wells Avenue, Suite 181
Fern Park FL 32730
Tel: (407)830-9226

THE CHRISTENSEN GROUP
4395 St. Johns Parkway
Sanford FL 32771
Tel: (407)302-2272

COCONUT GROVE TALENT AGENCY
3525 Vista Court
Coconut Grove FL 33133
Tel: (305)858-3002

THE DIAMOND AGENCY, INC.
The Historic District 204 W. Bay
Avenue
Longwood FL 32750
Tel: (407)830-4040

DIMENSIONS 3 MODELING
5205 S Orange Avenue Suite 209
Orlando FL 32809
Tel: (407)851-2575

FAMOUS FACES ENT. CO
3780 SW 30th Avenue
Fort Lauderdale FL 33312
Tel: (954)321-8883

FLORIDA STARS MODEL & TALENT
1020 NW 23rd Avenue Suite A
Gainesville FL 32609
Tel: (352)338-1086
Full Service

GREEN AGENCY, INC.
1329 Alton Road
Miami Beach FL 33139
Tel: (305)532-9225

THE HURT AGENCY, INC.
400 N New York Avenue Suite #207
Winter Park FL 32789
Tel: (407)740-5700

IN ANY EVENT
140 S. Atlantic Avenue 5th Floor
Ormond Beach FL 32176
Tel: (386)676-2223
Full Service

INTERNATIONAL ARTISTS GROUP,
INC.
2121 North Bayshore Drive Suite 2E
Miami FL 33137
Tel: (305)576-0001

LOUISE'S PEOPLE MODEL &
TALENT AGENCY
863 13th Avenue North
Saint Petersburg FL 33701
Tel: (727)823-7828
Full Service

IRENE MARIE AGENCY
728 Ocean Drive
Miami Beach FL 33139
Tel: (305)672-2929

MARTIN & DONALDS TALENT
AGENCY, INC.
2131 Hollywood Boulevard, # 308
Hollywood FL 33020
Tel: (954)921-2427
Full Service

ROXANNE MCMILLAN TALENT
AGENCY
12100 NE 16th Avenue Suite #106
Miami FL 33161
Tel: (305)899-9150

OUTLOOK ORLANDO, INC.
851 West State Road 436 Suite 1057
Altamonte Springs FL 32714
Tel: (407)788-6400
Full Service

PAGE PARKES MODELS
763 Collins Avenue 4th Floor
Miami Beach, FL 33139-6215
Tel: (305)672-4869

MARION POLAN TALENT AGENCY
10 NE 11th Avenue
Fort Lauderdale FL 33301
Tel: (954)525-8351

THE RUNWAYS TALENT GROUP, INC.
1688 Meridian Avenue Suite 500
Miami Beach FL 33139
Tel: (305)538-3529
Full Service

STELLAR TALENT AGENCY
407 Lincoln Road Suite 2K
Miami Beach FL 33139
Tel: (305)672-2217

EVELYN STEWART'S MODELING
911 Samy Drive
Tampa FL 33613
Tel: (813)968-1441

WILHELMINA-MIAMI
927 Lincoln Road Suite 200
Miami Beach FL 33139
Tel: (305)672-9344
Full Service

WORLD OF KIDS INC.
1460 Ocean Drive Suite 205
Miami Beach FL 33139
Tel: (305)672-5437
Full Service

Georgia

ATLANTA MODELS & TALENT, INC.
2970 Peachtree Road, NW Suite # 660
Atlanta GA 30305
Tel: (404)261-9627
Type: Full Service

AW/ATLANTA
887 West Marietta Street Suite # N-101
Atlanta GA 30318
Tel: (404)876-8555
Adults Full Service

TED BORDEN & ASSOCIATES
2434 Adina Drive, NE, Suite B
Atlanta GA 30324
Tel: (404)266-0664

THE BURNS AGENCY
3800 Bretton Woods Road
Decatur GA 30032
Tel: (404)303-8995
Adults Full Service

ELITE MODEL MANAGEMENT
CORP/ATLANTA
1708 Peachtree Street NW Suite # 210
Atlanta GA 30309
Tel: (404)872-7444
Adults Full Service

GENESIS MODELS AND TALENT, INC.
1465 Northside Drive Suite # 120
Atlanta GA 30318
Tel: (404)350-9212
Full Service

GLYN KENNEDY MODELS & TALENT
16 Willow Bend Drive
Cartersville GA 30121-4774
Tel: (770)607-2863
Full Service

L'AGENCE, INC.
5901-C Peachtree-Dunwoody Road
Suite 60
Atlanta GA 30328
Tel: (770)396-9015
Full Service

THE PEOPLE STORE
2004 Rockledge Road NE Suite 60
Atlanta GA 30324
Tel: (404)874-6448

DONNA SUMMERS' TALENT
8950 Laurel Way Suite #200
Alpharetta GA 30202
Tel: (770)518-9855

THE/HOT SHOT KIDS TALENT GROUP
561 West Pike Street
Lawrenceville GA 30045
Tel: (678)215-1500
Full Service

Hawaii

ADR MODEL & TALENT AGENCY
419 Waiakamilo Road Suite #204-205
Honolulu HI 96817
Tel: (808)842-1313
Full Service

KATHY MULLER TALENT AGENCY
619 Kapahulu Ave Penthouse
Honolulu HI 96815
Tel: (808)737-7917
Full Service

Hollywood

A S A
4430 Fountain Avenue Suite #A
Los Angeles CA 90029
Tel: (323)662-9787
Full Service

ABOVE THE LINE AGENCY
9200 Sunset Boulvard Suite 804
West Hollywood CA 90069
Tel: (310)859-6115
Adults

AGENCY WEST ENTERTAINMENT
6255 W Sunset Blvd Suite 908
Los Angeles CA 90028
Tel: (323)857-9050
Full Service

THE AGENCY
1800 Avenue of the Stars Suite # 1114
Los Angeles CA 90067
Tel: (310)551-3000
Adults Full Service

AIMEE ENTERTAINMENT
15840 Ventura Blvd. Suite 215
Encino CA 91436
Tel: (818)783-9115

ALLEN TALENT AGENCY
3832 Wilshire Blvd. 2nd Floor
Los Angeles CA 90010
Tel: (213)605-1110

AMATRUDA BENSON & ASSOC.
TALENT AGENCY
9107 Wilshire Blvd. Suite 500
Beverly Hills CA 90210
Tel: (310)276-1851
Full Service

ARTIST MANAGEMENT AGENCY
1800 E Garry St Suite 101
Santa Ana CA 92705
Tel: (949)261-7557

ARTISTS GROUP, LTD
10100 Santa Monica Blvd. Suite 2490
Los Angeles CA 90067
Tel: (310)552-1100
Adults Full Service

THE AUSTIN AGENCY
6715 Hollywood Blvd Suite 204
Los Angeles CA 90028
Tel: (323)957-4444
Type: Adults

AYRES TALENT AGENCY
1826 14th Street Suite 101
Santa Monica CA 90404
Tel: (310)452-0208
Adults Full Service

BADGLEY CONNOR TALENT AGENCY
9229 Sunset Boulevard Suite 311
West Hollywood CA 90069
Tel: (310)278-9313
Adults Full Service

BAIER-KLEINMAN INTERNATIONAL
3575 Cahuenga Blvd. West Suite 500
Los Angeles CA 90068
Tel: (323)874-9800
Adults

BALDWIN TALENT, INC
8055 West Manchester Ave Suite 550
Playa Del Rey CA 90293
Tel: (310)827-2422
Full Service

BARON ENTERTAINMENT, INC
5757 Wilshire Blvd Suite 659
Los Angeles CA 90036
Tel: (323)936-7600
Full Service

BERZON, MARIAN TALENT AGENCY
336 East 17th Street
Costa Mesa CA 92627
Tel: (949)631-5936

BICOASTAL TALENT INC
3489 A Cahunega Blvd West
Los Angeles CA 90068
Tel: (323)512-7755
Adults Full Service

BONNIE BLACKTALENT AGENCY
12034 Riverside Dr Suite 103
Valley Village CA 91607
Tel: (818)753-5424
Adults Full Service

THE BLAKE AGENCY
1327 Ocean Avenue Suite J
Santa Monica CA 90401
Tel: (310)899-9898
Adults

BLOC TALENT AGENCY, INC
5225 Wilshire Blvd Suite 311
Los Angeles CA 90036
Tel: (323)954-7730
Full Service

BRAND MODEL AND TALENT
1520 Brookhollow Suite 39
Santa Ana CA 92705
Tel: (714)850-1158
Full Service

CASSANDRA CAMPBELL MODELS &
TALENT
1617 El Centro Ave Suite 19
Los Angeles CA 90028
Tel: (323)467-1949
Full Service

CAREER ARTISTS INTERNATIONAL
11030 Ventura Blvd Suite # 3
Studio City CA 91604
Tel: (818)980-1315
Adults Full Service

CASTLE-HILL TALENT AGENCY
1101 S Orlando Avenue
Los Angeles CA 90035
Tel: (323)653-3535
Full Service

CAVALERI & ASSOCIATES
178 S Victory Blvd Suite #205
Burbank CA 91502
Tel: (818)955-9300
Full Service

NANCY CHAIDEZ AGENCY AND
ASSOCIATES, INC
6399 Wilshire Blvd Suite 424
Los Angeles CA 90048
Tel: (323)655-3455
Full Service

THE CHARLES AGENCY
11950 Ventura Blvd. Suite 3
Studio City CA 91604
Tel: (818)761-2224
Full Service

THE CHASIN AGENCY
8899 Beverly Blvd. Suite #716
Los Angeles CA 90048
Tel: (310)278-7505
Adults Full Service

CHATEAU BILLINGS TALENT AGENCY
5657 Wilshire Blvd. Suite 200
Los Angeles CA 90036
Tel: (323)965-5432
Type: Full Service

CINEMA TALENT AGENCY
2609 Wyoming Avenue Suite A
Burbank CA 91505
Tel: (818)845-3816
Full Service

RANDOLPH W. CLARK COMPANY
13415 Ventura Blvd. Suite 3
Sherman Oaks CA 91423
Tel: (818)385-0583
Full Service

COLLEEN CLER AGENCY, INC.
178 S Victory Suite # 108
Burbank CA 91502
Tel: (818)841-7943
Full Service

CONTEMPORARY ARTISTS, LTD.
610 Santa Monica Blvd Suite 202
Santa Monica CA 90401
Tel: (310)395-1800
Full Service

CORALIE JR. THEATRICAL AGENCY
4789 Vineland Avenue Suite # 100
North Hollywood CA 91602
Tel: (818)766-9501
Full Service

DDO ARTISTS AGENCY
8322 Beverly Blvd Suite 301
Los Angeles CA 90048
Tel: (323)782-0070
Adults Full Service

THE DANGERFIELD AGENCY
4063 Radford Ave Suite 201-C
Studio City CA 91604
Tel: (818)766-7717
Full Service

DRAGON TALENT INC.
8444 Wilshire Blvd Penthouse Suite
Beverly Hills CA 90211
Tel: (323)653-0366
Full Service

ELITE OF LOS ANGELES TALENT
AGENCY
345 N. Maple Drive Suite # 397
Beverly Hills CA 90210
Tel: (310)274-9395
Adults Full Service

ELLIS TALENT GROUP
4705 Laurel Canyon Blvd. Suite 300
Valley Village CA 91607
Tel: (818)980-8072
Adults

EQUINOX MODELS AND TALENT
8455 Beverly Blvd Suite 304
Los Angeles CA 90048
Tel: (323)951-7100
Adults

FERRAR MEDIA ASSOCIATES TALENT
AGENCY
8430 Santa Monica Blvd Suite 220
West Hollywood CA 90069
Tel: (323)654-2601
Adults

FILM ARTISTS ASSOCIATES
4717 Van Nuys Blvd Suite 215
Sherman Oaks CA 91403
Tel: (818)386-9669
Full Service

FLICK EAST & WEST TALENTS, INC.
9057 Nemo Street Suite # A
West Hollywood CA 90069
Tel: (310)271-9111
Adults Full Service

FONTAINE TALENT, FONTAINE MUSIC
205 South Beverly Drive Suite 212
Beverly Hills CA 90212
Tel: (310)471-8631

BARRY FREED COMPANY
468 N Camden Drive Suite 201
Beverly Hills CA 90210
Tel: (310)860-5627
Adults

ALICE FRIES AGENCY
1927 Vista Del Mar Avenue
Los Angeles CA 90068
Tel: (323)464-1404

DALE GARRICK INTERNATIONAL
8831 Sunset Boulevard Suite # 402
West Hollywood CA 90069
Tel: (310)657-2661

THE GEDDES AGENCY
8430 Santa Monica Blvd. # 200
West Hollywood CA 90069
Tel: (323)848-2700
Adults

LAYA GELFF AGENCY
16133 Ventura Boulevard Suite # 700
Encino CA 91436
Tel: (818)996-3100
Adults

PAUL GERARD TALENT AGENCY
11712 Moorpark Street Suite 112
Studio City CA 91604
Tel: (818)769-7015
Adults

DON GERLER AGENCY
3349 Cahuenga Blvd., West Suite # 1
Los Angeles CA 90068
Tel: (323)850-7386
Full Service

GORDON, MICHELLE & ASSOCIATES
260 S. Beverly Drive Suite 308
Beverly Hills CA 90212
Tel: (310)246-9930
Adults Full Service

GRANT, SAVIC, KOPALOFF AND
ASSOCIATES
6399 Wilshire Blvd. Suite 414
Los Angeles CA 90048
Tel: (323)782-1854
Adults Full Service

GREENE & ASSOCIATES
7080 Hollywood Blvd Suite 1017
Hollywood CA 90028
Tel: (323)960-1333
Adults Full Service

MITCHELL J. HAMILBURG AGENCY
11718 Barrington Court Suite 732
Los Angeles CA 90049
Tel: (310)471-4024

VAUGHN D. HART & ASSOCIATES
8899 Beverly Blvd. Suite # 815
Los Angeles CA 90048
Tel: (310)273-7887
Adults

HERVEY/GRIMES TALENT AGENCY
10561 Missouri # 2
Los Angeles CA 90025
Tel: (310)475-2010
Full Service

HILLTOP TALENT AGENCY
5225 Wilshire Blvd Suite 224
Los Angeles CA 90036
Tel: (323)857-1888
Full Service

DANIEL HOFF AGENCY
1800 N. Highland Avenue Suite # 300
Los Angeles CA 90028
Tel: (323)962-6643
Full Service

HOLLANDER TALENT GROUP, INC.
14011 Ventura Blvd Suite 202
Sherman Oaks CA 91423
Tel: (818)382-9800
Full Service

IFA TALENT AGENCY
8730 Sunset Blvd. Suite 490
West Hollywood CA 90069
Tel: (310)659-5522
Adults Full Service

ICON TALENT AGENCY
3800 Barham Blvd Suite 303
Los Angeles CA 90006
Tel: (323)845-1480
Full Service

J L A (JACK LIPPMAN AGENCY)
9151 Sunset Blvd
West Hollywood CA 90069
Tel: (310)276-5677
Full Service

JS REPRESENTS, TALENT AGENCY
6815 Willoughby Ave Suite 104
Los Angeles CA 90038
Tel: (323)462-3246
Adults Full Service

KM AND ASSOCIATES TALENT
AGENCY
4922 Vineland Ave North
Hollywood CA 91601
Tel: (818)766-3566
Adults

SHARON KEMP TALENT AGENCY
447 S. Robertson Blvd. Suite 204
Beverly Hills CA 90211
Tel: (310)858-7200

WILLIAM KERWIN AGENCY
1605 N. Cahuenga Boulevard
Suite # 202
Los Angeles CA 90028
Tel: (323)469-5155
Adults Full Service

ERIC KLASS AGENCY
139 S Beverly Drive Suite 331
Beverly Hills CA 90212
Tel: (310)274-9169
Adults

LJ AND ASSOCIATES
5903 Noble Avenue
Van Nuys CA 91411
Tel: (818)345-9274
Adults Full Service

LW 1, INC.
7257 Beverly Blvd 2nd Floor
Los Angeles CA 90036
Tel: (323)653-5700
Adults Full Service

LEAVITT TALENT GROUP
6404 Wilshire Blvd Suite 950
Los Angeles CA 90048
Tel: (323)658-8118

THE LEVIN AGENCY,
8484 Wilshire Blvd. Suite 750
Beverly Hills CA 90211
Tel: (323)653-7073
Adults Full Service

JANA LUKER TALENT AGENCY
1923 1/2 Westwood Blvd. Suite # 3
Los Angeles CA 90025
Tel: (310)441-2822
Full Service

LYNNE & REILLY AGENCY
Toluca Plaza Building
10725 Vanowen Street
North Hollywood CA 91605
Tel: (323)850-1984
Full Service

MGA/MARY GRADY AGENCY
221 E Walnut Street Suite 130
Pasadena CA 91101
Tel: (818)567-1400
Full Service

MADEMOISELLE TALENT AGENCY
10835 Santa Monica Blvd Suite 204-A
Los Angeles CA 90025
Tel: (310)441-9994
Full Service

MALAKY INTERNATIONAL
10642 Santa Monica Blvd. Suite 103
Los Angeles CA 90025
Tel: (310)234-9114
Adults Full Service

MARSHALL ENTERPRISES INC
22730 Hawthorne Blvd Suite 201
Torrance CA 90505
Tel: (310)378-1223
Full Service

MAXINE'S TALENT AGENCY
4830 Encino Avenue
Encino CA 91316
Tel: (818)986-2946
Adults Full Service

MEDIA ARTISTS GROUP
6404 Wilshire Blvd Suite 950
Los Angeles CA 90048
Tel: (323)658-5050
Full Service

MERIDIAN ARTISTS AGENCY
9229 Sunset Blvd Suite 310
West Hollywood CA 90069
Tel: (310)246-2600

MIRAMAR TALENT AGENCY
7400 Beverly Blvd. Suite 220
Los Angeles CA 90036
Tel: (323)934-0700
Adults Full Service

MORGAN AGENCY
7080 Hollywood Blvd Suite 1009
Los Angeles CA 90028
Tel: (323)469-7100
Full Service

DAVID H. MOSS & ASSOC.
733 North Seward Street Penthouse Los
Angeles CA 90038
Tel: (323)465-1234
Adults

N T A TALENT AGENCY
8899 Beverly Blvd Suite 612
Los Angeles CA 90048
Tel: (310)274-6297

NU TALENT AGENCY
117 N Robertson Blvd
Los Angeles CA 90048
Tel: (310)385-6907
Adults

OMNIPOP INC
10700 Ventura Blvd Second Floor
Suite 2C
Studio City CA 91604
Tel: (818)980-9267
Adults Full Service

ORIGIN TALENT AGENCY
4705 Laurel canyon Blvd Suite 306
Valley Village CA 91607
Tel: (818)487-1800

CINDY OSBRINK TALENT AGENCY
4343 Lankershim Blvd. Suite 100
North Hollywood CA 91602
Tel: (818)760-2488
Full Service

PACIFIC WEST ARTISTS TALENT
AGENCY
12500 Riverside Drive Suite 202
Valley Village CA 91607
Tel: (818)755-8544
Full Service

PAKULA KING & ASSOCIATES
9229 Sunset Blvd. Suite 315
West Hollywood CA 90069
Tel: (310)281-4868
Adults

THE PARTOS COMPANY
227 Broadway Suite 204
Santa Monica CA 90401
Tel: (310)458-7800
Adults Full Service

PEAK MODELS & TALENT
28065 Avenue Stanford
Valencia CA 91355
Tel: (661)288-1555
Adults Full Service

JOHN PIERCE AGENCY
8127 Melrose Ave Suite 3
Los Angeles CA 90027
Tel: (323)653-3976
Adults Full Service

PLAYERS TALENT AGENCY
13033 Ventura Blvd. Suite N
Studio City CA 91604
Tel: (818)528-7444
Full Service

PRIVILEGE TALENT AGENCY
14542 Ventura Blvd Suite 209
Sherman Oaks CA 91403
Tel: (818)386-2377
Adults Full Service

PROGRESSIVE ARTISTS
400 S Beverly Drive Suite #216
Beverly Hills CA 90212
Tel: (310)553-8561
Adults

Q MODEL MANAGEMENT
6100 Wilshire Blvd. Suite 710
Los Angeles CA 90048
Tel: (323)692-1700

QUALITA DELL' ARTE
5353 Topanga Canyon Road Suite 220
Woodland Hills CA 91364
Tel: (818)598-8073
Full service

CINDY ROMANO MODELING &
TALENT AGENCY
414 Village Square West
Palm Springs CA 92262
Tel: (760)323-3333
Full Service

S D B PARTNERS, INC
1801 Avenue of the Stars Suite 902
Los Angeles CA 90067
Tel: (310)785-0060
Adults

SAMANTHA GROUP TALENT
AGENCY
300 S. Raymond Avenue Suite 11
Pasadena CA 91105
Tel: (626)683-2444
Full Service

SARNOFF COMPANY, INC
3500 West Olive Ave
Burbank CA 91505
Tel: (818)753-2377
Adults

JACK SCAGNETTI TALENT AGENCY
5118 Vineland Avenue Suite 102
North Hollywood CA 91601
Tel: (818)762-3871
Adults Full Service

THE IRV SCHECHTER COMPANY
9460 Wilshire Blvd Suite 300
Beverly Hills CA 90212
Tel: (310)278-8070
Adults Full Service

SANDIE SCHNARR TALENT
8500 Melrose Avenue Suite 212
West Hollywood CA 90069
Tel: (310)360-7680
Adults

KATHLEEN SCHULTZ ASSOCIATES
6442 Coldwater Canyon Suite 206
North Hollywood CA 91606
Tel: (818)760-3100

DON SCHWARTZ ASSOCIATES
1604 N Cahuenga Blvd Suite 101
Los Angeles CA 90028
Tel: (323)464-4366
Full Service

SCREEN ARTISTS AGENCY, LLC
4526 Sherman Oaks Ave
Sherman Oaks CA 91403
Tel: (818)789-4896
Full Service

SHAPIRA & ASSOC
15821 Ventura Blvd Suite 235
Encino CA 91436
Tel: (818)906-0322
Adults Full Service

SHAPIRO-LICHTMAN TALENT
AGENCY, INC.
8827 Beverly Blvd
Los Angeles CA 90048
Tel: (310)859-8877
Adults

JEROME SIEGEL ASSOCIATES
1680 North Vine Street Suite 613
Los Angeles CA 90028
Tel: (323)466-0185

SIERRA TALENT AGENCY
14542 Ventura Blvd. Suite 207
Sherman Oaks CA 91403
Tel: (818)907-9645
Adults Full Service

SIGNATURE ARTISTS AGENCY
6700 W 5th Street
Los Angeles CA 90048
Tel: (323)651-0600
Full Service

MICHAEL SLESSINGER ASSOC
8730 Sunset Boulevard Suite 220
West Hollywood CA 90069
Tel: (310)657-7113
Adults

THE SOHL AGENCY
669 Berendo Street
Los Angeles CA 90004
Tel: (323)644-0500
Adults

CAMILLE SORICE TALENT AGENCY
13412 Moorpark Street Suite C
Sherman Oaks CA 91423
Tel: (818)995-1775
Full Service

SCOTT STANDER & ASSOCIATES INC.
13701 Riverside Drive Suite 201
Sherman Oaks CA 91423
Tel: (818)905-7000
Full Service

STARCRAFT TALENT AGENCY
1516 N Formosa Los Angeles CA
90046
Tel: (323)845-4784
Full Service

STARWILL TALENT AGENCY
433 N. Camden Drive 4th Floor
Beverly Hills CA 90210
Tel: (323)874-1239
Full Service

THE STEVENS GROUP
14011 Ventura Blvd Suite 201
Sherman Oaks CA 91423
Tel: (818)528-3674
Adults

SUPERIOR TALENT AGENCY
11425 Moorpark Street
Studio City CA 91602
Tel: (818)508-5627
Full Service

THOMAS TALENT AGENCY
6709 La Tijera Blvd. Suite 915
Los Angeles CA 90045
Tel: (310)665-0000
Full Service

ARLENE THORNTON & ASSOCIATES
12711 Ventura Blvd Suite 490
Studio City CA 91604
Tel: (818)760-6688
Adults Full Service

TILMAR TALENT AGENCY
4929 Wilshire Blvd Suite 830
Los Angeles CA 90010
Tel: (323)938-9815
Full Service

TISHERMAN AGENCY, INC.
6767 Forest Lawn Drive Suite 101
Los Angeles CA 90068
Tel: (323)850-6767
Adults

US TALENT AGENCY
485 S Robertson Blvd. Suite 7
Beverly Hills CA 90211
Tel: (310)858-1533
Adults Full Service

UNITED ARTISTS TALENT AGENCY
14011 Ventura Blvd. Suite 213
Sherman Oaks CA 91423
Tel: (818)788-7305

VISION ART MANAGEMENT
9200 Sunset Blvd. Penthouse 1
West Hollywood CA 90069
Tel: (310)888-3288
Adults

WALLIS AGENCY
4444 Riverside Dr Suite 105
Burbank CA 91505
Tel: (818)953-4848
Full Service

BOB WATERS AGENCY, INC
9301 Wilshire Blvd. Suite 300
Beverly Hills CA 90210
Tel: (323)965-5555
Adults

ANN WAUGH TALENT AGENCY
4741 Laurel Canyon Boulevard Suite
200
Valley Village CA 91607
Tel: (818)980-0141
Full Service

SHIRLEY WILSON & ASSOCIATES,
5410 Wilshire Boulevard Suite #806
Los Angeles CA 90036
Tel: (323)857-6977
Full Service

ZANUCK, PASSON & PACE
4717 Van Nuys Blvd Suite 102
Sherman Oaks CA 91403
Tel: (818)783-4890
Adults Full Service

Houston

ACTORS, ETC
2620 Fountainview Suite 210
Houston TX 77057
Tel: (713)785-4495

NEAL HAMIL AGENCY
7887 San Felipe Suite 204
Houston TX 77063
Tel: (713)789-1335
Type: Full Service

HOLLYWOOD & BROADWAY CON-
NECTIONS
1105 Holman Street
Houston TX 77004
Tel: (713)528-2306
Full Service

PAGE.713
2727 Kirby Penthouse
Houston TX 77098
Tel: (713)807-8222

PASTORINI BOSBY TALENT AGENCY
3013 Fountain View Drive Suite 240
Houston TX 77057
Tel: (713)266-4488

WILLIAMS TALENT, INC.
13313 Southwest Freeway Suite 194
Sugar Land TX 77478
Tel: (281)240-1080
Full Service

SHERRY YOUNG AGENCY
2620 Fountain View Suite #212
Houston TX 77057
Tel: (713)266-5800

Nashville

ACTOR AND OTHERS TALENT
AGENCY
6676 Memphis-Arlington Road
Memphis TN 38135
Tel: (901)384-6464
Full Service

ADVANTAGE MODELS & TALENT
230 Franklin Road Suite 802
Franklin TN 37064
Tel: (615)790-5001
Full Service

D S ENTERTAINMENT
4741 Trousdale Drive Suite 2
Nashville TN 37220
Tel: (615)331-6264
Full Service

DAN AGENCY MODELS & TALENT
209 10th Avenue South Suite 301
Nashville TN 37203
Tel: (615)244-3266
Full Service

BUDDY LEE ATTRACTIONS
38 Music Square East, SUITE 300
Nashville TN 37203
Tel: (615)244-4336

TALENT & MODEL LAND
4516 Granny White Pike
Nashville TN 37204
Tel: (615)321-5596

TALENT TREK AGENCY
5401 Kingston Pike Suite 450
Knoxville TN 37919
Tel: (865)977-8735

Nevada

J BASKOW, & ASSOCIATES
2948 E. Russell Rd.
Las Vegas NV 89120
Tel: (702)733-7818
Full Service

BEST AGENCY
5565 South Decatur Blvd. Suite 106
Las Vegas NV 89118
Tel: (702)889-2900
Full Service

CLASSIC MODELS, LTD.
3305 Spring Mountain Rd. Suite 12
Las Vegas NV 89102
Tel: (702)367-1444
Full Service

LENZ AGENCY
1591 East Desert Inn Road
Las Vegas NV 89109
Tel: (702)733-6888
Full Service

MCCARTY TALENT, INC.
4220 S. Maryland Pkwy Bldg. B, Suite 317
Las Vegas NV 89119
Tel: (702)944-4440
Adults Full Service

WAUHOB,DONNA AGENCY
5280 South Eastern Ave. Suite A3
Las Vegas NV 89119
Tel: (702)795-1523
Full Service

eNVy [Sic] MODEL & TALENT AGENCY
2121 Industrial Road Loft 211
Las Vegas NV 89102
Tel: (702)878-7368
Full Service

New Mexico

APPLAUSE TALENT AGENCY
225 San Pedro NE
Albuquerque NM 87108
Tel: (505)262-9733

CIMARRON TALENT AGENCY
10605 Casador Del Oso NE
Albuquerque NM 87111
Tel: (505)292-2314

EATON AGENCY, INC
3636 High Street N E
Albuquerque NM 87107
Tel: (505)344-3149

THE MANNEQUIN AGENCY
2021 San Mateo Blvd NE
Albuquerque NM 87110
Tel: (505)266-6823

THE PHOENIX AGENCY
8809 Washington Pl. NE
Albuquerque NM 87113-2715
Tel: (505)881-1209

SOUTH OF SANTA FE TALENT GUILD, INC.
6921-B Montgomery Boulevard, NE
Albuquerque NM 87109
Tel: (505)880-8550
Full Service

New York

AGENTS FOR THE ARTS, INC.
203 West 23rd Street 3rd Floor
New York NY 10011
Tel: (212)229-2562
Full Service

MICHAEL AMATO THEATRICAL ENTERPRISE
1650 Broadway Suite 307
New York NY 10019
Tel: (212)247-4456
Full Service

AMERICAN INTERNATIONAL TALENT
303 West 42nd Street Suite # 608
New York NY 10036
Tel: (212)245-8888
Full Service

ANDREADIS TALENT AGENCY, INC.
119 West 57th Street Suite # 711
New York NY 10019
Tel: (212)315-0303
Full Service

ARCIERI & ASSOCIATES, INC.
305 Madison Avenue Suite 2315
New York NY 10165
Tel: (212)286-1700

ARTISTS GROUP EAST
1650 Broadway Suite 610
New York NY 10019
Tel: (212)586-1452
Adults/Youth Full Service

ASSOCIATED BOOKING
CORPORATION
1995 Broadway
New York NY 10023
Tel: (212)874-2400
Full Service

RICHARD ASTOR AGENCY
250 West 57th Street Suite 2014
New York NY 10107
Tel: (212)581-1970
Full Service

BLOC AGENCY
41 East 11th Street, 11th Floor
New York NY 10003
Tel: (212)905-6236

BARRY HAFT BROWN ARTISTS
165 West 46th Street, Suite 908
New York NY 10036
Tel: (212)869-9310
Full Service

PETER BEILIN AGENCY
230 Park Avenue Suite 200
New York NY 10169
Tel: (212)949-9119
Full Service

BERMAN, BOALS & FLYNN, INC.
208 West 30th Street Suite 401
New York NY 10001
Tel: (212)868-1068
Full Service

BETHEL AGENCY
311 West 43rd Street, Suite 602
New York NY 10036
Tel: (212)664-0455
Full Service

CARLSON-MENASHE AGENCY
159 W. 25th Street Suite 1011
New York NY 10001
Tel: (646)486-3332
Adults Full Service

CARRY COMPANY
49 West 46th Street Fourth Floor
New York NY 10036
Tel: (212)768-2793
Full Service

THE CARSON ORGANIZATION, LTD.
234 West 44th Street Suite 902
New York NY 10036
Tel: (212)221-1517
Full Service

COLEMAN-ROSENBERG
155 E. 55th Street Apt. 5D
New York NY 10022-4039
Tel: (212)838-0734
Full Service

CORNERSTONE TALENT AGENCY
37 West 20th Street Suite 1108
New York NY 10011
Tel: (212)807-8344

GINGER DICCE TALENT AGENCY,
INC.
56 West 45th Street Suite 1100
New York NY 10036
Tel: (212)869-9650
Full Service

EASTERN TALENT ALLIANCE, INC.
1501 Broadway Suite 404
New York NY 10036
Tel: (212)220-9888
Adults Full Service

DULCINA EISEN ASSOCIATES
154 East 61st Street New York NY
10021
Tel: (212)355-6617
Full Service

FLAUNT MODEL MANAGEMENT,
INC.
114 East 32nd Street suite 501
New York NY 10016
Tel: (212)679-9011

GARBER AGENCY
2 Pennsylvania Plaza, Suite 1910
New York NY 10121
Tel: (212)292-4910
Adults Full Service

GENERATION TV, LLC
20 West 20th Street Suite 1008
New York NY 10011
Tel: (646)230-9491
Full Service

BARBARA HOGENSON AGENCY
165 West End Avenue, Suite 19C
New York NY 10023
Tel: (212)874-8084
Adults Full Service

ARCHER KING
317 West 46th Street Suite #3A
New York NY 10036
Tel: (212)765-3103
Full Service

KMA ASSOCIATES
11 Broadway Rm #1101
New York NY 10004-1303
Tel: (212)581-4610
Full Service

KOLSTEIN TALENT AGENCY
85 Lafayette Avenue
Suffern NY 10901
Tel: (845)357-8301
Full Service

THE KRASNY OFFICE, INC.
1501 Broadway Suite 1303
New York NY 10036
Tel: (212)730-8160
Full Service

LIONEL LARNER, LTD.
119 West 57th Street Suite 1412
New York NY 10019
Tel: (212)246-3105
Full Service

BRUCE LEVY AGENCY
311 West 43rd Street Suite 602
New York NY 10036
Tel: (212)262-6845
Full Service

NICOLOSI & COMPANY, INC.
150 W. 25th Street Suite 1200
New York NY 10011
Tel: (212)633-1010

NOUVELLE TALENT MANAGEMENT,
INC.
20 Bethune Street Suite 3B
New York NY 10014
Tel: (212)645-0940
Full Service

OMNIPOP, INC.
55 West Old Country Road
Hicksville NY 11801
Tel: (516)937-6011
Adults Full Service

THE MEG PANTERA AGENCY
1501 Broadway suite 1508
New York NY 10036
Tel: (212)278-8366
Full Service

PROFESSIONAL ARTISTS UNLTD.
321 West 44th Street Suite 605
New York NY 10036
Tel: (212)247-8770
Full Service

PYRAMID ENTERTAINMENT GROUP
89 Fifth Avenue
New York NY 10003
Tel: (212)242-7274
Adults Full Service

RADIOACTIVE TALENT, INC.
240-03 Linden Blvd.
Elmont NY 11003
Tel: (516)445-9595
Full Service

GILLA ROOS, LTD.
16 West 22nd Street 3rd Floor
New York NY 10010
Tel: (212)727-7820
Full Service Adults/Youth

SEM TALENT, INC.
113 Pavonia Avenue
Jersey City NJ 07310
Tel: (212)330-9146

SCHULLER TALENT, INC.
AKA NEW YORK KIDS
276 Fifth Avenue 10th Floor
New York NY 10001
Tel: (212)532-6005
Full Service

MICHAEL THOMAS AGENCY, INC.
134 East 70th Street
New York NY 10021
Full Service

TAMAR WOLBROM, INC.
130 West 42nd Street Suite #707
New York NY 10036
Tel: (212)398-4595
Full Service

HANNS WOLTERS INTERNATIONAL,
INC.
10 WEST 37TH STREET
New York NY 10018
Tel: (212)714-0100
Full Service

ANN WRIGHT REPRESENTATIVES,
INC.
165 West 46th Street Suite 1105 New
York NY 10036
Tel: (212)764-6770
Full Service

Pennsylvania Area

DOCHERTY, INC.
109 Market Street
Pittsburgh PA 15222
Tel: (412)765-1400
Full Service

EXPRESSIONS MODELING & TALENT
220 Church Street
Philadelphia PA 19106
Tel: (215)923-4420
Full Service

GOODMAN, VERONICA AGENCY
605 West Route 70, #1
Cherry Hills NJ 08002
Tel: (856)795-3133
Full Service

GREER LANGE TALENT AGENCY
40 Lloyd Avenue Suite 104
Malvern PA 19355
Tel: (610)647-5515
Adults

MARY ANNE CLARO TALENT
AGENCY, INC.
1513 West Passyunk Ave
Philadelphia PA 19145
Tel: (215)465-7788

MCCULLOUGH ASSOCIATES
8 South Hanover Avenue
Margate City NJ 08402
Tel: (609)822-2222
Full Service

MODELS ON THE MOVE
1200 Route 70 Barclay Towers, #6
Cherry Hill NJ 08034
Tel: (856)667-1060
Full Service

PLAZA 7
160 N Gulph Road
King Of Prussia PA 19406
Tel: (610)337-2693

REINHARD AGENCY
2021 Arch Street Suite 400
Philadelphia PA 19103
Tel: (215)567-2008
Full Service

THE T.G. AGENCY
2820 Smallman Street
Pittsburgh PA 15222
Tel: (412)471-8011
Full Service

G. WILLIAMS AGENCY
525 S. 4th Street #365
Philadelphia PA 19147
Tel: (215)627-9533
Full Service

San Diego

AGENCY 2 MODEL & TALENT
AGENCY
1717 Kettner Boulevard Suite #200
San Diego CA 92101
Tel: (619)461-2329

ARTIST MANAGEMENT TALENT
AGENCY
835 Fifth Avenue Suite #411
San Diego CA 92101
Tel: (619)233-6655
Full Service

ELEGANCE TALENT AGENCY
2763 State Street Carlsbad CA 92008
Tel: (760)434-3397
Full Service

JET SET TALENT AGENCY
2160 Avenida De La Playa
La Jolla CA 92037
Tel: (858)551-9393

NOUVEAU MODEL MANAGEMENT
909 Prospect Street Suite 230
La Jolla CA 92037
Tel: (858)456-1400
Full Service

SAN DIEGO MODEL MANAGEMENT
438 Camino Del Rio South, Suite #116
San Diego CA 92108-3546
Tel: (619)296-1018
Full Service

SHAMON FREITAS & COMPANY
9606 Tierra Grande Street Suite #204
San Diego CA 92126
Tel: (858)549-3955
Full Service

San Francisco

BOOM MODELS & TALENT
2325 3rd Street Suite #223 San
Francisco CA 94107
Tel: (415)626-6591
Full Service

MARLA DELL TALENT
2124 Union Street
San Francisco CA 94123
Tel: (415)563-9213

FILM THEATRE ACTORS EXCHANGE
3145 Geary Blvd. Suite 735
San Francisco CA 94118
Tel: (415)379-9308

GENERATIONS MODEL & TALENT
AGENCY
340 Brannan Street Suite 302
San Francisco CA 94107
Tel: (415)777-9099
Full Service

J E TALENT, LLC.
323 Geary Suite 302
San Francisco CA 94102
Tel: (415)395-9475
Full Service

LOOK MODEL & TALENT AGENCY
166 Geary Blvd Suite 1400
San Francisco CA 94108
Tel: (415)781-2841

PANDA AGENCY
3721 Hoen Avenue
Santa Rosa CA 95405
Tel: (707)576-0711

SAN FRANCISCO TOP MODELS AND
TALENT
2261 Market Street Suite 965
San Francisco CA 94114
Tel: (415)391-1800
Full Service

SHOW OFF TALENT, INC.
5050 El Camino Real Suite 104
Los Altos CA 94024
Tel: (650)903-1710
Full Service

TALENT PLUS AGENCY/LOS LATINOS
TALENT
2801 Moorpark Ave #11 Dyer Building
San Jose CA 95128
Tel: (408)296-2213

TONRY TALENT AGENCY
885 Bryant Street Suite 201
San Francisco CA 94103
Tel: (415)543-3797
Full Service

Seattle

ACTORS GROUP
603 Stewart Street Suite 214
Seattle WA 98121
Tel: (206)624-9465

COLLEEN BELL MODELING & TALENT
AGENCY
14205 SE 36th St., #100
Bellevue WA 98006
Tel: (425)649-1111
Full Service

DRAMATIC ARTISTS AGENCY, INC.
50 16th Avenue
Kirkland WA 98033
Tel: (425)827-4147
Full Service

TOPO SWOPE TALENT AGENCY
1932 1st Avenue Suite 700
Seattle WA 98101
Tel: (206)443-2021
Adults Full Service

Washington/Baltimore

THE BULLOCK AGENCY
5200 Baltimore Avenue Suite 102
Hyattsville, MD 20781
Tel: (301)498-9308
Full Service

KIDS INTERNATIONAL TALENT
AGENCY
938 East Swan Creek Rd. Suite 152
Fort Washington MD 20744
Tel: (301)292-6094
Type: Full Service

TAYLOR-ROYALL AGENCY
6247 Falls Road
Baltimore MD 21209
Tel: (410)828-6900

Appendix III | # Small Professional Theaters

This appendix contains a list of theaters that have signed a Small Professional Theatre (SPT) contract with Actors Equity Association. Many of them offer classes and have apprenticeship programs, where actors new to the business can earn points toward their union cards while watching professional actors work, learning as they go. I highly recommend that you patronize these theaters as both a spectator and a participant. Just think about how many of the casting directors quoted in this book recommend theater experience.

Eastern Region Equity Theaters

Connecticut

BRIDGEPORT FREE SHAKESPEARE
81 Humiston Drive
Bethany, CT 06524
(203) 393-3213, Fax: (203) 393-1173

CENTENNIAL THEATRE FESTIVAL
995 Hopmeadow
Simsbury, CT 06070
(860) 408-5300, Fax: (860) 408-5301

DOWNTOWN CABARET THEATRE
263 Golden Hill Street
Bridgeport, CT 06604
(203) 576-1634, Fax: (203) 576-1444

ELM SHAKESPEARE
P.O. Box 206029
New Haven, CT 06520
(203) 772-1474, Fax: (203) 785-1569

FAIRFIELD THEATRE COMPANY
739 Old Post Road, Box 320901
Fairfield, CT 06430
(203) 366-5900, Fax: (203) 366-4433

POLKA DOT PLAYHOUSE, INC.
DBA Playhouse on the Green
117 State Street
Bridgeport, CT 06604
(203) 333-3666, Fax: (203) 312-7529

SEVEN ANGELS THEATRE COMPANY
Hamilton Park Pavillion Plank Rd.
Waterbury, CT 06705
(203) 591-8223, Fax: (203) 598-7721

SHAKESPEARE ON THE SOUND
800 Connecticut Avenue
Norwalk, CT 06854
(203)299-1300, Fax: (203) 851-1491

STAMFORD CENTER FOR THE ARTS
307 Atlantic Street
Stamford, CT 06901
(203) 358-2305, Fax: (209) 358-2313

STAMFORD THEATREWORKS, INC
95 Atlantic Street
Stamford, CT 06901
(203) 359-4414, Fax: (203) 356-1846

THEATERWORKS, INC.
One Gold Street
Hartford, CT 06103
(860) 727-4027, Fax: (860) 525-0758

WHITE BARN THEATRE
FOUNDATION
452 Newton Road
Westport, CT 06880
(203) 227-6816

Delaware

HENLOPEN THEATER PROJECT, INC.
P. O. Box 606
Rehoboth Beach, DE 19911
(302) 226-4103, Fax: (302) 226-4104

Florida

ACTORS' PLAYHOUSE
280 Miracle Mile
Coral Gables, FL 33134
(305) 444-9293, Fax: (305) 444-4181

AMERICAN STAGE COMPANY
302 2nd Avenue South
St. Petersburg, FL 33101
(727) 823-1600, Fax: (727) 823-7529

BROWARD CENTER FOR THE
PERFORMING ARTS
201 SW Fifth Avenue
Fort Lauderdale, FL 33312
(954) 468-3295, Fax: (954) 468-3311

BROW ARD STAGE DOOR THEATER
COMPANY, INC.
8036 W. Sample Road
Coral Springs, FL 33065
(954) 344-7765, Fax: (954) 757-1735

CITY THEATRE, INC.
444 Brickell Avenue
Suite 229
Miami, FL 33131
(305) 755-9401, Fax: (305) 755-9404

THE DRAMA CENTER J & G MANN,
INC C/O WILTON PLAYHOUSE
1444 NE 26th Street
Ft. Lauderdale, FL 33305
(954) 567-3666, Fax: (954) 568-3001

FLORIDA REPERTORY THEATRE
2267 First Street POD 2483
Ft. Myers, FL 33902-2483
(941) 332-4665, Fax: (941) 332-1808

FLORIDA STUDIO THEATRE
1241 No. Palm Avenue
Sarasota, FL 34236
(941) 366-9017, Fax: (941) 955-4137

HIPPODROME STATE THEATRE
25 Southeast 2nd Place
Gainesville, FL 32601-6596
(352) 373-5968 Fax: (352) 371-9130

HOLLYWOOD BOULEVARD THEATRE
1865 Hollywood Boulevard, Studio 7
Hollywood, FL 33020
(954) 929-0111, Fax: (954) 929-0111

THE HOLLYWOOD PLAYHOUSE
2640 Washington Street
Hollywood, FL 33020
(954) 923-2623

KEYS COMMUNICATION GROUP,
DBA THEATRE KEY WEST
P.O. Box 992
Key West, FL 33041
(305) 295-9278, Fax: (305) 295-9936

KRAVIS CENTER FOR THE
PERFORMNG ARTS
RAYMOND F. KRAVIS CENTER
701 Okeechobee Blvd.
West Palm Beach, FL 33401

ORLANDO THEATRE PROJECT
SEMINOLE COMMUNITY COLLEGE
100 Weldon Blvd
Sanford, FL 32773
(407) 328-4722, Fax: (407) 322-1834

ORLANDO-UCF SHAKESPEARE
FESTIVAL
812 East Rollins Street - Suite 100
Orlando, FL 32803
(407) 893-4600 Fax: (407) 893-5643

NEW THEATRE, INC
4120 Laguna Street
Coral Gables, FL 33146
{305) 443-5373, Fax: (305) 443-1642

PIRATE PLAYHOUSE
J. HOWARD WOOD THEATRE
2200 Periwinkle Way
Sanibel, FL 33957
(941) 472-4109, Fax: (941) 472-0055

RIVERSIDE THEATRE
3250 Riverside Park Drive
Vero Beach, FL 32963
(561) 231-5860, Fax: (561) 234-5298

SHORES PERFORMING ARTS THEATRE
9806 NE 2nd Avenue
Miami Shores, FL 33138
(305) 751-0562, Fax: (305) 751-9159

THEATRE PROPERTY HOLDINGS, INC
201 Clematis Street
West Palm Beach, FL 33401
(561) 835-9221, Fax: (561) 339-8937

THEATRE WORKS OF SARASOTA, INC
1247 1st Street
Sarasota, FL 34236
(941) 952-9667 Fax: (941) 365-8088

Georgia

ACTORS THEATRE OF ATLANTA
4075 Paces Ferry Road NW
Atlanta, GA 30327
(404) 262-3032 x 1281
Fax: (404) 262-1967

ART STATION, INC.
P.O. Box 1998
5384 Manor Drive
Stone Mountain, GA 30086
(770) 469-1105, Fax: (770) 469-0355

ATLANTA SHAKESPEARE COMPANY
499 Peachtree Street
Atlanta, GA 30308
(404) 874-5299 x43
Fax: (404) 874-9219
Box Office: (404) 874-5299

GEORGIA ENSEMBLE THEATRE
950 Forest Street, 2nd Floor
Roswell, GA 30077-0607
(770) 641-1260, Fax: (770) 641-1360

HORIZON THEATRE COMPANY
P.O. Box 5376 Station E
Atlanta, GA 31107
1083 Austin Avenue NE
Atlanta, GA 30307
(404) 523-1477, Fax: (404) 584-8815

HOWARD AND KAFFATY, INC.
2730 Belaire Circle
Doraville, GA 30340
(770) 455-8472, Fax: (770) 451-5132

JOMANDI PRODUCTIONS
675 Ponce de Leon Avenue
City Hall East, 8th floor
Atlanta, GA 30308
(404) 876-6346, Fax: (404) 872-5764

SEVEN STAGES
1105 Euclid Avenue
Atlanta, GA 30307
(404) 522-0911/523-7647,
Fax: (404)522-0913

THEATRE DU REVE, INC.
1079 Milam Circle
Clarkston, GA 30021
(404) 508-4866

THEATER EMORY
EMORY UNIVERSITY
1602 Mizell Drive
Rich Building, Room 230
Atlanta, GA 30322
(404) 727-0523/0524,
Fax: (404) 727-6253

THEATRE IN THE SQUARE
11 Whitlock Avenue
Marietta, GA 30064
(770) 422-8369, Fax: (770) 424-2637

THEATRICAL OUTFIT
70 Fairlie Street, Suite 360
Atlanta, GA 30303
(404) 577-5257
Box Office: (404) 872-0665
Fax: (404) 577-5259

Maine

BAR HARBOR THEATRE
P.O. Box 574
Bar Harbor, ME 04609
(207) 827-5886, Fax: (207) 866-3444

THE PUBLIC THEATRE
2 Great Falls Plaza, #7
Auburn, ME 04201
(207) 782-2211, Fax: (207) 784-2942

THEATER AT MONMOUTH
P.O. Box 385
Monmouth, ME 04259
(207) 933-2952, Fax: Same

Maryland

CUMBERLAND THEATRE
101-103 N. Johnson Street
Cumberland, MD 21502
(301) 759-4990

EVERYMAN THEATRE
1727 N. Charles Street
Baltimore, MD 21201-5801
(410) 752-0111, Fax: (410) 752-5891

MARYLAND STAGE COMPANY
UNIVERSITY OF MARYLAND
FOUNDATION, INC.
DEPARTMENT OF THEATRE, UMBC
1000 Hilltop Circle
Baltimore, MD 21250
(410) 455-2917, Fax: (410) 455-1046

NATIONAL PLAYERS, INC.
2001 Olney-Sandy Spring Road
Olney, MD20832
(301) 924-5908, Fax: (301) 924-2654

POTOMAC THEATRE PROJECT
2001 Olney-Sandy Spring Rd.
Olney, MD 20832
(301) 924-4485, Fax: (301) 924-2654

THE REP STAGE COMPANY
at HOWARD COMMUNITY COLLEGE
HOWARD COLLEGE PERFORMING
ARTS
10901 Little Patuxent Parkway
Smith & Outback
Columbia, MD 21044
(410) 772-4959, Fax: (410) 772-4040

ROUND HOUSE THEATRE CO
12210 Bushey Drive, #101
Silver Spring, MD 20902
(301) 933-9530, Fax: (301) 933-2321

SHAKESPEARE PROJECT, INC.
15 W. Patrick Street
Frederick, MD 21701
(301) 668-4090, Fax: (301) 622-1064

Massachusetts

BARRINGTON STAGE COMPANY
P.O. Box 1205
Great Barrington, MA 01257
(413) 528-8806, Fax: (413) 528-8807

BOSTON PLAYWRIGHTS' THEATRE
BOSTON UNIVERSITY
949 Commonwealth Avenue
Boston, MA 02215
(617) 353-5899, Fax: (617) 353-6196

BOSTON THEATRE WORKS
325 Commonwealth Ave. Suite 11
Boston, MA 02116
Phone and Fax: (617) 728-4321

COMMONWEALTH SHAKESPEARE
COMPANY
125 Kingston Street, #2
Boston, MA 02111
Summer: 1697 Cambridge Street, #14
Cambridge, MA 02138
(617) 423-7600, Fax: (617) 423-7600

FIREFLY PRODUCTIONS, INC.
36 Broomfield Street, #408
Boston, MA 02108
(617) 423-7600, Fax: (617) 423-7077

FOXBORO REGIONAL CENTER FOR
THE PERFORMING ARTS
P.O. Box 266
Foxboro, MA 02035
(508) 543-4434, Fax: (508) 261-7202

GLOUCESTER STAGE COMPANY
267 East Main Street
Gloucester, MA 01930
(978) 281-4099, Fax: (978) 282-1393

JEWISH THEATRE OF NEW ENGLAND
LEVENTHAL SIDMAN
JEWISH COMMUNITY CENTER
333 Nahanton Street
Newton Center, MA 02159
(617) 558-6481, Fax: (617) 244-8290

LYRIC STAGE
140 Clarendon Street
Boston, MA 02116
(617) 437-8819, Fax: (617) 536-2830

LYRIC WEST THEATRE COMPANY,
INC.
50 Oakland Street
Wellesley, MA 02481
(781) 235-0488, Fax: (781) 239-1047

MINIATURE THEATRE OF CHESTER
P.O. Box 722
Chester, MA 01011
(413) 354-7770, Fax: (413) 354-7825

NEW REPERTORY THEATRE
P.O. Box 610418
1155 Walnut Street
Newton Highlands, MA 02161
(917) 332-7058, Fax: (617) 527-5217

NORA THEATRE COMPANY
P.O. Box 382034
Cambridge, MA 02238
(617)491-2026, Fax: (617) 491-1887

PLAYKILL II INC.
1205 Statler Office Building
Boston, MA 02116
(617) 426-9211, Fax: (617) 426-7443

PROVINCETOWN REPERTORY
THEATRE
PO Box 812
Provincetown, MA 02657
or: 336 Commercial Street, Suite 7
Provincetown, MA 02657
(508) 487-0600, Fax: (508) 487-2482

THE PUBLICK THEATRE
165 Friend Street
Boston, MA 02114
(617) 782-5425, Fax: (617) 782-2855

REAGLE PLAYERS
617 Lexington Street
Waltham, MA 02154
(781) 894-0703 Fax: (781) 647-5584

SHAKESPEARE & CO.
70 Kemble Street
Lenox, MA 01240
(413) 637-1199, Fax: (413) 637-4274

STONEHAM THEATRE & ENSEMBLE
395 Main Street
Stoneham, MA 02180
(781) 279-2200, Fax: (781) 279-2374

WORCESTER FOOTHILLS THEATRE
110 Front Street, Suite 137
Worcester, MA 01608
(508) 754-3314, Fax: (508) 767-0676

WORCESTER FORUM THEATRE
ENSEMBLE
6 Chatham Street
Worcester, MA 01609
(508) 799-9166, Fax: (508) 795-0640

SUGAN THEATRE COMPANY
75 Garfield Street
Cambridge, MA 02138
(617) 497-5134, Fax: (617) 373-2501

VINEYARD PLAYHOUSE COMPANY,
INC.
24 Church Street
Vineyard Haven, MA 02568
(508) 693-6450, Fax: (508) 693-3431

WELLFLEET HARBQRACTORS
THEATER
67 Eric's Way
Well Fleet Harbor, MA 02667
(508) 349-7871, Fax : (508) 349-1703

WHEELOCK FAMILY THEATRE
200 The Riverway
Boston, MA 02215
(617) 734-5200 x235
Fax: (617) 734-7103

Mississippi

NEW STAGE THEATRE
1100 Carlisle Street
Jackson, MS 39202
(601) 948-0142, Fax: (601) 948-3533

New Hampshire

AMERICAN STAGE FESTIVAL
14 Court Street
Nashua, NH 03060
(603) 889-2330, Fax: (603) 889-2336

New Jersey

ACTORS' SHAKESPEARE COMPANY
STEVENS INSTITUTE OF
TECHNOLOGY
Castle Point on Hudson
Hoboken, NJ 01047
(201) 216-8960, Fax: (201) 216-8937

ARTS MAPLEWOOD/OUR HOUSE
PRODUCTIONS
WHAT EXIT? THEATRE COMPANY
482 Summit Avenue
Maplewood, NJ 07040
(973) 763-0805, Fax: (973) 763-4029

BICKFORD THEATRE - MORRIS
MUSEUM
6 Normandy Heights Road
Morristown, NJ 07960
(973) 917-3700 x3707
Fax: (973) 538-7945

CAPE MAY STAGE COMPANY
31 Perry Street
Cape May, NJ 08204
(609) 884-1341, Fax: (609) 884-4686

CENTENARY STAGE COMPANY
Centenary College
400 Jefferson Street
Hackettstown, NJ 07840
(908) 979-0900, Fax: (908) 979-4297

DREAM CATCHER REPERTORY
THEATRE, INC.
Bloomfield College
B1oomfield, NJ 07003
(973) 748-9008, Fax: (908) 273-6848

FOUNDATION THEATRE
Burlington County College Foundation
Route 530
Pemberton, NJ 08068
(609) 894-9311 x7423
Fax: (609) 894-4597

THE GARAGE THEATRE GROUP
161 Newcomb Road
Tenafly, NJ 07670
(201) 569-7710, Fax: Same

LUNA STAGE COMPANY
695 Bloomfield Avenue
Montclair, NJ 07042
(973) 744-3309, Fax: (973) 509-2388

NEW JERSEY REPERTORY COMPANY
179 Broadway
Long Branch, NJ 07740
(732) 229-3166

PASSAGE THEATRE COMPANY
PO Box 967
Trenton, NJ 08605-0967
(609) 392-0766, Fax: (609) 392-0318

PLAYWRIGHTS THEATRE OF
NEW JERSEY, INC.
33 Green Village Road
Madison, NJ 07940
(973) 514-1787, Fax: (973) 514-2060

PRINCETON REPERTORY COMPANY
One Palmer Square, Suite 541
Princeton, NJ 08542
(609) 921-3682, Fax: (212) 989-433]

SIMULATIONS, INC.
P. O. Box 399
Martinsville, NJ 08836
(732) 356-7800, Fax: (732) 356-5833

SURFLIGHT THEATRE SHOWPLACE
INCORPORATED
P.O. Box 1155
Beach Haven, NJ 08008
(609) 492-9477, Fax: (609) 492-4469

THEATREFEST
MONTCLAIR STATE UNIVERSITY
Upper Montclair, NJ 07043
(973) 655-7496, Fax: (973) 655-5366

TWO RIVER THEATRE COMPANY
223 Maple Avenue.
Red Bank, NJ 07701
(732) 345-1400 (732) 345-1414

New York

ADIRONDACK THEATRE FESTIVAL
PO Box 3203
Glens Falls, NY 12801
(518) 798-7479, Fax: (518) 739-1334

BROOKLYN LYCEUM
227 4th Avenue
Brooklyn, NY 11215
(646) 208-9877, Fax: (718) 398-7301

COMPASS ROSE THEATRE COMPANY
409 Union Street, #3
Brooklyn, NY 11231
(212) 726-1441, Fax: (718) 726-2861
At ROUND LAKE AUDITORIUM
Wesley Circle
Round Lake, NY 12151
(518) 899-7141

C-R PRODUCTIONS INC
18 Columbia Gardens
Cohoes, NY 12407
(518) 237-7999, Fax: (518) 237-0029

DEPOT THEATRE
P.O. Box 414
Westport, NY 12993
(518) 962-4449, Fax: (518) 962-2022

EAST LYNNE THEATRE COMPANY
121 Madison Avenue, #3M
New York, NY 10016
(609) 884-5898

THE EMELIN THEATRE
153 Library Lane
Mamaroneck, NY 10543
(914) 698-3045 X12
Fax: (914) 698-1404

FLEETWOOD STAGE COMPANY
44 Wildcliff Drive
New Rochelle, NY 1080S
(914) 654-8533, Fax: (914) 235-4459

FORESTBURGH PLAYHOUSE
Theatre AMDG Inc.
39 Forestburgh Road
Forestburgh, NY 12777
(914) 794-2005, Fax: (845) 794-3747

GATEWAY PLAYHOUSE
Allan & Allan Arts, Ltd.
P.O. Box 5
Bellport, NY 11713
(631) 286-0555, Fax: (631) 486-5806

GUILD HALL OF EAST HAMPTON, INC.
JOHN DREW THEATRE
58 Main Street
East Hampton, NY 11937
(631) 324-0806, Fax: (631) 329-5043

HANGAR THEATRE
AKA CENTER FOR THE ARTS
DeWitt Mall
P.O. Box 205
Ithaca, NY 14851
(781) 273-8588, Fax: (781) 273-4516

HUDSON STAGE COMPANY
P.O. Box 835
Croton-On-Hudson, NY 10520
(914) 271-2811, Fax: (914) 737-7511

HUDSON VALLEY SHAKESPEARE
FESTIVAL
155 Main Street
Cold Spring on Hudson, NY 10516
(914) 265-7858, Fax: (914) 465-7865

INTERACT THEATRE COMPANY
THE ADRIENNE
2030 Sansom Street
Philadelphia, PA 19103
(215) 568-8077, Fax: (215) 568-8095

JEAN COCTEAU REPERTORY
330 Bowery
New York, NY 10012
(212) 677-0060, Fax: (212) 777-6151

JOSHUA KANE'S
651 10th Street, #3
Brooklyn, NY 11215
(718) 965-6694, Fax: (118) 369-2006

LYCIAN CENTER LIMITED - KINGS
THEATRE
P.O. Box F
Sugarloaf, NY 10981
(914) 469-2185, Fax: (914) 469-5355

NEW YORK STAGE & FILM COMPANY
151 W. 30th St., Suite 905
New York, NY 10001
or: POWER HOUSE THEATRE
124 Raymond Avenue
Vassar College
Poughkeepsie, NY 12604
(845) 437-7021 (212) 239-2334
Fax: (212) 239-2996

QUEEN CITY STAGE COMPANY
P.O. Box 154
La Grangeville, NY 12540
(914) 473-1325, Fax: (914) 486-4648

QUEENS THEATRE IN THE PARK
P.O. Box 52006
Flushing, NY 11352
(718) 760-0686, Fax: (718) 760-1972

R. E. PRODUCTIONS, INC.
420 E. 79th Street, #17B.
New York, NY 10021
(212) 861-5648 Fax: (212) 861-5648

RIVER REP
100 East 4th Street
New York, NY 10003
(212) 674-8181
or: Summer Address: P.O. Box 637
Ivoryton, CT 06442
(860) 167-3085

SARATOGA SHAKESPEARE
COMPANY, INC.
P.O. Box 5059
Saratoga Springs, NY 12866
(518) 884-4947

SARATOGA STAGES
P.O. Box 475
Saratoga Springs, NY 12866
(518) 584-8870, Fax: (518) 584-8871

SCHOOLHOUSE THEATRE
3 Owens Road
Croton Falls, NY 10519
(914) 277-8477, Fax: (914) 277-2269

SHADOWLAND ARTISTS INC.
157 Canal Street
Ellenville, NY 12428
(845) 647-5511, Fax: (845) 647-3510

STAGEWORKS ON THE HUDSON
133 Warren Street
Hudson, NY 12534
(518) 828-7843, Fax: (518) 828-4026

STATUE OF LIBERTY - ELLIS ISLAND
FOUNDATION, INC.
Vital Theatre Company
432 West 42nd Street
New York, NY 10036
(212) 268-2040, Fax: (212) 268-0474

TOURING CIRCUIT, LTD
1501 Broadway, #309
New York, NY 10036
(212) 840-5564, Fax: (212) 391-1546

WOMEN'S THEATRE COOPERATIVE
P.O. Box 5924
Parsippany, NY 07054
(973) 443-9125, Fax: (201)335-3038

North Carolina

BLOWING ROCK STAGE COMPANY
PO Box 2170
Blowing Rock, NC 28805
(828) 295-9168, Fax: (828) 295-9104

NORTH CAROLINA THEATRE
One East South Street
Raleigh, NC 27601
(919) 831-6941, Fax: (919) 831-6951

TRIAD STAGE
232 South Elm Street
Greensboro, NC 27401
(336) 274-0067, Fax: (336) 274-1774

Ohio

ACTORS' SUMMIT
86 Owen Brown Street
Hudson, OH 44236
(330) 142-0800, Fax: (330) 650-4880

CAIN PARK SUMMER THEATRE
C/O City Of Cleveland Heights
40 Severance Circle
Cleveland Heights, OH 44118
(216) 371-3000, Fax: (216) 371~1152

ENSEMBLE THEATRE
3275 Hyde Park Avenue
Cleveland Heights, OH 44118
(216) 321-2930, Fax: (216) 56.1.-1992

Pennsylvania

ACT II PLAYHOUSE LTD.
56 E. Butler Avenue
Ambler, PA 19002
(215) 654-0200, Fax: (215) 654-5001

BUSHFIRE THEATRE OF
PERFORMIING ARTS
224 South 52nd Street
Philadelphia, PA 19139
(215) 747-9230, Fax: (215) 747-9236

CARNEGIE MELLON NEW PLAYS
SHOWCASE
School Of Drama
Purnell Center Of Fine Arts
Pittsburgh, PA 15213-3890
(412) 268-3292, Fax: (412) 621-0281

BRISTOL RIVERSIDE THEATRE
P.O. Box 1250
Bristol, P A 19007
(215) 785-6664, Fax: (215) 785-2762

1812 PRODUCTIONS
525 South 4th Street, Suite 479
Philadelphia, PA 19147
(215) 592-9560, Fax: (215) 592-9580

FULTON OPERA HOUSE
12 N. Prince Street
Lancaster, PA 17603
(717)394-7133, Fax: (717) 397-3780

GRETNA PRODUCTIONS
P.O. Box 578
Mt. Gretna, PA 17064
(717) 964-3322, Fax: (717) 964-2189

HEDGEROW THEATRE
JASPER DEETER CORPORATION
146 West Rose Valley Rd.
Wallingford, PA 19086
(610) 565-4211, Fax: (610) 565-1672

LANTERN THEATRE
6604 Wayne Avenue
Philadelphia, PA 19119
(215) 844-3150, Fax: (215) 829-1151

PENNSYLVANIA SHAKESPEARE
FESTIVAL
AT DeSALES UNIVERSITY
2755 Station Avenue
Center Valley, PA 18034
(610) 282-9455, Fax: (610) 282-2084

PHILADELPHIA SHAKESPEARE
FESTIVAL
2111 Sansom Street
Philadelphia, PA 19103
(215) 496-9722, Fax: (215) 469-0663

PITTSBURGH IRISH & CLASSICAL
THEATRE
P. O. Box 23607
Pittsburgh, PA 15222
(412) 561-6000

PITTSBURGH MUSICAL THEATRE
207 S. Main Street
Pittsburgh, PA 15220
(412) 539-0999, Fax: (412) 539-0998
Box Office: (421) 539-0900

RAUH CONSERVATORY
STUDENT COMPANY
Richard E. Rauh Conservatory
327 S. Main Street
Pittsburgh, PA 15220
(412) 539-0110

PITTSBURGH PLAYHOUSE
Point Park College
222 Craft Avenue
Pittsburgh, PA 15213
(412) 621-4445
Fax: (412) 621-4762

SAINT VINCENT THEATRE
St. Vincent College
300 Fraiser Purchase Road
Latrobe, PA 15650
(724) 537-8900, Fax: Same

SOCIETY FOR THE
PERFORMING ARTS
321 W. State Street
Media, PA 19063
(610) 891-0100, Fax: (610) 891-0247

Rhode Island

COLONIAL THEATRE
P.O. Box 762
Street address: 4 High Street
Westerly, RI 02891
(401) 596-7909

THEATRE BY THE SEA
Fourquest Entertainment, Inc.
P.O. Box 5240
Wakefield, RI 02880
(401) 782-3644, Fax: (401) 782-2900

South Carolina

THE SELF FAMILY ARTS CENTER
14 Shelter Cove Lane
Hilton Head Island, SC 29928
(843) 686-3945, Fax: (843) 842-7877

Tennessee

MOCKINGBIRD PUBLIC THEATRE
800 4th Avenue South
Nashville, TN 37210
(615) 463-0071 Fax: (515) 279-8003

NASHVILLE SHAKESPEARE FESTIVAL
800 4th Avenue South
Nashville, TN 37210
(615) 255-2273, Fax: (615) 248-2273

PARNASSUS PRODUCTIONS
118 Deer Run
Altamont, TN 37301
(931) 692-2480, Fax: (931) 692-2680

Vermont

BREADLOAF SCHOOL OF ENGLISH
Tilden House/Freeman International
Center
Middlebury College
Middlebury, VT 05750
(802) 443-5360, Fax: (802) 443-2060

DORSET THEATRE FESTIVAL
American Theatre Works
P.O. Box 510
Dorset, VT 05251
(802) 867-2223/5777
Fax: (802) 867-0144

OLDCASTLE THEATRE COMPANY
Route 9 & Gypsy Lane
Bennington, VT 05201
(802) 447-1261, Fax: (802) 442-3074

VERMONT STAGE COMPANY
P.O. Box 874
Burlington, VT 05402
(802) 656-4351, Fax: (802) 656-0349

WESTON PLAYHOUSE THEATRE
CORPORATION
703 Main Street
Weston, VT 05161-0216
(802) 824-8167, Fax: (304) 824-5099

Virginia

INTERACT THEATRE CO
1221 Mottrom Drive
McLean, VA 22101
(703) 848-2632, Fax: (703) 848-2665

MILL MOUNTAIN PLAYHOUSE
One Market Square SE, 2nd Floor
Roanoke, VA 24011-1437
(540) 342-5730, Fax: (540) 342-5745

SIGNATURE THEATRE
3806 South Four Mile Run Drive
Arlington, VA 22206
(703) 845-1724, Fax: (703) 820-7790

THEATER AT LIME KILN
Lime Kiln Arts, Inc.
14 S. Randolph Street
Lexington, VA 24450
(540) 463-7088, Fax: (540) 463-1082

THEATER OF THE FIRST AMENDMENT
George Mason University
(Center For The Arts)
Mail Stop 3E6
Fairfax, VA 22030-4444
(703) 993-2195, Fax: (703) 993-2191

WAYSIDE THEATRE CO
7853 Main Street
Middletown, VA 22645
(540) 869-1776, Fax: (540) 869-1746

Washington

FOLGER SHAKESPEARE LIBRARY
201 E. Capitol Street, S.E.
Washington, DC 20003
(202) 544-4600, Fax: (202) 544-7520

SOURCE THEATRE COMPANY
1835 14th Street, NW
Washington, DC 20009
(202) 462-1073, Fax: (202) 462-2300

STUDIO THEATRE, INC.
1333 P Street, NW
Washington, DC 20005
(202) 232-7267, Fax: (202) 588-5262

THEATER OF THE
JEWISH COMMUNITY CENTER
1529 16th Street, NW
Washington, DC 20036
(202) 518-9400 x229
Fax: (202)518-9420/9421

WASHINGTON STAGE GUILD
(T/A), THEATRE DOWNTOWN, INC
4018 Argyle Terrace, NW
Washington, DC 20011
(202) 529-2084, Fax: (301) 529-2740

WOOLLY MAMMOTH
917 M Street, NW
Washington, DC 20001
(202) 312-5267, Fax: (202) 289-2446

West Virginia

WEST VIRGINIA PUBLIC THEATRE
CREATIVE ARTS CENTER
453 Oakland Street, Suite 1
Morgantown, WV 26505
(304) 598-0144, Fax: (304) 598-0145

Central Region Equity Theaters

Arkansas

ARKANSAS REPERTORY THEATRE
P.O. Box 110
Little Rock, AR 72203
www.therep.org

Illinois

A RED ORCHID THEATRE
1531 N. Wells St.
Chicago, IL 60610
www.a-red-orchid.com

THE AARDVARK
2523 N Maplewood
Chicago, IL 60647
www.aardvarktheatre.com

ABOUT FACE THEATRE COLLECTIVE
1222 W. Wilson, 2nd Floor West
Chicago, IL 60640
www.aboutfacetheatre.com

AMERICAN THEATER COMPANY
1909 W Byron St.
Chicago, IL 60613
www.atcweb.org

AMERICAN WRITERS' THEATRE OF
CHICAGO, INC
c/o Books On Vernon
Glencoe, IL 60022
www.Illyria.com/writers.html

AMERICANA PRODUCTIONS
915 Linden Ave.
Wilmette, IL 60091

APOLLO FINE ARTS & ENT CENTRE
311 Main St.
Peoria, IL 61602
www.apollofinearts.com

ARTISTIC CIRCLES
P.O. Box 511-24117
Chicago, IL 60654

THE ARTISTIC HOME
1420 W. Irving Park Rd
Chicago, IL 60613
www.theartistichome.org

APOLLO FINE ARTS & ENT CENTRE
311 Main St.
Peoria, IL 61602
www.apollofinearts.com

APPLE TREE THEATRE
595 Elm Pl Ste 210
Highland Park, IL 60035
www.appletreetheatre.com

ASSOCIATED COLLEGES
OF THE MIDWEST
3340 N. Clark Street
Chicago, IL 60657

BUFFALO THEATRE ENSEMBLE
425 22nd & Park Arts Center
Glen Ellyn, IL 60137
www.cod.edu/artscntr

CHICAGO ASSOCIATES OF
STRATFORD
4138 Woodland Ave.
Western Springs, IL 60558

CHICAGO CENTER PERFORMING
ARTS
777 N. Green St.
Chicago, IL 60622
www.theatreland.com

CHICAGO DRAMATISTS
1105 W. Chicago Ave.
Chicago, IL 60622
www.chicagodramatists.org

CHICAGO SHAKESPEARE THEATER
aka Shakespeare Repertory
800 E Grand Ave.
Chicago, IL 60611
www.chicagoshakes.com

CHICAGO THEATRE CO
500 E 67th St.
Chicago, IL 60637

CIRCA 21 DINNER PLAYHOUSE
1828 3rd Avenue
Rock Island, IL 61201

COLLABORACTION THEATRE
COMPANY
2046 West Caroll Street
Chicago, IL 60608

COMFORTABLE SHOES
CHICAGO LLC
1006 S. Michigan Ave., Suite 800
Chicago, IL 60605

CONGO SQUARE THEATRE CO
1501 W. Randolph
Chicago, IL 60607

COURT THEATRE
University of Chicago
5535 S Ellis
Chicago, IL 60637
www.courttheatre.org

DEFIANT THEATRE COMPANY
P.O. Box 138052
Chicago, IL 60613

DREAM TEAM PRODUCTIONS LLC
c/o Landon Shaw
1347 N. Dearborn, Suite 602
Chicago, IL 60610

DRURY LANE DINNER THEATRE
2500 W 95th St.
Evergreen Park, IL 60642
www.drurylane.com

DRURY LANE OAKBROOK THEATRE
100 Drury Lane
Oakbrook, IL 60181

DUNCAN YMCA
Cherin Center
1001 West Roosevelt Road
Chicago, IL 6060S

EUROPEAN REPERTORY COMPANY
2936 N. Southport 3rd Floor
Chicago, IL 60657

FAMOUS DOOR THEATRE
P.O. Box 57029
Chicago, IL 60657

FIRST FOLIO SHAKESPEARE FEST
146 Juliet Court
Clarendon Hills, IL 60514
www.firstfolio.org

GOODMAN THEATRE
a/k/a Chicago Theatre Group
170 N. Dearborn
Chicago, IL 60601
www.goodman-theatre.org

GREASY JOAN & CO
P.O. Box 13077
Chicago, IL 60613

HEALTHWORKS THEATRE
3171 N. Halsted St.
Chicago, IL 60657

ILLINOIS COLLEGE
1101 West College Avenue
Jacksonville, IL 62650

ILLINOIS SHAKESPEARE FESTIVAL
Illinois State University
Campus Box 5700
Normal, IL 61790
www.thefestival.org

ILLINOIS THEATRE CENTER
P.O. Box 397
371 Artists' Walk
Park Forest, IL 60466

KIRKLAND AND ELLIS
200 East Randolph Street
Chicago, IL 60601

LA VIE ENNUI CHICAGO
P.O. Box 577676
Chicago, IL 60657
www.lavieenui.com

LIGHT OPERA WORKS
927 Noyes St.
Evanston, IL 60201

LITTLE THEATRE ON THE SQUARE
P.O. Box 288
Sullivan, IL 61951

LIVE BAIT THEATRICAL CO
3914 N Clark
Chicago, IL 60613
www.livebaittheater.org

LOOKINGGLASS THEATRE CO.
2936 N South port, 3rd floor
Chicago, IL 60657
www.lookingglasstheatre.org

LOYOLA UNIVERSITY
Kathleen Mullady Theatre
Chicago, IL 60626

LOYOLA UNIVERSITY THEATRE
6525 N. Sheridan Road
Chicago, IL 60626

MARRIOTT'S LINCOLNSHIRE
North Dury Lane Productions
10 Marriott Dr.
Lincolnshire, IL 60069

MCLEAON COUNTY HISTORICAL
200 N Main St.
Bloomington, IL 61701

METROPOLIS PERFORMING ARTS
111 W. Campbell St.
Arlington Heights, IL 60005

MIMI AYERS PRODUCTIONS
6935 S. Crandon Avenue, #30
Chicago, IL 60649

MOVING DOCK THEATRE CO
2970 N. Sheridan Rd., #1021
Chicago, IL 60657

NAKED EYE THEATRE CO
1454 W Hollywood, #3E
Chicago, IL 60660

NEW AMERICAN THEATRE
118 N Main St.
Rockford, Il 61101

NEXT THEATRE CO
927 Noyes St.
Evanston, IL 60201
www.nexttheatre.org

NOBLE FOOL THEATRE
8 E. Randolph
Chicago, IL 60601
www.noblefoot.com

NORTHLIGHT THEATRE
9501 N.Skokie Blvd
Skokie, IL 60076
www.northlight.org

OAK PARK FESTIVAL THEATRE
P.O. Box 4114
Oak Park, Il 60303
www.oprf.com/festival

ORGANIC THEATRE CO.
P.O. Box 578189
Chicago, IL 60657

OTG PRODUCTIONS
5650 N. Sheridan Rd., #19F
Chicago, IL 60660

OVER THE TAVERN LLC
6446 Thunderbird Drive
Indian Head Park, IL 60525

PAGEANT CHICAGO LLC
2031 W. Dickens
Chicago, IL 60647
www.pageanttheamusical.com

PERFORMING ARTS AT METROPOLIS
111 West Campbell Street
Arlington Heights, IL 60005

PIVEN THEATRE WORKSHOP
927 Noyes
Evanston, IL 60201
www.piventheatreworkshop.com

POWERSUASION
a/k/a Karolus Inc
400 E Randolph St., Suite 503
Chicago, IL 60601

QUINCY COMMUNITY THEATRE
300 Civic Center Plaza, Suite 118
Quincy, IL 62301

RED HEN PRODUCTIONS
5123 N. Clark
Chicago, IL 60640
www.redhenproductions.com

REMY BUMPO PRODUCTIONS
3717 N. Ravenswood, Suite 245
Chicago, IL 60613

RICHARD FRIEDMAN PRODUCTIONS
5819 N. Sacramento
Chicago, IL 60659

RIVENDELL THEATRE ENSEMBLE
1711 W. Belle Plaine, #3B
Chicago, IL 60613

ROADWORKS PRODUCTIONS
1144 W. Fulton
Chicago, IL 60607
www.roadworks.org

RUNNING WITH SCISSORS
P.O. Box 408438
Chicago, IL 60640

SEANACHAI THEATRE CO
2206 N. Tripp Ave.
Chicago, IL 60639
www.seanachai.org

SECOND CITY INC.
1616 N Wells St.
Chicago, IL 60614
www.secondcity.com

SHAKESPEARE ON THE GREEN
700 E. Westleigh
Lake Forest, IL 60045

SHATTERED GLOBE THEATRE
2856 N. Halsted
Chicago, IL 60657
www.shatteredglobe.org

SOUTHERN ILLINOIS UNIVERSITY
Department of Theatre
Carbondale, IL 62901

SPLINTER GROUP THEATRE CO
DBA Irish Repertory Theatre
5875 N. Lincoln
Chicago, IL 60659

STAGE LEFT INC
3408 N. Sheffield
Chicago, IL 60657

STEPPENWOLF THEATRE COMPANY
758 W North Ave., 4th Floor
Chicago, IL 60610
www.steppenwolf.org

STILL POINT THEATRE COLLECTIVE
1337 West Ohio
Chicago, IL 60622

TEATRO VISTA
3712 N. Broadway, #275
Chicago, IL 60613
www.teatrovista.org

SUMMERNITE
Northern Illinois Univeristy
Stevens Bldg.
DeKalb, IL 60115
www.niu.edu

TERRAPIN THEATRE
444 North Wabash, Suite 410
Chicago, IL 60611

TIMBER LAKE PLAYHOUSE
P.O. Box 29
Mount Carroll, IL 61053

V MONOLOGUES CHICAGO INC
916 S. Wabash, Suite 503
Chicago, IL 60605
www.apollochicago.com

VICTORY GARDENS THEATER
2257 N. Lincoln Ave.
Chicago, IL 60614

WORKING WOMEN HISTORY PRO-
JECT
3161 N Cambridge
Chicago, IL 60657

WALKABOUT THEATRE COMPANY
3241 North Ravenswood Avenue
Chicago, IL 60657

Indiana

BEEF & BOARDS DINNER THEATRE
a/k/a Lark Productions
9301 N Michigan Rd.
Indianapolis, IN 46268
www.beefandboards.com

BROWN COUNTY PLAYHOUSE
Indiana University
Bloomington, IN 47405

CHILDRENS MUSEUM OF
INDIANAPOLIS
3000 N Meridian
Indianapolis, IN 46206

INDIANA REPERTORY THEATRE, INC.
140 W Washington St.
Indianapolis, IN 46204

INDIANA STATE UNIVERSITY
540 S 7th St
Terre Haute, IN 47807

INDIANAPOLIS CIVIC
1200 W 38th St.
Indianapolis, IN 46208

NEW HARMONY THEATRE
8600 University Blvd.
Evansville, IN 47712
www.usi.edu

PHOENIX THEATRE INC.
749 N Park Ave.
Indianapolis, IN 46202
www.phoenixtheatre.org

PURDUE UNIVERSITY
2101 E Coliseum Blvd.
Fort Wayne, IN 46805

RIDGEWOOD ARTS FOUNDATION
INC.
907 Ridge Rd
Munster, IN 46321

SHADOWAPE THEATRE COMPANY
5549 North Haverford Avenue
Indianapolis, IN 46220

UNIVERSITY OF NOTRE DAME
Summer Shakespeare
202 Decio Faculty Hall
Notre Dame, IN 46556

WAGON WHEEL PRODUCTIONS INC
2517 E Center St.
Warsaw, IN 46580

WEST SIDE THEATRE GUILD
9th Avenue & Gerry Street
Gary, IN 46406

Iowa

CLINTON AREA SHOWBOAT
P.O. Box 764
Clinton, IA 52733

DORIAN OPERA THEATRE
Luther College
700 E. Judisch
Decorah, IA 52101

THE DRAMA WORKSHOP
P.O. Box 8237
Des Moines, IA 50301

IOWA SUMMER REPERTORY
University of Iowa
N. Riverside Dr., 107 TB
Iowa City, IA 52242

NEW GROUND THEATRE
1821 Sunset Drive
Bettendorf, IA 52722

OLD CREAMERY THEATRE
39 38th Ave., Suite 200
Amana, IA 52203

RIVERSIDE THEATRE
213 North Gilbert Street
Iowa City, IA 52245

RIVERSIDE THEATRE SHAKESPEARE
213 N. Gilbert St.
Iowa City, IA 52245
www.riversidetheatre.org

STAGE WEST THEATRE COMPANY
P.O. Box 12127
Des Moines, IA 50312

Kansas

CABARET OLD TOWN
412 1/2 E Douglas Ave.
Wichita, KS 67202
www.cabertoldtown.com

CHESTNUT FINE ARTS CENTER
234 North Chestnut Street
Olathe, KS 66061

ACCESSIBLE ARTS INC
1100 State Avenue
Kansas City, KS 66102
www.accessbilearts.org

GREAT PLAINS THEATRE FESTIVAL
P.O. Box 476
Abilene, KS 67410

HEART OF AMERICA SHAKESPEARE
4800 Main St., # 302
Kansas City, MO 64112

MOSLEY STREET MELODRAMA
234 N Mosley St.
Wichita, KS 67202
www.mosleystreet.com

JOHNSON COUNTY COMMUNITY
COLLEGE
12345 College Blvd.
Overland Park, KS 66210

MUSIC THEATRE OF WICHITA
225 W Douglas Ave., Suite 202
Wichita, KS 67202
www.musictheatreofwichita.org

NEW THEATRE RESTAURANT
1116 W. 24th St.
Kansas City, KS 64108

STAGE ONE PRODUCTIONS
1710 E Douglas Ave.
Wichita, KS 67214

STORM ENTERTAINMENT
2034 North Amidon
Wichita, KS 67203

THEATRE FOR YOUNG AMERICA
4881 Johnson Dr.
Mission, KS 66205
www.tya.org

UNICORN THEATRE
3820 Main St.
Kansas City, MO 64111

UNIVERSITY OF MO-KANSAS CITY
5100 Rockhill Road
Department of Theatre
Kansas City, MO 64110

UNIVERSITY OF KANSAS
1530 Naismith Drive
Lawrence, KS 66045

Kentucky

ACTORS THEATRE OF LOUISVILLE
316-320 W. Main St.
Louisville, KY 40202
www.actorstheatre.org

HORSE CAVE THEATRE
P.O. Box 215
Horse Cave, KY 42749

MADISONVILLE COMMUNITY AND
TECHICAL COLLEGE
2000 College Drive
Madisonville, KY 42431

STAGE FIRST CINCINNATI
118 16th Street
Newport, KY 41071

STAGE ONE:
LOUISVILLE CHILDREN'S THEATRE
501 W Main
Louisville, KY 40202

STEPHEN FOSTER DRAMA
P.O. Box 546
Bardstown, KY 40004

Louisiana

BEEFIELD PRODUCTIONS
1204 Smith Drive
Metairie, LA 70005

DOG & PONY THEATRE COMPANY
P.O. Box 71234
New Orleans, LA 70172

EPISCOPAL SCHOOL
3200 Woodland Ridge Blvd.
Baton Rouge, LA 70816

FIRST UNITED METHODIST CHURCH
500 Common Street
Shreveport, LA 71165

FPN PRODUCTIONS
2735 Canal Street
New Orleans, LA 70119

JEFFERSON PERFORMING ARTS
1118 Clearview Pkwy
Metairie, LA 70001

LE PETIT THEATRE DU VIEUX
701 S. Peters St., Suite 300
New Orleans, LA 70130

NEW ORLEANS CLASSIC THEATRE
1778 Gentilly Boulevard
New Orleans, LA 70119

NEWTON AND ASSOCIATES
3001 Division Street, Suite 118
Metairie, LA 70065

SHAKESPEARE FESTIVAL AT TULANE
Tulane University
Dept of Theatre & Dance
New Orleans, LA 70118

THE PRODUCER'S CIRCLE LLC
1111 S. Peters St. #207
New Orleans, LA 70130

SOUTHERN REPERTORY THEATRE
333 Canal St., Box 34
New Orleans, LA 70119

SOUTHERN REPERTORY THEATRE
1437 S Carrollton Avenue
New Orleans, LA 70118

SWINE PALACE PRODUCTIONS
Reilly Theatre
Tower Drive - LSU
Baton Rouge, LA 70803
www.swinepalace.org

THEATRICKS LLC
3900 Canal Street
New Orleans, LA 70119

TULANE SUMMER LYRIC THEATRE
104 Dixon Hall
New Orleans, LA 70118

Michigan

20TH CENTURY CLUB INC
2111 Woodward Ave., Suite 910
Detroit, MI 48201

BARN THEATRE INC
13351 W. M-96
Augusta, MI 49012
www.barntheatre.com

BIG PICKLE PRODUCTIONS
P.O. Box 331
Chelsea, MI 48118

CENTER FOR RESEARCH ON
LEARNING
610 University Street
Ann Arbor, MI 48109

CHERRY COUNTY PLAYHOUSE
Western Michigan's
425 W Western Ave., Suite 406
Muskegon, MI 49440
www.cherrycountyplayhouse.org

CHIMERA THEATRE
800 West Huron, Apt. 2
Ann Arbor, MI 48104

CROSWELL OPERA HOUSE
129 E Maumee Street
Adrian, MI 49221

DETROIT ACTORS GUILD PROD. INC
DJK Operating LLC
5707 Hillcrest
Detroit, MI 48236

DETROIT REPERTORY THEATRE
13101 Woodrow Wilson St.
Detroit, MI 48238

GRAND VALLEY STATE U
School of Communications
Allendale, MI 49401

HOPE COLLEGE SUMMER THEATRE
P.O. Box 9000
Holland, MI 49422

JEWISH ENSEMBLE THEATRE
6600 W Maple Rd.
West Bloomfield, MI 48322

MEADOW BROOK THEATRE
Oakland University
Rochester, MI 48309

MICHIGAN SHAKESPEARE FESTIVAL
123 Fieldcrest St., #304
Ann Arbor, MI 48103

MICHIGAN THEATER
603 East Uberty Street
Ann Arbor, MI 48104

MUSKEGON COMMUNITY COLLEGE
221 S Quarterline Road
Muskegon, MI 49442

OLYMPIA ENTERTAINMENT INC
a/k/a Second City Detroit
2301 Woodward Ave.
Detroit, MI 48201

PLOWSHARES THEATRE
2870 E. Grand Blvd., Suite 600
Detroit, MI 48202

PERFORMANCE NETWORK
120 E. Huron
Ann Arbor, MI 48104

PLANET ANT THEATRE
2357 Caniff
Hamtramck, MI 48212

PRITCHARD THEATREICAL PRODS
Box 693
Marshall, MI 49068

PROSPERA THEATRE COMPANY
116 South Seventh Street
Ann Arbor, MI 48103

PURPLE ROSE THEATRE
P.O. Box 220
Chelsea, MI 48118
www.home.earthlink.net/purplerose/

UNIVERSITY OF MICHIGAN
2512 Frieze Bldg.
105 State St.
Ann Arbor, MI 48109

WESTSHORE CC
3000 S Stiles Rd.
Scottville, MI 49454

ZEITGEIST GALLERY
2661 Michigan Ave.
Detroit, MI 48226

WATER WORKS THEATRE COMPANY
510 West Houstonia
Royal Oak, MI 48073

Minnesota

ACTORS THEATRE OF MINNESOTA
1043 Grand Ave., #291
St. Paul, MN 55105

ANNE BERTRAM COMPANY
3616 45th Avenue South
Minneapolis, MN 55406

BALLET OF THE DOLLS
820 18th Avenue NE
Minneapolis, MN 55418

BARTH ENTERPRISES, LLP
22 Fifth Avenue South
St. Cloud, MN 56301

ASSOC. OF UNIVERSALIST WOMEN
16733 Camborne Place
Eden Prairie, MN 55346

BRYANT LAKE BOWL THEATER
810 West Lake Street
Minneapolis, MN 55408

BUFFALO GAL PRODUCTIONS
3024 Bryant Avenue South
Minneapolis, MN 55408

CARLYLE BROWN & COMPANY
P.O. Box 4731
St. Paul, MN 55401

CHANHASSEN DINNER THEATRES
International Theatres Corp
P.O. Box 100
Chanhassen, MN 55317
www.chanhassentheatres.com

CHILDREN'S THEATRE COMPANY
2400 Third Ave. S
Minneapolis, MN 55404

EYE OF THE STORM THEATRE
3600 16th Avenue
Minneapolis, MN 55407

FRANK THEATRE
3156 23rd Ave. South
Minneapolis, MN 55407

THE GLOBE OF AMERICA
608 Juliet Avenue
St. Paul, MN 55105

GREAT AMERICAN HISTORY THEATRE
30 E. 10th St.
St. Paul, MN 55101

GREAT RIVER REVIEW
211 West Wabasha Street
Winona, MN 55987

GUTHRIE THEATRE FOUNDATION
725 Vineland Pl.
Minneapolis, MN 55403
www.guthrietheater.org

HEY CITY THEATRE
a/k/a SJC Minneapolis LLLP
824 Hennepin Ave.
Minneapolis, MN 55403
www.heycity.com

ILLUSION THEATRE
528 Hennepin Ave., Suite 704
Minneapolis, MN 55403
www.illusiontheater.org

JUNGLE THEATRE
2951 Lyndale Ave. S
Minneapolis, MN 55408
www.jungletheater.com

KLS PRODUCTIONS
3425 Girard Ave. S
Minneapolis, MN 55408

MICHAEL BRINDISI
P.O. Box 100
Chanhassen, MN 55317

MINNESOTA FESTIVAL THEATRE
P.O. Box 1134
Albert Lea, MN 56007

MINNESOTA SHAKESPEARE PROJECT
3608 Pillsbury Ave.
Minneapolis, MN 55409

MIXED BLOOD THEATRE CO
1501 S. Fourth St.
Minneapolis, MN 55403
www.mixedblood.com

OLD LOG THEATER
P.O. Box 250
Excelsior, MN 55331

ORDWAY CENTER FOR THE
PERFORMING ARTS
345 Washington St.
St. Paul, MN 55102
www.ordway.org

PARK SQUARE THEATRE
408 Saint Peter St., Suite 110
St. Paul, MN 55102
www.parksquaretheatre.org

PENUMBRA THEATRE
270 N. Kent St.
St. Paul, MN 55102

PILLSBURY HOUSE THEATRE
3501 S. Chicago Ave.
S. Minneapolis, MN 55407
www.11uswest.users.net

PIONEER PRODUCTIONS
22 Fifth Avenue South
St. Cloud, MN 56301

THE PLAYWRIGHTS' CENTER
2301 Franklin Ave.
E Minneapolis, MN 55406
www.pwcenter.org

RURAL AMERICA ARTS PARTNERSHIP
P.O. Box 276
412 Broadway
Plainview, MN 55964

SJC MIRTNEAPOLIS, LLLP
824 Hennepin Avenue
Minneapolis, MN 55404

SUNSHINE BOYS, LLC
c/o Troupe America Inc.
528 Hennepin Ave #206
Minneapolis, MN 55403

STAGES THEATRE COMPANY
1111 Main Street
Hopkins, MN 55343

TEN THOUSAND THINGS
3153 36th Avenue
So Minneapolis, MN 55406

THE BURNING HOUSE GROUP
1304 University Ave., NE Suite 306
Minneapolis, MN 55413

THEATRE DE LA JEUNE LUNE
Ford Center
420 North 5th Street
Minneapolis, MN 55401

THEATRE MU
711 W Lake St., Suite 212
Minneapolis, MN 55408

TRIPLE ESPRESSO LLC
1410 Nicollet Avenue
Minneapolis, MN 55403

TROUPE AMERICA INC
528 Hennepin Ave., Suite 206
Minneapolis, MN 55403
www.troupeamerica.com

Missouri

AMERICAN HEARTLAND THEATRE
2450 Grand Ave., Suite 314
Kansas City, MO 64108

ARROW ROCK LYCEUM THEATRE
5 S Ninth, Suite 204
Columbia, MO 65201
www.lyceumtheatre.org

BROADWAY ON YOUR DOORSTEP
P.O. Box 2010
Florissant, MO 63032

CITY PLAYERS OF ST. LOUIS
7558 Woodland Dr.
St. Louis, MO 63143

THE COTERIE THEATRE
2450 Grand Ave., Suite 144
Kansas City, MO 64108

DRAMARAMA THEATRE CO
7627 Mission Valley Dr.
St. Louis, MO 63123
www.worldzone.net/family/dramarama

HISTORYONICS THEATRE CO
P.O. Box 2938
St. Louis, MO 63130
www.historyonics.org

HOT HOUSE THEATRE CO
P.O. Box 430
Saint Louis, MO 63143

(MOSTLY) HARMLESS THEATRE
6614 Clayton Rd., #274
St. Louis, MO 63117

IMAGINARY THEATRE COMPANY
clo Rep. Theatre of St. Louis
130 Edger Rd.
St. Louis, MO 63119

MISSOURI REPERTORY THEATRE
4949 Cherry St.
Kansas City, MO 64110
www.missourireptheatre.org

MUNICIPAL THEATRE ASSOCIATION
OF ST LOUIS
The Muny
St. Louis, MO 63112
www.muny.com

NEW JEWISH THEATRE
2 Millstone Campus Drive
St Louis, MO 63146

OFF CENTER THEATRE COMPANY
4841 Colony Church, #1
St. Louis, MO 63129

O'FALLON COMMUNITY THEATER
100 North Main Street
O'Fallon, MO 63366

OZARK ACTORS THEATRE
P.O. Box K
Rolla, MO 65402

QUALITY HILL PRODUCTIONS
DBA Quality Hill Playhouse
303 W. 10th St.
Kansas City, MO 64105
www.qhpkc.org

REPERTORY THEATRE OF ST. LOUIS
130 Edgar Rd.
P.O. Box 191730
St. Louis, MO 63119

SHAKESPEARE FESTIVAL ST. LOUIS
14 S. Euclid Ave.
St. Louis, MO 63108

ST. LOUIS BLACK REPERTORY
634 N Grand, #10-F
St. Louis, MO 63103

ST. LOUIS SHAKESPEARE COMPANY
5535 Waterman Boulevard
St. Louis, MO 63112

STAGES ST. LOUIS
104 N. Clay
St. Louis, MO 63122

STARLIGHT THEATRE ASSOCIATION
OF KANSAS CITY
6601 Swope Pkwy.
Kansas City, MO 64132
www.kcstarlight.com

UNIVERSITY OF MISSOURI ALUMNI
123 Reynolds Alumni Center
Columbia, MO 65211

Nebraska

BRIGIT SAINT BRIGIT THEATRE
1901 South 72nd Street
Omaha, NE 68124

HAYMARKET THEATRE
803 Q Street
Lincoln, NE 68508

NEBRASKA REPERTORY THEATRE
University of Nebraska
215 Temple
Lincoln, NE 68588

NEBRASKA SHAKESPEARE FESTIVAL
Creighton University
2500 California Plaza
Omaha, NE 68178
www.neshakespeare.creighton.edu

OMAHA COMMUNITY PLAYHOUSE
Nebraska Theatre Caravan
6915 Cass Street
Omaha, NE 68132

ONE'S COMPANY
2240 Lake St.
Lincoln, NE 68502

OPERA OMAHA INC
1625 Street, Suite 100
Omaha, NE 68102

SWAN THEATRE AT WYUKA
3600 "0" Street
Lincoln, NE 68510

UNIVERSITY OF NEBRASKA
215 Temple 12th &. R
Lincoln, NE 68588

WEST NEBRASKA ART CENTER
P.O. Box U2
Scottsbluff, NE 69361

Ohio

ACT OUT PRODUCTIONS
2517 North Fourth St.
Columbus, OH 43202

THEATRICAL SKETCH COLLECTIVE
56 W. Russell Street
Columbus, OH 43215
(614) 224-6346, Fax: (412) 363-4799

CHILDRENS THEATRE
1349 E McMillan Street
Cincinnati, OH 45206

CINCINNATI OPERA
1241 Elm Street
Cincinnati, OH 45202

CINCINNATI PLAYHOUSE IN THE
PARK
P.O. Box 6537
Cincinnati, OH 45206

CINCINNATI SHAKESPEARE FEST
717-719 Race Street
Cincinnati, OH 45202
www.cincyshakes.com

CINCINNATI SYMPHONY
1241 Elm Street
Cincinnati, OH 45210

CINCINNATI YOUNG PEOPLES
THEATRE
P.O. Box 5255
Cincinnati, OH 45205

CONTEMPORARY AMERICAN
THEATRE
775 High St., 2nd Floor
Columbus, OH 43215

ENSEMBLE THEATRE OF CINCINNATI
1127 Vine St.
Cincinnati, OH 45210

FIRST FRONTIER INC
P.O. Box C
105 E Market St.
Xenia, OH 45385

HUMAN RACE THEATRE CO
126 N. Main St., Suite 300
Dayton, OH 45402

MIAMI UNIVERSITY
125 Center for the Performing Arts
Oxford, OH 45056

NEW EDGECLIFF THEATRE
3972 Trevor Avenue
Cincinati, OH 45211

OTTERBEIN COLLEGE THEATRE
Dept. of Theatre
Westerville, OH 43081

RED HERRING THEATRE CO
617 E 3rd Ave.
Columbus, OH 43201

RHYTHM IN SHOES
126 North Main Street, Suite 420
Dayton, OH 45402

SENIOR REPERTORY OF OH
THEATRE CO
51 Jefferson Avenue
Columbus, OH 43215

STAGE 5 REP
2517 N. 4th St.
Columbus, OH 43202

WILMINGTON COLLEGE OHIO
251 Ludovic Street
Wilmington, OH 45177

UNIVERSITY OF DAYTON
300 College Park Avenue
Dayton, OH 45469

Oklahoma

JEWEL BOX THEATRE
3700 North Walker
Oklahoma City, OK 73118

LIGHT OPERA OKLAHOMA
2210 South Main Street
Tulsa, OK 74114

LYRIC THEATRE OF OKLAHOMA
1727 NW 16th Street
Oklahoma City, OK 73106
www.lyrictheatreok.com

OK REP!
450 W. Seventh St. #710
Tulsa, OK 74119
www.okreptheatre.com

OKLAHOMA CITY THEATRE
P.O. Box 18226
Oklahoma City, OK 73154

OKLAHOMA SHAKESPEARE FESTIVAL
P.O. Box 1074
Durant, OK 74702

SYNCHRONICITY THEATRE
COMPANY
P. O. Box 18226
Oklahoma City, OK 73154

THEATRE ARTS CHILDREN'S THEATRE
2034 West Houston
Broken Arrow, OK 74012

THEATRE TULSA
450 West 7th Street, Suite 1101
Tulsa, OK 74119

TRT "THE REP"
309 E. 2nd Street
Tulsa, OK 74120

Wisconsin

AMERICAN PLAYERS THEATRE
P.O. Box 819
Spring Green, WI 53588
www.americanplayers.org

BRAVO PRODUCTIONS
33 South Main Street
Fond du lac, WI 54935

BRUMDER MANSION
3046 West Wisconsin Avenue
Milwaukee, WI 53208

CEDAR CREEK REPERTORY COMPANY
P.O. Box 154
Cedarburg, WI 53012

CORNERSTONE THEATRE COMPANY
3046 W. Wisconsin Avenue
Milwaukee, WI 53208

DICK KLOPCIC PRODUCTIONS
1131 Janesville Ave.
Fort Atkinson, WI 53538

DOOR SHAKESPEARE
P.O. Box 351
Baileys Harbor, WI 54202

EASTBROOK CHURCH
4555 N. 150th St.
Brookfield, WI 53005

FIRST STAGE MILWAUKEE
DBA First Stage Children's
929 N. Water St.
Milwaukee, WI 53202

HANSBERRY-SANDS THEATRE CO
P.O. Box 511367
Milwaukee, WI 53203

KLOPCIC FAMILY PRODUCTIONS LLC
1131 Janesville Ave.
Ft. Atkinson, WI 53538

LAKE PEPIN PLAYERS
P.O. Box 163
Pepin, WI 54759

LOVE LETTERS LIMITED
1520 West Greenbriar Lane
Mequon, WI 53092

MADISON REPERTORY THEATRE
122 State St., Suite 201
Madison, WI 53703

MILWAUKEE CHAMBER THEATRE
158 N. Broadway, 5th Floor
Milwaukee, WI 53202
www.chamber-theatre.com

MILWAUKEE REPERTORY THEATRE
108 E. Wells St.
Milwaukee, WI 53202

MILWAUKEE SHAKESPEARE
COMPANY
225 E. St. Paul Ave., Suite 205
Milwaukee, WI 53202
www.milwaukeeshakespeare.com

NEW COURT THEATRE
136 West Grand Avenue
Beloit, WI 53511

NEXT ACT THEATRE
P.O. Box 394
Milwaukee, WI 53201
www.nextact.org

OLD GEM
116 S Knowles Avenue
New Richmond, WI 54017

PENINSULA PLAYERS THEATRE
W4351 Peninsula Players Rd.
Fish Creek, WI 54212

RENAISSANCE THEATRE WORKS
10324 W Vienna Ave.
Wauwatosa, WI 53222

SKYLIGHT OPERA THEATRE CORP
158 N Broadway
Milwaukee, WI 53202

STAGE DOOR THEATER
3703 Town Park Road
Sturgeon Bay, WI 54235

STEPPING OUT PRODUCIONS
2515 Lefeber Avenue
Wauwatosa, WI 53213

THEATRE X INC
158 North Broadway
Milwaukee, WI 53202

THIRD AVENUE PLAYHOUSE
239 North 3rd Avenue
P.O. Box 843
Sturgeon Bay, WI 54235

UNIVERSITY OF WISCONSIN
P.O. Box 413
Milwaukee, WI 53201

Western Region Equity Theaters

Arizona

ACTORS THEATRE OF PHOENIX
911 North 4th Street
Phoenix, AZ 85004

ARIZONA JEWISH THEATRE
COMPANY
444 West Camelback Road, # 208
Phoenix, AZ 85013

INVISIBLE THEATRE
1400 North 1st Avenue
Tucson, AZ 85719

PHOENIX THEATRE
100 East McDowell Road
Phoenix, AZ 85004

SHAKESPEARE SEDONA
6858 North 85th Street
Scottsdale, AZ 85250

California

COLONY THEATRE COMPANY
555 North 3rd Street
Burbank, CA 91502

ENSEMBLE THEATRE COMPANY
914 Santa Barbara Street
Santa Barbara, CA 93101

FOOTHILL THEATRE COMPANY
P.O. Box 1812
Nevada City, CA 95959

HERMOSA BEACH PLAYHOUSE
2226 Artesia Boulevard
Redondo Beach, CA 90278

INTERNATIONAL CITY THEATRE
"One World Trade Center," Suite 300
P.O. Box 32069
Long Beach CA 90832

KINGSMEN SHAKESPEARE COMPANY
P.O. Box 1772
Thousand Oaks, CA 91358

PALM CANYON THEATRE
538 North Palm Canyon Drive
Palm Springs, CA 92262

RUBICON THEATRE COMPANY
1006 East Main Street, Suite 300
Ventura, CA 93001

SACRAMENTO THEATRE COMPANY
1419 H Street
Sacramento, CA 95814

SAN DIEGO REPERTORY THEATRE
79 Horton Plaza
San Diego, CA, 92101

SANTA SUSANA REPERTORY
COMPANY
P.O. Box 1923
Thousand Oaks, CA 91358

SHAKESPEARE SANTA CRUZ
Theatre Arts Center/UCSC
1156 High Street
Santa Cruz, CA 95064

SIERRA REPERTORY THEATRE
PO Box 3030
Sonora, CA 95370

THEATRE FOR CHILDREN
B Street Theatre
P.O. Box 19206
Sacramento, CA 95816

Colorado

CURIOUS THEATRE COMPANY
1080 Acoma Street
Denver, CO 80204

FLYOVER PRODUCTIONS
10081 South Blackbird Circle
Higlands Ranch, CO 80130

LIZARD HEAD THEATRE COMPANY
P.O. Box 1557
Telluride, CO 81435

Idaho

IDAHO SHAKESPEARE FESTIVAL
P.O. Box 9365
Boise, ID 83707

NEW THEATRE COMPANY INC
P.O. Box 1163
Sun Valley, ID 83353

Nevada

NEVADA SHAKESPEARE
454 Glenmanor Drive
Reno, NV 89509

ROYAL STRATFORD SHAKESPEARE
PLAYERS
Starbright Theatre Company
2215 Thomas Ryan Boulevard
Las Vegas, NV 89134

New Mexico

ZYGOTE PRO-CREATIONS
700 1st Street NW
Albuquerque, NM 87102

Oregon

ARTISTS REPERTORY THEATRE
1516 SW Alder
Portland, OR 97205

Texas

ALLIED THEATRE GROUP INC.
1300 Gendy Street
Fort Worth, TX 76107

AUSTIN PLAYHOUSE
P.O. Box 50533
Austin, TX 78763

AUSTIN SHAKESPEARE FESTIVAL
P.O. Box 683
Austin, TX 78767

CIRCLE THEATRE INC.
P.O. Box 470456
Fort Worth, TX 76147

DALLAS CHILDREN'S THEATRE
5938 Skillman
Dallas, TX 75231

GRANBURY OPERA HOUSE
133 East Pearl Street
Granbury, TX 76048

LYRIC STAGE INC
3333 North MacArthur Boulevard
Irving, TX 75062

MAIN STREET THEATRE
2540 Times Boulevard
Houston, TX 77005

PLANO REPERTORY THEATRE INC.
P.O. Box 861859
Plano, TX 75086

STAGES REPERTORY THEATRE
3201 Allen Parkway #101
Houston, TX 77019

STATE THEATER COMPANY
719 Congress Avenue
Austin, TX 78701

THEATRE THREE INC.
2800 South Street, Suite 168
Dallas, TX 75201

WATER TOWER THEATRE
15650 Addison Road
Addison, TX 75001

ZACHARY SCOTT THEATRE CENTER
1510 Toomey Road
Austin, TX 78704

Utah

SALT LAKE ACTING COMPANY
168 West 500 N
Salt Lake City, UT 84103

TUACAHN CENTER FOR THE ARTS
1100 Tuacahn Drive
Ivins, UT 84738

Washington

BOOK-IT REPERTORY THEATRE
305 Harrison Street
Seattle, WA 98109

EMPTY SPACE THEATRE
3509 Fremont Ave. North
Seattle, WA 98103

HARLEQUIN PRODUCTIONS
202 Fourth Avenue E
Olympia, WA 98501

REBOUND ONE PRODUCTIONS -
ACT THEATRE
Kreielsheimer Place
700 Union Street
Seattle, WA 98104

SEATTLE SHAKESPEARE COMPANY
P.O. Box 19595
Seattle, WA 98109

TACOMA ACTORS GUILD
901 Broadway, 6th Floor
Tacoma, WA 98402

Appendix IV |

Combined Regional Theater Auditions

Illinois Theater Association

1225 W. Belmont Ave.
Chicago, IL 60657-3205
Ph: 773-929-7288, x 18 and 19
Fax: 773-327-1404
www.iltheassoc.org
Application Deadline: Mid-February
Audition Date: Early March
Registration Fee: $30

Auditions are open to students enrolled in college and university programs, college and university students who intend to move to Chicago, non-professional members of an Illinois community theater and freelance, non-union actors.

Applicants must first audition at a preliminary screening audition. Screening evaluations will be done by a committee of professional actors and directors and representatives from the League of Chicago Theaters and the Illinois Theater Association.

Approximately sixty individuals will be selected for the final callback auditions, held a day after the preliminaries. Attending the callbacks will be representatives of Chicago and national casting directors, resident theaters, summer stock companies, and academic assistantship programs.

Indiana Theatre Association/Algonquin Project (ITAP)
Wheeler Arts Community
Room #227
1035 Sanders Street
Indianapolis, IN 46203
Ph: 317-634-4670
Email: itap@intheatre.org
intheatre.org
Deadline: varies (see website)
Audition/Interview Date: varies (see website)
Fee: $20

Auditions/Interviews are for union and nonunion actors, designers, and technicians seeking summer and year-round paid acting or design/technical theatre positions. Nonunion applicants and applicants with little professional experience must be recommended by a professional director or a director working in academia.

Applications will be available online at *intheatre.org*.

The Indianapolis Theatre Fringe Festival
PO Box 532355
Indianapolis, IN 46253
Email: kmr@speaksure.com
www.indyfringe.org
Deadline: Mid-February
Audition Date: Late February
Fee: $20

Auditions are for union and nonunion actors seeking summer and year-round paid acting positions. Nonunion applicants and applicants with little professional experience must be recommended by a professional director or a director working in academia.

Send your completed application with your photo and fee to the above address.

Midwest Theater Auditions
Webster University
470 East Lockwood
St. Louis, MO 63119-3194
Ph: 314-968-6937
Fax: 314-963-6048
Email: mwta@webster.edu
www.webster.edu/depts/finearts/theater/mwta

Application Deadline: Mid-December
Audition Date: Mid-February
Fee: $30

These auditions are for Equity and non-Equity performers looking for paid positions in summer stock theaters, outdoor dramas, Shakespeare festivals, year-round theaters, college and professional training programs, and internships.

Although there are more than 450 audition slots available, audition slots are limited and are assigned on a first-come basis. All applicants do not get a slot, so apply ASAP.

National Dinner Theatre Association
NDTA
P.O. Box 726,
Marshall, MI 49068
Ph: 517-857-3851
Fax: 517-857-2017
www.ndta.com
Fee is $35.00.

National Outdoor Drama Auditions
Institute of Outdoor Drama
CB #3240 1700 Airport Rd.
University of North Carolina
Chapel Hill, NC 27599-3240
Ph: 919-962-1328
Email: outdoor@unc.edu
www.unc.edu/depts/outdoor
Application Deadline: Early March
Audition Date: Mid-March
Fee: $30

Applicants must be at least eighteen years old to audition, have had previous experience in theater and be available for a nine to twelve week commitment during the summer, which includes two weeks of rehearsal.

Outdoor dramas are historical plays performed in large, scenic outdoor amphitheaters across the country. Broad and welldefined defines the style for these shows. They are stories of dramatic historic events or represent the lives of historic figures through music, dance, and theatrical spectacle. Casts are large and require good acting, singing, and dance skills. Performers with stunt, stage combat, and horseback skills are often needed also.

Typically, 150 – 200 people from fifty or more colleges and universities in twenty states compete for jobs offered by fifteen to twenty theaters recruiting from around the country.

Positions pay in the range of $150/week to $500/week ($200 – $300 per week on average) depending on the theater company and position. Worker's comp insurance, housing, and some meals are often included in the compensation plan.

New England Theatre Conference, Inc.
198 Tremont Street # 502
Boston, MA 02116-4750
Ph: 617-851-8535
Email mail@netonline.org
www.netonline.org
Application Deadline: Late January
Audition dates: Mid-March
Fee: $30.00 – $55.00

These auditions are open to non-Equity performers and college students, not to Equity members, high school students or anyone under eighteen years old. All applicants become NETC members. The fee is nonrefundable; however, applicants who not selected for an audition slot will have their application and résumé information forwarded to the casting people who do hire directly from the applications.

About sixty producers, talent agents, and representatives from training institutions will audition prescreened applicants in acting and/or musical talent. Both job-in and full-season openings are available in Equity and non-Equity theaters, college-based theaters, repertory companies, Shakespeare festivals, Renaissance festivals, outdoor dramas, musical theater, touring companies, children's theater, dinner theater, and intern or apprentice programs.

Approximately 750 of over 1,000 applicants will be given appointments for an audition. Only experienced and trained performers should apply for an audition slot.

New Jersey Theatre Alliance
163 Madison Ave, Suite 500
Morristown, NJ 07960
Ph: 973-540-0515 x11
Fax: 973-540-9799
Email: info@njtheatrealliance.org
www.njtheatrealliance.org
Application deadline: late June
Audition date: late August

The New Jersey Theatre Alliance, the association of professional Equity Theatres of New Jersey, conducts combined lottery auditions for both Equity and non-Equity actors and actresses once a year, by appointment only.

Northwest Drama Conference Auditions
University of Idaho—Moscow
David Lee-Painter, Chair
Department of Theatre and Film
Moscow, ID 83844-3074
Ph: 208-885-6197
Fax: 208-885-2558
Email cvasek @uidaho.edu
www.cwu.edu/~nwdc
Application Deadline: Late January
Audition Date: Mid February
Fees: $45 - $75

The Northwest Drama Conference takes place in a different location each year, so consequently these auditions rotate to different locales each year. In 2005, the conference will be held in Ashland, Oregon.

The Ohio Theatre Alliance
North Central Regional Auditions and Interviews
c/o Theatre Department
Muskingum College
New Concord OH 43762
Ph: 740-826-8373
Fax: 740-826-8109
Email: drao@muskingum.edu
www.ohiotheateralliance.org
Application Deadline: Mid-January
Audition Date: Early February
Fee: Approx. $35

These auditions are open to Equity and non-Equity performers and students who are eighteen years or older. Positions available include summer, year-round, paying and non-paying positions, as well as graduate training programs, apprenticeships, internships, touring groups, children's theater, outdoor drama, and summer stock.

Rocky Mountain Theater Association
Summer Theater Auditions
Western Wyoming College
P.O. Box 428/C-564
Rock Springs, WY 82902-0428
www.rmta.net
Application Deadline: Mid-January
Audition Date: Early February
Fee: $70 - $85 which includes required registration fee for convention and membership.

Southeastern Theatre Conference
PO Box 9868
Greensboro, NC 27429-0868
Ph: 336-272-3645
www.setc.org
General Email: setc@setc.org

SETC hosts two sets of auditions for Equity and non-equity actors and dancers seeking positions with professional companies.

FALL PROFESSIONAL AUDITIONS: Auditions for Professional Actors only for full-time/year round employment take place the first Sunday and Monday AFTER LABOR DAY each fall. These auditions take place in Charlotte, NC (Sept 12 and 13, 2004).

Actors must apply to receive an audition slot. Application deadline is approximately 4 weeks prior to auditions (August 15, 2004).

Cost is $25.00

To be Qualified to apply as a professional you must:
- Be 19 years of Age
- Not be enrolled in school
- Be available to work full-time
- Have a minimum of 2 professional acting positions with SETC approved professional company(ies)
- Supply a recommendation, in the form of signature, by a professional director who has directed applicant at a professional theatre listed on the application. Full Equity members are exempt from this requirement.

Auditions slots are granted based on qualification(s). Applicants with greater experience and qualifications are given priority.

SPRING AUDITIONS: Auditions for Pre-professionals and Professional for summer or full-time/year round employment. Some summer apprentice/internship positions also available.

Undergraduate Students and other pre-professionals are required to qualify via a state audition in the state in which they are

1) a student, or if non-student,

2) state in which they reside.

Applications vary for each state. Contact SETC for state contact information. SETC registration and application forms are due at time of state audition.

Professionals must apply and qualify for an audition slot:

Application deadline: 2nd Friday of January each year (January 14, 2005).

Auditions take place Thur-Sat during the SETC Annual Convention - the first full Wed - Sunday of each March (Greensboro, NC March 2-6 for 2005).

To attain an audition slot you must:

• Meet the necessary qualifications

• Complete the convention registration form & audition application

• Include the necessary fees to pay SETC membership and audition fee

To be Qualified to apply as a professional you must:

• Be 18 years of Age

• Not be enrolled in school. Note: Graduate Students have the option to go through the state screening procedure or apply as a professional if possessing the necessary experience

• Be available to work summer or full-time

• Have a minimum of 2 professional acting positions with SETC approved professional company(ies)

• Supply a recommendation, in the form of signature, by a professional director who has directed applicant at a professional theatre listed on the application. Full Equity members are exempt from this requirement.

Auditions slots are granted based on qualification(s). Applicants with greater experience and qualifications are given priority.

Fees: $85 for student applicants, or $145 for adults. Fee covers SETC membership, conference registration and auditions.

Conference meals and lodging fees are separate.

Visa, Master Card and money orders or certified checks are accepted with applications/registration.

Southwest Theater Association

3000 General Pershing Blvd.
Oklahoma City, OK 73107-6202
Ph/Fax: 405-946-9380
Email: swtajimmyv@theshop.net
www.southwest-theater.com

Professional auditions are usually held in mid-February. See web page for further information.

SWTA is not doing Professional auditions this spring SWTA will be doing the SETC out-of-region auditions at Plano, TX, November 5, 2004. Contact *www.setc.org* for further information.

StrawHat Auditions

1771 Post Rd. East, # 315
Westport, CT 06880
www.strawhat-auditions.co
Auditions are held in late March in New York
Application Deadline: Mid-February
Registration Fee: $28
Audition Fee: $40

The registration fee is non-refundable. If accepted to audition, then the additional $40 applies: the $40 fee is returned if applicant is not selected.

This audition is open to non-Equity actors, dancers, and singers eighteen or older, who are beginning or continuing professional careers in the theater. Most auditions are for summer stock theaters, but some regional theaters offer year-round positions. Approximately 500 performing positions are usually offered.

Applicants are screened in a competitive process, and accepted applicants have their picture and résumé published in the Straw Hat National Resource Book, which is distributed to all attending theaters.

All applicants, including those who are not selected to audition, have their picture and résumé posted in the StrawHat Casting OnLine database as part of a searchable online profile created from their application information.

Theater Auditions in Wisconsin

721 Lowell Center
610 Langdon St.
Madison, WI 53703-1195
Ph: 608-263-6736
Email liberalarts@dcs.wisc.edu
www.dcs.wisc.edu/lsa/theater/auditions
Registration Deadline: End of January
Audition Date: Second Saturday in February
Fee: $35.00

These auditions are open to non-Equity performers, dancers, designers, technicians, and support staff. Positions offered include full-time, part-time, and summer work, paid and un-paid with touring companies, professional theater, graduate training, outdoor drama, musical theater, children's and youth theater, and intern or apprentice programs.

Theater Bay Area General Auditions
657 Mission St., Ste. 402
San Francisco, CA 94105
Ph: 414-957-1557
Fax: 415-957-1556
Email: dale@theaterbayarea.org
www.theaterbayarea.org
Application Deadline: Varies but usually Mid-December
Audition Dates: Varies but usually late January – early February

Auditions are open to all Equity and non-Equity actors.

Non-Equity actors must be TBA (Theater Bay Area) members.

Membership Fee: $61/yr.

The deadline to join or renew membership is Mid-December. Non-Equity actors must also fulfill one of the following:

- Have accumulated the equivalent of one year of full-time acting training
- Performed in at least eight non-academic stage productions

Guidelines change slightly each year, so check *www.theatrebayare.org* for the most current information.

Send application, membership/renewal application form and fee (unless you are a current, paid-up member), headshot, résumé and proof of Equity membership (if applicable)

Incomplete application packets will not be considered.

Applications are screened by a panel composed of Bay Area casting and theater directors and qualified applicants are entered in a lottery drawing for audition slots. Applicants are notified by early January as to whether or not they have received an audition slot.

Actors new to the Bay Area, actors of color, physically challenged actors, actors under eighteen years or over fifty years are actively encouraged to apply.

These auditions are very competitive. Slightly more than half of the applications receive audition slots.

Unified Professional Theatre Auditions (UPTA)
Playhouse on the Square
51 S. Cooper St.
Memphis, TN 38104
Ph: 901-725-0776
Fax: 901-272-7530
Email: upta@upta.org
www.upta.org
Early Deadline Date: End of December

Audition Dates: Early February
Fee: $25 – $40

UPTA is a set of auditions and interviews organized for actors, production personnel, and producers so that the greatest number of quality actors and production personnel who are available year-round can be seen by quality professional theater companies

For actors and production personnel, the auditions will provide access to professional companies who offer:
- paid year-round employment, OR
- paid job-in employment, OR
- paid internships

For theaters and production companies, the auditions will provide access to actors who will be:
- available for employment YEAR-ROUND!
- auditioning in a proper theater atmosphere—onstage at Playhouse on the Square

It will also provide companies access to production personnel who are available year-round.

Criteria for our Actors and Production Personnel are as follows:

Pre-Professional Auditions
- Actor must receive UNDERGRADUATE degree (BA, BFA, etc.) in theatre by September 1 of the year they audition, AND
- Actor must be available for work year-round (in other words, not going back to school in the Fall or Spring), AND
- Actor must have registration signed by the department head of their theatre program.

Regular Auditions
- Actor must be available for work year-round (in other words, not going back to school in the Fall or Spring), and
- Actor must have a post-graduate degree (MA, MFA, Ph.D., etc.) in theatre by September 1 of the year they audition, or
- Have registration signed by a registered UPTA theatre, or
- Have registration signed by a current Theatre Communications Group (TCG) member theatre, or
- Have attended previous UPTAs, or
- Be a member of Equity or EMC program.

Production Interviews

- Production personnel must be available for work year-round (in other words, not going back to school in the Fall or Spring), and
- Production personnel must have an undergraduate degree (BA, BFA, etc.) in their respective technical, administrative, or artistic field by September 1 of the year they audition, or
- Have registration signed by a registered UPTA theatre, or
- Have registration signed by a current Theatre Communications Group (TCG) member theatre, or
- Have attended previous UPTAs, or
- Be an Equity stage manager.

Registration Information

Actors & Production Personnel = $25 through 12/31, $40 thereafter
Companies = $90 through 10/31, $140 thereafter
For more information, visit us online at *www.upta.org* or send SASE to:
Michael Detroit, Audition Coordinator
Unified Professional Theatre Auditions,
51 S. Cooper St.
Memphis, TN, 38104
Ph: 901-725-0776
Fax: 901-272-7530

University/Resident Theater Association (U/RTA)

National Unified Auditions/Interviews and MAPs
1560 Broadway, Ste. 712
New York, NY 10036
Ph: 212-221-1130
Fax: 212-869-2752
www.urta.com
National Unified Auditions and Interviews (NUA/Is)
Application available on-line at www.urta.com
Application Deadline: November
Application fee $80-$100
No Applications Will Be Accepted After Early December.

Screening Auditions for Acting Candidates, but Open Call Auditions guarantee all actors the opportunity to appear before interested school recruiters.

January - New York City
February - Chicago, IL
February - San Francisco, CA
September (MAPS) - New York City

NUA/I process is designed for graduating, degree candidates who are seeking advanced training through graduate school. Several hundred positions are offered annually primarily through acceptance in M.F.A. graduate programs. Casting opportunities are also available in Shakespeare Festivals, resident theater companies both on and off campus, and various seasonal activities.

The Master Audition Programs (MAPS) is for Master of Fine Arts candidates about to graduate, or who have graduated in the preceding two years. Graduation from an U/RTA member program is required. Select graduates will audition for casting directors, talent agents, and other representatives from participating professional theater organizations.

For further information, go to *www.urta.com*.

Appendix V | # Theater- Related Websites

Below is a list of sites of interest to theater buffs, professionals, and academics. The desciptions of each site comes directly from its pages.

Sit down for an hour or so and just look at all the information that's out there. Try a couple of word searches and see what comes up. I recommend this because I want to send educated actors into the breach!

memory.loc.gov American Memory Collection of the Library of Congress: Photographs of American theaters.

www.tonisant.com/aitg Applied and Interactive Theater Guide: Many links, e.g., to improvisation pages, drama therapy, psychodrama, theater of the oppressed, etc.

www.artswire.org "ArtsWire is an 'online communication for the arts,' a program of the New York Foundation for the Arts."

www.vl-theater.com "Whether your interests are the London theater of the 17th century or Korean mask dramas and puppetry, this site . . . is a tremendously authoritative guide to quality theater and drama resources on the web. There is an exhaustive range of links to international online articles, journals, museums, organizations and theater companies and annotated links to a rich and truly fascinating series of collections of theater images. This site is a valuable first stop for theater studies scholars." —CTI Centre for Textual Studies, Oxford

www.msstate.edu/Fineart_Online "Fineart Forum Resource Directory: Online Hotlinks directory of over one thousand online resources, exhibits, scholarly works, and interactive art projects."

www.carnegielibrary.org/subject/theater/indexes.html "Intuitions is maintained by a student-run experimental theater company at the University of Pennsylvania. This site focuses on college theater and has hundreds of links."

www.stetson.edu/departments/csata/thr_guid.html "McCoy's Guide to Theater and Performance Studies has significant stagecraft and technical theater resources and includes many little-known links."

www.playbill.com/theatrecentral/sites "Theatre Central contains resources, a directory of theater professionals, theater listings from around the world, an online journal, call board, and discussion forum."

usinfo.state.gov/usa/infousa/arts "U.S. State Department. Their guide to theater resources on the Internet that also contains information on how to use the Internet, explanation of different types of documents, etc., which includes listservs and newsgroups."

www.uky.edu/Subject/theater.html "World Wide Web Arts Resources compiles information about government, local, and academic sources available via the Internet. The performing arts section includes information and links to dozens of independent theater and many online journals."

www.wmich.edu/theatre/directions/assoc.php This site has links to most academic theater associations, a must if you are thinking about teaching.

Online Journals

www.aislesay.com *Aisle Say* is the Internet magazine of stage reviews and opinion. Includes reviews from the United States and around the world.

artdeadlineslist.com *Art Deadlines* is a list of deadlines for publications, contests, grants, etc. focusing mostly on the visual arts.

www.artsreach.com *Arts Reach* is an online journal dedicated to increasing funding to the arts.

www.chronicle.com *The Chronicle of Higher Education:* "Academe This Week" is a supplement to the print journal.

How to Get a Visa to Work as an Actor in the United States

by Edward C. Beshara

Actors: Coming to America

Actors are an essential and integral part of the entertainment industry in the United States. American films, television shows, and theatrical performances are shown and distributed not only in the United States but worldwide. Today we are seeing an increase in more and more foreign actors who are coming to America to work in the entertainment industry. When we think of actors we also refer to them as artists and entertainers. Sometimes we use the words interchangeably. The scope of this chapter is to show how actors, artists, or entertainers who are nationals of other countries may obtain the appropriate visa to work and live in the United States.

Terminology

The immigration laws and rules govern what types of visas may be obtained by foreign nationals in seeking entry to work and live in the United States. An actor may obtain what is called a nonimmigrant visa so that they may work in the United States for a temporary period of authorized stay. Other actors may obtain immigrant visas so that they may permanently reside and work in the United States.

If the intent of the actor is to only temporarily live and work in the United States, then a nonimmigrant visa is appropriate. When the actor intends to permanently live and work in the United States, then the appropriate visa to obtain is the immigrant visa.

Students

Foreign nationals who wish to further their studies in the theater and the arts and further their acting education may obtain a student visa to enter and study in the United States.

First, the foreign national student will have to obtain permission from the American university or college to enter a course program comprised of either a two-year diploma, a four-year degree, or a master's degree. The course or study programs can be in a number of different areas, namely the dramatic arts, theater, television, and motion picture areas.

The American college or university needs to have the authority by the immigration service agency (USCIS, which is under the Department of Homeland Security) to be able to issue and sign a form called an I-20. This I-20 form is the school's acceptance of the foreign national to be permitted to attend their course program full-time. One of the requirements is that the foreign national student has the financial ability to pay for the coursework, room and board, and course program for at least one academic year. The foreign national student will then present the I-20 form and a nonimmigrant application form to the U.S. consulate where they reside so that they may obtain an F-1 student visa to enter and study in the United States.

For the first academic year the student is permitted to work on school grounds for not more than twenty hours per week. If as part of their coursework professors require the students to work off campus at theaters or on television or in film, then as part of their coursework off campus they may be able to be paid by the employers at the various locations where they are completing their curricular training for work.

After the first academic year, based upon economic ability and the need to continue to pay for the cost of courses and living, the foreign national student may apply for employment authorization so that they can work off campus for not more than twenty hours per week or full-time during official school breaks. Of course, to maintain their permission to be employed, the foreign national student needs to be continually enrolled full-time to complete their course of study. After completing the diploma or degree courses, the foreign national students are permitted to obtain work authorization for one year to complete practical training within an industry that covers their major study. In this instance, they are foreign national students during this practical year working in theater, television, or film.

Extraordinary Ability Actors or Entertainers

Foreign national actors or entertainers who have extraordinary abilities and who wish to enter the United States temporarily to live and work may obtain a nonimmigrant visa known as the O-1 visa.

To obtain an O-1 visa the actor must demonstrate that they have sustained national or international acclaim. In addition, the foreign national actor must submit documentation showing that they are coming to the United States to continue work by using their extraordinary abilities.

In obtaining the O-1 visa the foreign national actor may offer evidence by documentation showing their extraordinary abilities and distinction. The evidence or documentation would show that the foreign national actor has a degree of skill and recognition substantially above other actors in the field and, of course, are prominent or renowned.

The type of evidence or documentation to show that the foreign national actor may qualify for the O-1 visa may include nomination for or achievement of well-known national or international awards such as the Academy Award, Emmy, or Grammy.

At least three major types of evidence would be needed to obtain an O-1 visa. Besides national or international awards, the types of evidence may include the following:

- The foreign national has received or may demand a high fee for their performance
- has obtained nationally or internationally known success
- has been nationally or internationally recognized through publications especially in their field, which may include critical reviews, stories, or written interviews
- has obtained substantial recognition from critics, industry groups, and peers
- the foreign national actor has performed in well-known plays, movies, or television productions
- such performances have been recognized by distinguished writers or publications in the industry.

The foreign national actor may present other documentation to show distinction or extraordinary ability.

Accompanying Employees

Foreign nationals who need to accompany O-1 foreign national actors may obtain an O-2 visa. To obtain an O-2 visa the employee accompanying the O-1 foreign national actor must:

- show that they are coming to the United States just to assist in the O-1's performance
- be an integral part in assisting the O-1 national actor in their performance in the United States

- have essential skills and experience in assisting the O-1 national actor
- show that these skills and experience cannot be performed by U.S. workers
- show that they do have a foreign home that they have no intention of abandoning.

Usually the accompanying employee has had a preexisting long-standing relationship with the O-1 foreign national actor.

Family Members

Spouses and minor children under twenty-one years of age are all considered dependents of the O-1 foreign national actor and may accompany the O-1 actor to the United States by obtaining the O-3 visa.

Consultations

Before the foreign national actor can obtain the O-1 visa, a statement from a union in the industry known as a *consultation* will have to be obtained. The union or collective bargaining representative will provide an advisory statement consultation referring to the nature of the foreign national actor's work, the foreign national's extraordinary or distinguished qualifications, and a statement making it clear that they have no objection to the foreign national actor working in the United States.

U.S. Government Steps in Obtaining the O Visa

The U.S. employer, which may include the motion picture company, television company or U.S. agents, or theatrical group, will file a form (petition) with the U.S. government's immigration service center having jurisdiction over the location where the foreign national actor will be employed.

As stated above, the petitioner may be a U.S. agent and may include traditional management or booking agents or other authorized individuals or companies that may serve as a foreign national actor's employer's agent for a limited purpose.

The supporting evidence, which includes documentation showing extraordinary ability or distinction, and the consultation statement is filed with the petition.

The petition must be filed within six months of the start date of the foreign national actor's starting employment. If the foreign national actor is going to be employed or provide services at a number of different locations throughout the United States, then the petition must be filed with the immigration service center having jurisdiction over the petitioner's address as specified on the petition. In addition, if the foreign national actor works for more than one employer, then the U.S. employers must file separate petitions unless a U.S. agent files the petition.

Expedited Procedure

In certain circumstances the U.S. petitioner and or foreign national actor may desire to have the U.S. government immigration service make a quick decision on the petition. The foreign national actor or U.S. employer may have certain deadlines or start dates for the production or performance, so time, of course, is of the essence. For expedited processing by the U.S. immigration service, a filing fee of $1,000 is required, while a filing fee of $2,000 is required for accompanying employee foreign nationals who wish to obtain the O-2 visa.

Temporary Period of Authorized Stay

The O petitions may be approved for an initial temporary authorized period of three years, while extensions of stay to continue or complete the performance or event may be obtained for one year at a time.

U.S. Consulate Processing

If the O petition is approved, then the approval notice is wire-transferred to the U.S. consulate having jurisdiction over where the foreign national actor, accompanying employees, or dependents reside. The foreign nationals will prepare and submit nonimmigrant application forms with photographs for submission to the U.S. consulate for review. Currently every nonimmigrant application will require a personal interview by the U.S. consulate. There will be security checks performed on each nonimmigrant application. It is important to have the application forms and supporting documentation in order to make sure the process is handled efficiently by the U.S. consulate.

Once approved, the appropriate O visa is issued and stamped in the passport. The visa stamp will include the photograph of the foreign national, the issuance date, and expiration date of the visa and usually will allow multiple entries. That is, the visa is the document that allows a foreign national to apply for entry into the United States at the port of entry, for example, seaports, airports, or land ports.

Once the foreign national arrives at the port of entry, the O visa is presented to the U.S. immigration service for review and possible questions. The U.S. immigration service will then issue an I-94 card, "the arrival/departure" card, which will state the date of entry and the period of authorized stay.

Acting Groups

Foreign national actors in artistic groups (not individuals) who are internationally known may obtain P-1 visas to enter and work in the United States.

To be considered for the P-1 visa, the acting groups must show that they are internationally recognized through evidence of documentation indicating the following:

- that the acting group has received a high level of achievement and has been recognized above other acting groups for a sustained and substantial period of time
- that the acting group has performed regularly for a period of one year
- and proof that each member of the acting group has been employed on a regular basis by the group.

The foreign national acting group under the P-1 category will be coming to the United States to perform certain events and/or to conduct tours. In addition, the foreign national group may show that they:

- have received international recognition to obtain the P-1 visa by showing the group has been nominated for or received major international awards for outstanding achievement in their field
- will be coming to the United States to continue to perform in productions or events with distinguished reputations
- will continue to command a high salary or substantial remuneration
- or by coming to the United States and performing certain productions or events will gain significant recognition from critics and recognized industry publications.

The United States Citizenship and Immigration Services (USCIS) has recently developed beneficial policies for the entering of foreign national acting groups. That is, the immigration service only requires that 75 percent of the acting group's members must have had a sustained and substantial relationship with the acting group for at least a year, and as long as the foreign national acting group is recognized nationally as being outstanding in their discipline, the international recognition requirement is waived.

Reciprocal Exchange Programs

Foreign national actors either individually or part of a group under the direction of a reciprocal exchange program between U.S. organizations and their own country organizations will provide for the temporary exchange of actors or acting groups by allowing the foreign national actor or group to obtain a P-2 visa. In the United States, Actors Equity has been involved in establishing a reciprocal exchange program.

Culturally Unique Actors

Foreign national actors either individually or as a group who are to interpret, coach, or teach a culturally unique acting experience or performance that is influenced by the country of origin, ethnicity, or religion to the American public may obtain a P-3 visa to enter and work in the United States. The culturally unique acting experience or performance may be part of either a commercial or noncommercial program. The P-3 visa category may cover such performances as English Shakespearean actors performing at college or university theaters, as an example.

Accompanying Aliens

All foreign national essential support personnel who are highly skilled and are an integral or important part of the performance of the P-1, P-2, or P-3 foreign nationals can qualify for the P-4 visa to enter and accompany the P foreign nationals.

U.S. Government Steps in Obtaining the P Visa

The U.S. employer, which may include corporations, organizations, or agents (management and booking agents), may file the petition for P status with the immigration service centers having jurisdiction over the petitioner's address as specified on the form. The petitions are filed with supporting documentation such as evidence showing that the foreign national actors either individually or in groups qualify for the specific P status categories. In addition to the supporting evidence, as stated above, the petitioner will submit a consultation, which is a written advisory opinion from an appropriate labor union stating their recommendation that the foreign national actor or group qualifies to enter the United States under the various P status categories. Basically, the consultation is a recommendation and also serves as a no-objection letter to the issuance of P status for the foreign national actor or group.

Temporary Period of Authorized Stay

The P petitions may be approved for the time needed to complete the event or performance, in either case not to exceed one year. P petitions for accompanying foreign nationals' essential support personnel may be authorized to enter the United States for one year. Extensions of stay to continue or complete the performance or event may be obtained for one year at a time.

Expedited Procedures

For expedited processing by the U.S. immigration service, a filing fee of $1,000 is required, while a fee of $2,000 is required for accompanying employee foreign nationals.

U.S. Consulate Processing

The procedure to obtain a P visa at the U.S. Consulate is the same procedure as obtaining the O visas as stated above.

Permanent Residency (Green Card) for Actors

Foreign national actors may self-petition for the approval of permanent residency or an immigrant visa that will allow them to live and work permanently in the United States without time limitations.

Foreign national actors who may qualify for the O-1 visa category on the basis of extraordinary abilities may use the same evidence and documentation for submission of a self-petition for their permanent residency.

If the foreign national actor is currently in the United States under a nonimmigrant status, during this period of legal status the foreign national actor may concurrently file the self-petition and the individual application (including family members, spouse, and minor children) for permanent residency. The filing of the individual application for permanent residency will also include formal requests for permission to obtain employment that allows them to work anywhere and formal request for permission to leave and reenter the United States, both for periods of one-year increments.

Obtaining Permanent Residency through Family Relationships

Foreign national actors who are engaged to be married to U.S. citizens may obtain fiancé visas that will allow them to enter the United States, marry the U.S. citizen within ninety days of entry, and while in the United States apply for U.S. residency. As stated above, the filing of the individual permanent residency application also allows a request to be made for work authorization and permission for travel to leave and return to the United States, while foreign national actors who have previously entered the United States legally and subsequent to their entry into the United States who now decide to marry U.S. citizens may also apply for permanent residency in the United States. After marriage to the U.S. citizen, the foreign national actor's spouse may file the individual application for permanent residency concurrently with the U.S. citizen's spouse's petition or request for the foreign spouse to become a permanent resident of the United States.

Reality Not Fiction

The reality is that the U.S. entertainment industry has and will continue to need foreign national actors. The success of the industry in the United States has been as result of a hiring of foreign national actors. This appendix has shown that there are legal ways and means for foreign national actors to obtain visas to work in the United States in the entertainment industry either on a temporary or permanent basis. Once the foreign national actor or U.S. employer decides that there is a need for a foreign national actor to participate in the performance or event, then the planning process should start immediately. Currently with unusual time delays associated with U.S. government processing and the uncertainty and inconsistency of questions concerning the petition by the United States immigration service, there is a need to spend as much time as possible in the preparation and filing of the respective petitions.

Edward C. Beshara, who wrote this appendix, is an internationally respected immigration lawyer and former president of the American Immigrations Lawyers Association, Central Florida Chapter. He can be contacted at the offices listed below.

Aviewtrans, P.A.
Attorneys at Law
A Full-Service U.S. Immigration Law Firm—Since 1983
Edward C. Beshara
President and CEO/Attorney at Law

Main Corporate Offices: Lee World Center
1850 Lee Rd., Ste. 300
Orlando/Winter Park, FL 32789
Ph: 1-407-629-6455
Fax: 1-407-629-4569
Email: admin@aviewtrans.com
www.aviewtrans.com

Other Offices:
303 Collins St., Level 28
Melbourne, Victoria 3000
Australia
Ph: 61.3.9678.9214
Fax: 61.3.9678.9009

259 George St., Level 22
Sydney CBD, New South Wales 2000
Australia
Ph: 61.2.9255.7742
Fax: 61.2.9247.2417

Appendix VII |

Useful Addresses

Acting World Books
P.O. Box 3899
Hollywood, CA 90078
(818) 905-1345

Actors Equity Association
165 West 46th St.
15th Floor
New York, NY 10019-5214
(212) 869-8530
www.actorsequity.org

AFTRA
260 Madison Ave.
New York, NY 10016
(212) 532-0800
www.aftra.com

Back Stage & Back Stage West
1515 Broadway, 14th Floor
New York, NY 10036
(800) 634-6810
www.backstage.com

Breakdown Services Ltd.
P.O. Box 69277
Los Angeles, CA 90069
(310) 276-9176
www.breakdownservices.com

Daily Variety
5700 Wilshire Blvd., Ste. 120
Los Angeles, CA 90036
(323) 857-6600
www.variety.com

David Nations Photography
1000 Universal Studios Plaza,
B22a, Ste. 132
Orlando, FL 32819
(407) 224-6399
www.davidnationsphotography.com

Photoscan
646 Bryn Mawr St.
Orlando, FL 32804
(800) 352-6367
www.ggphotoscan.com

Producers Masterguide
60 Est 8th Street, 34th Floor
New York, NY 10003-6514
(212) 777-4002
www.producers.masterguide.com

Ross Reports
770 Broadway, 6th Floor
New York, NY 10003
Attn: Blanca
(646) 654-5708
www.ccgdata.com

Samuel French Bookstore
76223 Sunset Blvd.
Hollywood, CA 90046
(213) 876-0570

Samuel French, Inc.
45 West 25th St., Dept. W
New York, NY 10010
(212) 206-8990
www.samuelfrench.com

Screen Actors Guild
5757 Wilshire Blvd.
Los Angeles, CA 90036
(213) 954-1600
Conservatory (213) 856-7736
www.sag.org

Appendix VIII | # Recommended Reading

Adler, Stella. *The Technique of Acting,* Bantam Books, 1990

Charles, Jill. *Directory of Professional Theater Training Programs, Regional Theatre Theatre Directory, Summer Theater Directory,* Theatre Directories, 2004

Friedman, Ginger. *The Perfect Monologue,* Limelight Editions, 1998

Goldman, William. *Adventures in the Screen Trade,* Warner Books, 1989

Henry, Mari Lyn & Rogers, Lynne. *How to be a Working Actor,* Back Stage Books, 1994

Hooks, Ed. *The Ultimate Scene and Monologue Sourcebook,* Back Stage Books, 1994

Hornby, Richard. *The End of Acting.* Applause Books, 2000

Jaroslaw, Mark. *The Actor's Handbook: Seattle & The Pacific Northwest,* Niche Press, 1989

Kondazian, Karen. *The Actor's Encyclopedia of Casting Directors,* Lone Eagle Publishing, 2000

Lewis, M.K. and Rosemary. *Your Film Acting Career,* Gorham House, 1997

Linklater, Kristin. *Freeing the Natural Voice,* Drama Publishers, 1976

Litwak, Mark. *Reel Power,* William Morrow, 1986

McGaw, Charles. *Acting is Believing,* HBJ College and School Division, 1995

Monos, Jim. *Professional Actor Training in New York City,* Broadway Press, 1989

Shurtleff, Michael. *Audition!* Bantam Books, 1979

Stanislavski, Konstantin. *An Actor Prepares, My Life in Art, Building a Character,* Theatre Arts Books, 2002

About the Author

Andrew Reilly is an actor, director, writer, and teacher of acting. He has worked extensively in theater, film, and television. He began acting as an amateur in community theater before deciding in middle age to pursue acting as a career. While completing a Master of Fine Arts degree at University of South Carolina, he was admitted into SAG, AEA, and AFTRA, the three professional actors' unions, and was also awarded a fellowship to the Folger Conservatory in Washington, DC.

After acting in regional theater as well as in New York and Los Angeles, he was awarded a Rotary International Fellowship to the Sorbonne in Paris for French theater studies. Reilly has directed productions in France, Russia and Hong Kong, as well as in Los Angeles. In 2001 he was awarded a Fulbright grant to lecture in Russia on American theater and film, and became the founding artistic director of the English Language Theatre of Orenburg, the Russian sister city of Orlando, Florida, where he now lives and works.

Andrew Reilly offers lectures and workshops and can be contacted by email at *anreilly@yahoo.com* for further information.

SENTIENT PUBLICATIONS, LLC publishes books on cultural creativity, experimental education, transformative spirituality, holistic health, new science, and ecology, approached from an integral viewpoint. Our authors are intensely interested in exploring the nature of life from fresh perspectives, addressing life's great questions, and fostering the full expression of the human potential. Sentient Publications' books arise from the spirit of inquiry and the richness of the inherent dialogue between writer and reader.

We are very interested in hearing from our readers. To direct suggestions or comments to us, or to be added to our mailing list, please contact:

SENTIENT PUBLICATIONS, LLC
1113 Spruce Street
Boulder, CO 80302
303.443.2188
contact@sentientpublications.com
www.sentientpublications.com